T0301252

Successes and Failures in Regulating and Deregulating Utilities

Successes and Failures in Regulating and Deregulating Utilities

Evidence from the UK, Europe and the USA

Edited by

Colin Robinson

Emeritus Professor of Economics, University of Surrey, UK

In Association with the Institute of Economic Affairs and the London Business School

Edward Elgar

Cheltenham, UK • Northampton, MA, USA

Published by
Edward Elgar Publishing Limited
Glensanda House
Montpellier Parade
Cheltenham
Glos GL50 1UA
UK

Edward Elgar Publishing, Inc.
136 West Street
Suite 202
Northampton
Massachusetts 01060
USA

A catalogue record for this book
is available from the British Library

Library of Congress Cataloguing in Publication Data
Successes and failures in regulating and deregulating utilities : evidence from the UK, Europe, and the US / edited by Colin Robinson.
    p. cm.
   "In association with the Institute of Economic Affairs and the London Business School."
   Includes bibliographical references and index.
    1. Public utilities—Government policy—Great Britain. 2. Public utilities—Deregulation—Great Britain. 3. Public utilities—Government policy—Europe. 4. Public utilities—Deregulation—Europe. 5. Public utilities—Government policy—United States. 6. Public utilities—Deregulation—United States. I. Robinson, Colin, 1932– II. Institute of Economic Affairs (Great Britain) III. London Business School.

   HD2768.G74S83 2004
   363.6—dc22

2004043515

ISBN   1 84376 770 8

Printed and bound in Great Britain by MPG Books Ltd, Bodmin, Cornwall

Contents

Figures and tables

FIGURES

TABLES

The authors

Doug Andrew has economics and public policy degrees from Princeton and Auckland Universities. He is a consultant and was Group Director of Economic Regulation at the Civil Aviation Authority in London from 1997 to 2003 and Commissioner for Eurocontrol's Performance Review Commission. Previously, he was Branch Manager and Deputy Secretary in the New Zealand Treasury specializing in microeconomic and regulatory reform and corporatization in sectors such as energy, telecommunications and transport.

Frits Bolkestein who is Dutch, is the European Union Internal Market Commissioner. He was educated at Barlaeus Gymnasium in Amsterdam, Oregon State College, USA, where he studied mathematics and the Gemeentelijke Universiteit Amsterdam, where he studied mathematics and physics, philosophy and Greek. He also studied economics at the University of London and completed a Master at Law at the University of Leiden.

Bolkestein worked for the Shell Group from 1960 to1976, with posts in East Africa, Honduras, El Salvador, London, Indonesia and Paris, and from 1973 to 1976 he was Director of Shell Chimie in Paris.

Between 1978 and 1999 Bolkestein was a Member of Parliament for the V.V.D. (Liberals) and from 1982 to 1986 he was Minister for Foreign Trade. He was Chairman for the Atlantic Commission (in the Netherlands) from 1986 to 1988 and from 1988 to 1989, he was Minister of Defence. He was Chairman of the V.V.D. Parliamentary Group between 1990 and 1998 and since 1996 he has been President of Liberal Internationale.

Bolkestein is also Chairman of the Amsterdam Bach Soloists, member of the Royal Institute of International Affairs (London) and the author of books and articles on a wide range of topics.

Martin Cave is Professor and Director of the Centre for Management under Regulation at the Warwick Business School. Until 2001, he was Professor of Economics at Brunel University. He specializes in regulatory economics, especially of the communications sector. As well as his academic work, Cave advises OFTEL, OFCOM and other regulators in the UK and was a member of the UK Competition Commission from 1996 to 2002. He has also undertaken studies for the European Commission. He is the author of the *Independent Review of Spectrum Management* (2002) for the UK Government, co-author of *Understanding Regulation* (1999) and co-editor of the *Handbook of Telecommunications Economics* (2002).

Graham Corbett was appointed Chairman of the Postal Services Commission in March 2000. He was previously a Deputy Chairman of the Competition Commission. He is also Chairman of Ricability, a charity concerned with research and information for consumers with disabilities.

Corbett was born in 1934. He qualified as a chartered accountant and was for 12 years the Senior Partner of Peat Marwick's Continental European firm based in Paris. He then moved to the commercial world to become the chief financial officer and a main board director of Eurotunnel. He was awarded a CBE in 1994 for services to transport.

David Edmonds has been Director General of Telecommunications at Oftel, the UK telecommunications regulatory agency, since 1998.

In September 2002 he was appointed as a Board member of Ofcom, the new regulator for the communications sector. He will continue to hold his current responsibilities as Director General of Telecommunications until Oftel is merged with the other communications regulators to form Ofcom in December 2003.

Between 1991 and 1997 he was Managing Director of Group Central Services at NatWest, responsible for the development, operation and management of the Group's £2.8 billion property portfolio, and the Group's support services.

From 1984 to 1991 David Edmonds was Chief Executive of the Housing Corporation, the major instrument for delivery of the Government's social housing programme.

Edmonds' career in the Civil Service includes two years as Head of the Division in the Department of Environment, dealing with housebuilding and mortgage finance, four years as Principal Private Secretary to the Secretary of State for the Environment, and one year as Under Secretary of the Inner Cities Directorate, responsible for policy and management of Government's Inner Cities Programme.

David Edmonds spent six years as a Council Member and Treasurer of Keele University, five years as a Board Member of English Partnerships, and Chairman of its Property, Planning and Projects Committee, and has been a Member of the Board of Hammerson Plc since 2003. He was a Chair of CRISIS, the charity for the single homeless for six years, and he is currently a Member of the Board of the Social Market Foundation.

Philip Fletcher was appointed for a renewable five-year term as Director General of Water Services on 1 August 2000.

His previous career was based mainly in central government public service, with an emphasis on financial issues.

Born in 1946, Philip's immediate previous post was as Receiver for the Metropolitan Police District from 1996. The Receiver had statutory responsibility for the administration of the Metropolitan Police Fund. He was a full member of the Commissioner's management team but was separately accountable to the Home Secretary. He was in charge of finance, procurement, internal audit and property services, and the legal owner of all Metropolitan Police property. In that role, he managed projects to improve financial management and review and outsource support services.

Earlier, he was a founder member of the Department of the Environment from 1970. His work there covered such issues as planning and land use, urban regeneration, rural issues, local government, finance and private housing. As Director of Central Finance there, he took part in the issues leading up to the privatization of the water industry in England and Wales in 1989.

Fletcher was appointed Chief Executive of PSA Services (the former Property Services Agency) in 1993. When he had completed its privatization, he transferred to head the Cities and Countryside Group in DoE in 1994.

Educated at Marlborough College and Oxford University, Philip Fletcher is married with one daughter. He is a lay reader in the Church of England and his hobbies include walking and bird-watching.

Callum McCarthy joined the FSA in September 2003 from the Office of Gas and Electricity Markets where he was Chairman and Chief Executive. He had previously held senior positions in Barclays Bank, BZW and Kleinwort Benson, as well as in the Department for Trade and Industry.

He is an economist and graduate of the School of Business at Stanford University, where he was a Sloan Fellow.

McCarthy's early career was in the chemical industry, and in the DTI where he held several posts including Principal Private Secretary to Roy Hattersley when he was Secretary of State for Prices and Consumer Protection and to Norman Tebbit when he was Secretary of State for Trade and Industry.

In 1985 he left the DTI and joined Kleinwort Benson as Director of Corporate Finance. In 1989 he joined Barclays' investment banking arm, BZW, as Managing Director and Deputy Head of Corporate Finance, later becoming Chief Executive Officer of Barclays Bank group operations in Japan before moving to head the Bank's businesses in North America.

McCarthy left Barclays to become Director General of the gas regulator Ofgas in 1998. When the new energy super-regulator Ofgem was set up the following year, he became Chief Executive before becoming executive Chairman in 2000. At Ofgem he oversaw the introduction of greater competition into the gas and electricity markets.

Callum McCarthy is married with two sons and one daughter. He was born on 29 February 1944.

Sir Derek Morris is Chairman of the Competition Commission (formerly the Monopolies and Mergers Commission). He first joined the MMC in 1991 as a member, becoming a deputy chairman in 1995 and chairman in 1998. Having studied Politics, Philosophy and Economics at Oxford from 1964 to 1967, and then for a D.Phil in economics at Nuffield College, he took up a Research Fellowship at the Centre for Business and Industrial Studies at Warwick University. Then, from 1970 until 1998, he was fellow and tutor in economics at Oriel College, Oxford.

During this time he wrote numerous book and articles, primarily in the field of Industrial economics. Books included *The Economic System in the UK* (third edition, Oxford University Press, 1985); *Unquoted Companies* (Macmillan, 1984); *Industrial Economics and Organisation* (Oxford University Press, 1979, second edition, 1991); and *Chinese State Owned Enterprises and Economic Reform* (the last three written by D. Hay). Other academic activities included chairmanship of the economics sub-faculty and then Social Studies faculty at Oxford and editorial board responsibilities for the *Journal of Industrial Economics,* the *Oxford Review of Economic Policy, Oxford Economic Papers*, among others.

Other activities have included three years on secondment as economic Director of the National Economic Development Council, and Chairman of Oxford Economic and Social Research. He has also been involved for over 20 years in various types of advisory and consultancy work, initially in the field of competition policy but more recently for the Asian Development Bank, in helping to design and implement economic reform measures in China and Central Asia.

Derek Morris was knighted in the 2002 New Year Honours List.

Chris Nash has a BA in Economics with First Class Honours from Reading University and a PhD in Transport Economics from Leeds. He joined the Institute for Transport Studies at Leeds University in 1974 as BR Lecturer in Rail Transport. He was promoted to Senior Lecturer in 1988 and to Professor of Transport Economics in 1989. He spent seven years as Director of the Institute. He is author or co-author of four books and around 100 other published papers and has managed many European, Research Council and industry-financed research projects, particularly in the fields of rail transport, public transport economics and project appraisal. He has acted as Advisor to many committees, including the Transport Committee of the British House of Commons, the EC High Level Group on Infrastructure Charging and the International Railways Union Economics Committee. His overseas experience includes projects in Egypt, India, China and Australia.

Colin Robinson was educated at the University of Manchester, and then worked for 11 years as a business economist before being appointed, in 1968, to the Chair of Economics at the University of Surrey where he founded the Department of Economics and is now Emeritus Professor.

He is a Fellow of the Royal Statistical Society, Fellow of the Society of Business Economists and Fellow of the Institute of Energy. He is a past member of the Monopolies and Mergers Commission and of the Secretary of State for Energy's Advisory Council on Research and Development (ACORD). He was named British Institute of Energy Economics 'Energy Economist of the Year' in 1992 and in 1998 received the award of 'Outstanding Contribution to the Profession and its Literature' from the International Association of Energy Economics.

Robinson is sole or joint author of 23 books and monographs and over 150 papers, including studies of North Sea oil and gas, the British coal industry, energy policy, nuclear power, energy privatization programmes and the international oil, gas and coal markets. He has appeared as expert witness in numerous legal proceedings in Britain and abroad.

He was Editorial Director of the Institute of Economic Affairs from 1992 to 2002 and is a member of the Institute's Academic Advisory Council and a Trustee of the Wincott Foundation.

Ian Senior has been an economic consultant for over 30 years. He has a BA degree in French and German from Oxford University and an MSc(Econ) from University College London. Following five years at Post Office HQ and two years at Liberal Party HQ, he worked for the Economist Intelligence Unit, Economists Advisory Group, REMIT Consultants and National Economic Research Associates (NERA). He is now an Associate Director with Triangle Management Services.

In 1970 he authored an IEA monograph in which he was the first to argue that the letter monopoly should be abolished. At the time this was considered to be heresy but today the monopoly has been reduced in the UK and abolished in Sweden and New Zealand. In the UK the letter monopoly will be abolished in 2007.

Since 1970 Senior has published a considerable number of papers and articles about postal matters and has completed a wide range of postal consultancy assignments for the European Commission and other clients. In February 2002 his monograph 'Consigned to oblivion: what future for Consignia?' was published by the Adam Smith Institute and in May 2003 the IEA published his 'Penny on the post: too little, too late, too intrusive' in the Current Controversies series. A further monograph is forthcoming to be published by Triangle Management Services: 'The UK's post offices: time's up?'. He is regularly interviewed on radio and TV about postal matters.

Andrew Sentance is Chief Economist and Head of Environmental Affairs at British Airways plc. His current responsibilities include advising the company on global economic developments, formulating and implementing corporate environmental policy and providing an economic and environmental perspective on major strategic and regulatory issues affecting British Airways.

He joined BA in January 1998 from London Business School, where he was Director of the Centre for Economic Forecasting. Previous positions held include Head of Economic Policy (1986–88) and Director of Economic Affairs (1989–93) at the CBI. While at the CBI, he was a founder member of the Treasury's Panel of Independent Forecasters (formerly known as the seven 'wise men') which provided advice to the Chancellor of the Exchequer under the last government.

Dr Sentance was educated at Eltham College, Clare College, Cambridge and the London School of Economics, where he gained his MSc and his PhD.

He holds visiting professorships at Royal Holloway, University of London and Cranfield University. He is Deputy Chairman of the Council of the Society of Business Economists, having served as Chairman of the Society from 1995 until 2000. He is also a trustee of the Anglo-German Foundation and of Harvest Help which is a development charity.

Dr Sentance is an established commentator on global and national economic issues, environmental issues and airline industry developments. He is a frequent speaker at conferences on economic and airline industry issues and the author of numerous articles and reports.

Dr Sentance is 45 years old and is married with two children.

J. Gregory Sidak studies regulatory and antitrust policy concerning network industries. He is the F.K. Weyerhaeuser Fellow in Law and Economics Emeritus at the American Enterprise Institute for Public Policy Research (AEI) and the President and Chief Executive Officer of Criterion Economics, L.L.C., an economic consulting firm based in Washington, DC. His research concerns regulation of network industries, antitrust policy, the Internet, intellectual property, and constitutional issues concerning economic regulation. He has directed AEI's Studies in Telecommunications Deregulation since the project's inception in 1992.

Sidak served as Deputy General Counsel of the Federal Communications Commission from 1987 to 1989 and as Senior Counsel and Economist to the Council of Economic Advisers in the Executive Office of the President from 1986 to 1987. He is the author of about 50 scholarly articles in law reviews or economics journals, including the *American Economic Association Papers and Proceedings, Antitrust Law Journal, California Law Review, Columbia Law Review, Harvard International Law Journal, Journal of Network Industries, Journal of Political Economy, New York University Law Review, Stanford Law*

Review, University of Chicago Law Review, Yale Law Journal, and *Yale Journal on Regulation*, as well as opinion essays in the *Wall Street Journal* and other business periodicals.

David Starkie is Managing Director of Economics-Plus Limited, and Director of transport programmes at the Regulatory Policy Institute, Hertford College, Oxford. Apart from a period with the Western Australian Government, when he served as deputy to the Director-General of Transport, he followed a mainly academic career until 1985 and was, latterly, Professorial Fellow at the University of Adelaide. In Australia, he was adviser to the Australian National Road Freight Inquiry, a member of the Road Transport Committee of the Australian Road Research Board and a member of the Western Australian Government's Transport Strategy Committee. Since returning to the UK in the mid-1980s, he has worked on early road PFIs and undertook a peer review of the National Roading Account proposals for the New Zealand Ministry of Transport. Between 1972 and 1997 he also advised Select Committees of the House of Commons on more than a dozen inquiries covering wide-ranging subjects including *Charging for Motorways*. A graduate and post-graduate of the London School of Economics, he is a member of the Royal Economic Society and of the Institute of Directors. He is the author of many books and papers, including *The Economic Value of Peace and Quiet* (with David Johnson) and *Privatising London's Airports* (with David Thompson) and is co-editor of the *Journal of Transport Economics and Policy*.

Irwin Stelzer is a Senior Fellow and Director of Hudson Institute's regulatory studies program. Prior to joining Hudson Institute in 1998, Stelzer was resident scholar and director of regulatory policy studies at the American Enterprise Institute. He is also the US economic and political columnist for *The Sunday Times* (London) and *The Courier Mail* (Australia), a contributing editor of *The Weekly Standard,* a member of the Publication Committee of *The Public Interest,* and a member of the board of the Regulatory Policy Institute (Oxford).

He founded National Economic Research Associates, Inc (NERA) in 1961 and served as its president until a few years after its sale in 1983 to Marsh & McLennan. He has also served as Managing Director of the investment banking firm Rothschild Inc. and a Director of the Energy and Environmental Policy Center at Harvard University.

His academic career includes teaching appointments at Cornell University, the University of Connecticut, and New York University, and an associate membership of Nuffield College, Oxford. He is a former member of the Litigation and Administrative Practice Faculty of the Practicing Law Institute. He served on the Massachusetts Institute of Technology Visiting Committee for the Department of Economics, and has been a teaching member of Columbia University's Continuing Legal Education Programs.

Stelzer received his bachelor and master-of-arts degrees from New York University and his doctorate in economics from Cornell University. He has written and lectured on economic and policy developments in the United States and Britain. He has written extensively on policy issues such as America's competitive position in the world economy, optimum regulatory policies, the consequences of European integration, and factors affecting and impeding economic growth. He has served as economics editor of the Antitrust Bulletin and is the author of *Selected Antitrust Cases: Landmark Decisions* and *The Antitrust Laws: A Primer*.

Leonard Waverman is Professor of Economics at the University of Toronto and currently a visiting Professor in the Regulation Initiative at the London Business School. He is also Director for the Global Forum for Competition and Trade Policy. He was editor of the *Energy Journal* for eight years and has been a Board member of both the Ontario Telephone Service commission and the Ontario Energy Board, and a member of NARUC (National Association of Regulatory Utility Commissioners) for five years. Waverman specializes in energy economics, the economics of telecommunications systems and antitrust economics. He has published and consulted on these issues in Canada, the USA, Europe and Asia, to firms, governments and international organizations. Recent books include, *Talk is Cheap: The Promise of Regulatory Reform in North America* (with Robert Crandall for the Brookings Institution, 1996) and *Competition Policy in a Global Economy: Modalities for Co-operation* (edited with William Comanor and Akira Goto, Rutledge Press, 1997). Forthcoming books include, *Global Speak: The Revolution in International Telecommunications* and *Universal Service: For Whom the Bells Used to Toll* (with Robert Crandall for the Brookings Institution). Professor Waverman has been awarded the Honor of Chevalier dans les Ordres des Palmes Academiques by the Government of France.

Tom Winsor was appointed Rail Regulator and International Rail Regulator with effect from 5 July 1999.

He was born in 1957 and brought up in Broughty Ferry, Dundee. He was educated at Grove Academy, Broughty Ferry and then at the University of Edinburgh, where he graduated with an LL.B. (Scots Law) in 1979. As a solicitor, he qualified first in Scotland, where he is a Writer to the Signet, and subsequently in England and Wales. After general practice in Dundee, he took a postgraduate qualification in oil and gas law at the Centre for Energy, Petroleum and Mineral Law and Policy of the University of Dundee.

In the course of his legal career, Tom Winsor specialized first in UK and international oil and gas law, later adding electricity, regulation, railways and public law. He joined Denton Hall as a partner in 1991, where he was responsible for the design of the regulatory regime for the electricity industry in Northern Ireland. In 1993 he was seconded to the Office of the Rail Regulator as Chief Legal Adviser and later as General Counsel. He returned to his partnership at Denton Hall in 1995 as head of the railways department, part of the firm's energy and infrastructure practice.

Tom Winsor is an honorary lecturer at the Centre for Energy, Petroleum and Mineral Law and Policy of the University of Dundee, where he directed the UK Oil and Gas Law summer course from 1993 to 1997. He is married, with one daughter, and lives in Kent, travelling daily to his office in London by train.

George Yarrow is Director of the Regulatory Policy Institute, Oxford and an economic adviser to Ofgem. He is also a visiting Professor at the University of Newcastle and an Emeritus Fellow of Hertford College, Oxford.

After graduating from St John's College, Cambridge, he held appointments at the Universities of Warwick, Newcastle and Oxford. His principal research activities have covered a broad range of issues in the economics of competition and regulation, but he has also written monographs and papers on welfare reform and on aspects of environmental policy.

In addition to his advisory work for Ofgem, he has recently served on expert panels advising on the Communications White Paper and on the regulatory impact assessments now widely utilized across Government departments.

George Yarrow has previously given lectures in the IEA/LBS series on social obligations in telecoms, progress in gas competition, the Monopolies and Mergers Commission, and economic assessments under the Competition Act.

Introduction

Colin Robinson

A series of lectures on regulatory issues is held in the autumn of each year, organized by the London Business School and the Institute of Economic Affairs and named the 'Beesley Lectures' after the late Professor Michael Beesley who originated the series in 1991. The twelfth series of lectures, in the autumn of 2002, again attracted distinguished speakers and chairmen: the chairman of each lecture also acts as discussant, commenting on the paper after it is given. Both the lectures and the chairmen's comments, revised by the speakers, are reprinted in this volume.

Since the series began, a huge amount of experience has accumulated regarding how and how not to regulate privatized industries. In the early days, lecturers would usually speak in broad terms about how regulation was developing in one of the British regulated utilities. Now, however, the issues have become more specific; some of them cross the boundaries of particular industries, and international experience of regulation is a significant element in the series.

One of Michael Beesley's aims in establishing these lectures was to provide a forum in which utility regulation could be discussed, in which best practice could be established and in which the regulators themselves, as well as academic and other commentators, could have their say. He was concerned also that regulation should have a liberal inclination, promoting competition wherever possible. His aims have largely been fulfilled. The annual volumes in which the lectures are reprinted are an important historical record of how both regulators and expert observers of regulation, from Britain and overseas, have seen the practice of utility regulation evolve over the years. Moreover, they reflect the tensions which exist between deregulation, the introduction of competition and the tendency to reregulate.

The papers in this volume begin with a chapter by J. Gregory Sidak, of the American Enterprise Institute, in which he takes a critical look at deregulation of telecommunications in the United States. He argues that deregulation has increased regulation, with considerable administrative costs. Moving from regulation to a 'truly deregulated market is costly, and the alternative of managed competition is surely costlier'. It would have been better to have applied a consumer-welfare, rather than competitor-welfare, standard. Sidak also contends that the Federal Communications Commission was at fault over WorldCom:

the FCC was 'oblivious to the largest accounting fraud in history'. Regulators 'should not interfere if WorldCom soon ceases to exist'.

David Edmonds, Britain's Director-General of Telecommunications, agrees with Sidak that regulation should be about promoting the consumer interest, but argues that, in a market such as Britain's with a powerful incumbent, regulation will often have to be intrusive as the market evolves towards competition. He is more cautious than Sidak about dealing with company failures. It is difficult, says Edmonds, not to become involved if there is the possibility of some consumers suffering loss of supply.

Chapter 2 is by David Starkie of Economics-Plus Limited who examines roads from a network point of view. He emphasizes the importance of introducing a market approach into road services 'by integrating pricing and investment decisions and by offering road users a choice of different road services at different prices'. Starkie says that, at the margin, the unit costs of widening motorways are increasing and it would not be efficient to proceed with a number of such schemes. Capacity might be better used if the length of time taken by road works could be curtailed and if speed differentials could be reduced. He would also like to see the price mechanism integrated into the design of new road schemes. An economic regulator for roads could promote efficient pricing and provision of road services.

Leonard Waverman of London Business School discusses David Starkie's paper and asks, what is the optimal level of congestion? On the demand side, the value of time is crucial. If, for example, time savings were ignored except for business trips, there would be few additions to the roads network. Leisure time should be included, argues Waverman, because it has an opportunity cost, though including all leisure time lost, valued at the wage, would probably produce too many highways. He is sceptical of the idea of speed governors to reduce speed differentials.

In Chapter 3, George Yarrow of the Regulatory Policy Institute, Oxford, assesses the Enterprise Bill, which he thinks, on balance, 'represents continued, albeit limited, progress towards a more well designed competition policy'. In particular, he approves of the underlying approach of avoiding detailed political supervision. His reservations concern the reluctance he perceives to permit judicial supervision of the substance of enforcement decisions, the failure to address aspects of public policy that hinder competition (such as environmental and health and safety regulation), and the lack of coherence in Britain's framework of competition policy which now incorporates some elements of the US and EU systems.

Sir Derek Morris, Chairman of the Competition Commission, commenting on George Yarrow's critique, is not persuaded that the Bill raises real procedural problems. Nor does he agree that the Competition Commission's role is primarily regulatory. He agrees that Britain has incorporated elements of other systems into its new competition legislation but 'Absorbing what appears to be the best of the rest is probably not an unsound benchmark for action in any walk of life.' Britain's new legislation should, for example, provide a 'more robust merger regime than in Europe' without the very time-consuming procedures of the United States.

Martin Cave, of Warwick University, considers in Chapter 4 the extent to which Ofcom can apply 'light touch' regulation, as it is enjoined to do by the 2002 Communications Bill, to the telecommunications, pay-TV and public service broadcasting markets. He discusses also the arrangements for the allocation of spectrum. He expects deregulation of BT's retail activities but '*ex ante* regulatory oversight of some of its network or wholesale activities … in the medium term'. BSkyB's market power will be dealt with through competition law. The BBC's advantageous position, because of the licence fee, means that regulation will be required to ensure it does not distort competition when it goes beyond its public service broadcasting remit. Ofcom should, he thinks, be looking at and, if necessary, implementing innovatory ideas about the allocation of spectrum.

Irwin Stelzer, of Irwin M. Stelzer Associates, remarks on the absence of clear regulatory procedures in Britain. He is even more concerned than Martin Cave about the difficulty of regulating vertically integrated companies with market power at one horizontal level and suggests that vertical disintegration may be required. Similarly, as regards the BBC, he sees great difficulty in drawing the boundary between public service and commercial activities: 'really rigid vertical separation' may be necessary. Stelzer maintains also that there is more overlap between the BBC and BSkyB than is generally recognized, thus complicating the regulator's task.

The fifth chapter, by Christopher Nash of the University of Leeds, discusses the future of the railways. He stresses the differences between the railways and other network industries which were, he contends, not sufficiently recognized at the time of privatization and which have led to some of the many problems that have been encountered. Economic analysis can be helpful in dealing with these but there are major political difficulties in implementing the necessary changes. Independent regulation is still required, in his view, though solutions to many of the problems will have to be sought by the Strategic Rail Authority. The most important area where progress is required is providing adequate incentives to train operating companies 'to develop their services in the most socially desirable way, and to make the most efficient use of track capacity'.

Tom Winsor, the rail regulator, comments on each of the issues raised by Nash. On timetabling and capacity use he argues that the decision criteria applied by his office are simpler and give more predictable results than Nash suggests. As regards cost increases, Winsor argues that Railtrack is too ready to accept increases claimed by the Train Operating Companies. Now there is an 'engaged and competent' Strategic Rail Authority (SRA), he expects better and faster decisions about capacity utilization: he criticizes Railtrack for its failure to produce a long-term strategy, thus making invention of the SRA necessary. He agrees with Nash about the need for 'strong accountability between infrastructure user and infrastructure provider'.

Chapter 6, by Frits Bolkestein, the European Union's Internal Market Commissioner, points out that the internal market is by no means complete. As part of its completion, the aim is to liberalize large parts of European utility markets. Energy liberalization is under way, though 'two big players, Germany and France, lag behind'. There are, says Bolkestein, fears that energy liberalization will cause similar problems to those in California in 2000. However the European situation is fundamentally different and, in any case, California's problems were not the result of liberalization. Bolkestein argues that increased use of nuclear power would increase diversification of energy sources and help meet Kyoto commitments. He also examines the prospects for liberalization of water markets, arguing that 'steps towards market opening of the water sector are feasible'.

Commenting on Bolkestein's paper, Philip Fletcher, the water regulator for England and Wales, concentrates his remarks on water. He points to some of the problems in liberalizing water markets, arguing that, in the nineteenth century, when London had a free market in water in its 'rudest and rawest form', malpractices and health problems abounded. Privatization of water without liberalization has, however, brought major benefits in terms of improved quality of drinking water and river water in England and Wales. A massive investment programme underlies these improvements. The British government wants more competition for business users but is unwilling to move to full competition in the domestic sector.

Postal regulation is the subject of Chapter 7, by Ian Senior, of the consultancy, Triangle Management Services. The Postal Services Act 2000 is, in his view, on the right lines in aiming for liberalization but it is flawed by attempts at social engineering. The main part of his paper proposes a set of criteria by which to judge good postal regulation. In particular, postal regulators should be independent of government, they should issue licences freely, they should not intervene on service quality, they should set access charges to former incumbents' 'final mile' networks, they should intervene to prevent predatory pricing, a clear date for full market liberalization should be set and, once that date is reached, they should phase out their roles as 'specialist regulator and watchdog'. Senior assesses Postcomm against these criteria and finds some 'passes' and some 'serious failures'.

Graham Corbett, Chairman of Postcomm, agrees that postal regulation should have the 'shortest life practicable' but takes issue with Senior's assessment of Postcomm's performance so far. The criticism that Postcomm failed to institute a liberal licensing policy is inappropriate, says Corbett, because Postcomm first had to carry out an investigation to ensure there would be no material damage to the universal service. Nor could Postcomm have avoided intervention on service standards because competition might have taken too long to produce standards that were acceptable. Finally oversight of Royal Mail prices is also justifiable so long as Royal Mail remains the dominant player in the market.

In Chapter 8, Doug Andrew, of the Civil Aviation Authority (at the time he gave the lecture), examines the aviation industry as an example of the problems of providing incentives for investment in a regulated industry, considering the effects of both market failure and government failure. He points out the substantial benefits to consumers that have arisen through aviation market liberalization and argues that further benefits could be achieved through more liberalization. The 'commercial model has worked well in aviation,' he concludes. Public policy problems now lie principally in upstream infrastructure markets where excess demand is a significant issue in parts of the UK: lessons from the downstream markets about the advantages of the commercial approach are only slowly being learned.

Andrew Sentance, of British Airways, agrees that commercial models are the right way forward, but, he says, the market will not solve all problems: in particular, the airline industry is plagued by periodic overcapacity. Sentance argues that Doug Andrew is 'trying to promote a form of deregulation without a significant injection of competition' which will create problems for airlines. He is concerned about the CAA's proposal to substitute a 'dual till' for the present 'single till' because it is complex and is likely to increase prices. He wants stability in the regulatory structure. He also emphasizes the need for a clearer airport strategy, effective action on environmental issues and a streamlined planning system.

Colin Robinson, in the last chapter, argues that the government has not learned the lessons of history, in particular the disadvantages of a centralized, prescriptive energy policy which in the past has produced unintended and unwelcome results. The proposals made by the government's Performance and Innovation Unit, despite their emphasis on the benefits of liberalized markets, are, he says, in practice a recipe for significant old-style intervention in energy markets. There may be reasons to intervene on environmental grounds but it would be better done by general instruments, such as a carbon tax, rather than 'the mix of interventionist ideas in the PIU report'. He claims also that the PIU approach runs the risk of encroaching on the system of independent regulation of the gas and electricity industries which has produced such good results.

Callum McCarthy, Chairman of the Gas and Electricity Markets Authority, accepts that the 'frailties of planning' should be avoided and draws attention to the dangers of 'gapology'. He is less certain, however, of Robinson's rejection of government planning. He argues that, rather than reject it entirely, we should think about ways in which intervention might successfully be achieved. He agrees that general rather than specific measures are preferable and would like to see any such measures as comprehensive as possible. Government will always be under pressure to act, he says, and it is important to develop guidance to make any actions as productive as possible.

The host of issues examined in this volume illustrate the changing nature of utility regulation in Britain and overseas as, where markets are in place, they evolve and as, where regulators still attempt to control, they battle with new and complex issues. The respective roles of governments and regulators are still not clearly defined (and may never be), and so the future of 'independent' regulation is not plain. Regulators' roles now differ markedly as between the different privatized utilities in Britain. Some, such as water and the railways, are little touched by liberalization and are primarily under the supervision of a regulator, whereas in the energy utilities there are now well established competitive markets and most price controls have been removed, leaving relatively 'light-touch' regulation. Another issue is whether in Britain, in the medium to long term, regulation will remain primarily of the 'home-grown' variety or whether it will conform to an EU-harmonized norm. It is this constantly changing scene that will be under discussion in future series of Beesley Lectures.

1. The failure of good intentions: the collapse of American telecommunications after six years of deregulation

J. Gregory Sidak

The United States has spent more than six years trying to deregulate telecommunications. We are not in the 'transition' any longer. It is time to take stock. I address three topics. The first is the administrative cost of deregulation. Next, I examine the consequences of the Federal Communications Commission's use of a competitor-welfare standard when formulating its policies for local competition. Finally, I speculate about how the WorldCom bankruptcy will affect the telecommunications industry and its regulation.

THE ADMINISTRATIVE COST OF DEREGULATION

My first point is a simple one: deregulation has actually increased regulation. That is not a reason to reject deregulation, but it may be a useful indicator of whether we are on the right trajectory for true deregulation. Consider first the growth of regulatory inputs.

Figure 1.1 shows the FCC's annual budget in inflation-adjusted dollars. Real expenditures quickly rose by about one-third after enactment of the Telecommunications Act of 1996, from $158.8 million to $211.6 million, and they have stayed at that higher level. The increase is 37 per cent if one includes 1995 in the post-deregulation period, perhaps on the rationale that Congress and the FCC both saw new legislation coming and sought to get an early jump on some of the expected regulatory detail.

What happened to regulatory output? The FCC, of course, produces many regulatory products. Some, such as inaction, are particularly difficult to quantify. But a simple, albeit imperfect, measure of output is the number of pages per year of the *FCC Record*, the official compendium of all FCC decisions, proposed rulemakings, adjudications and the like. As Figure 1.2 shows, the number of pages per year nearly tripled in the post-1996 period. During that period, the *FCC Record* averaged 23 838 pages per year.

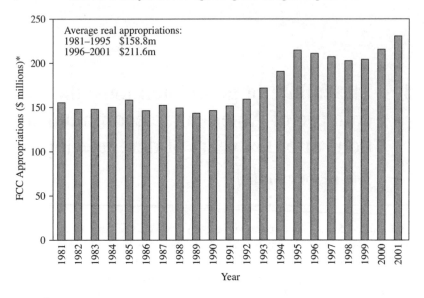

Note: * Adjusted for inflation using the CPI-U in 2001 dollars.

Source: 1997 FCC Record, Congressional Appropriations findings, 1999–2002.

Figure 1.1   FCC appropriations, in constant dollars

So, at a very crude level of analysis, it would appear that deregulation permanently increased the inputs and outputs of the FCC. Indeed, on the back of the envelope, it appears that a 1 per cent increase in real expenditures for the FCC would produce about a 9 per cent increase in output.

How did the near tripling of the FCC's output in the post-1996 period affect the transactions costs that private firms incurred in connection with telecommunications deregulation? This question is hard to answer because the relevant data are by definition private rather than public. One anecdotal measure that is publicly available is the number of lawyers who belong to the Federal Communications Bar Association. As Figure 1.3 shows, this measure of the number of telecommunications lawyers grew by 73 per cent between December 1994 and December 1998. If one assumes (very conservatively) that the average income of an American telecommunications lawyer is $100000, then the current membership of the FCBA represents an annual expenditure on legal services of at least $340 million.

Of course, some of these telecommunications lawyers may have been laid off by now, and others may have redeployed their talents in more promising specialties, such as bankruptcy, securities litigation and white-collar criminal

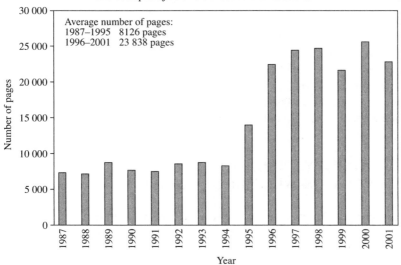

Note: The first year of the *FCC Record*'s publication 1986, was excluded because of its small value (1368 pages).

Figure 1.2   Number of pages of annual FCC Record

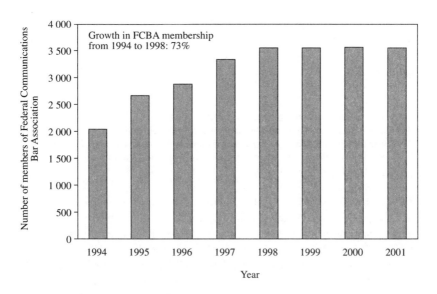

Source: *Fed. Comm. L.J.* (various years).

Figure 1.3   Growth in the number of telecommunications lawyers

defence. But the data do suggest that the stock of telecommunications lawyers experienced a substantial and enduring shift upward after 1996 that tracked the increase in the FCC's real budget and the increase in its annual output as measured by the size of the *FCC Record*.

Regardless of whether one considers particular FCC policies to be good or bad, there can be no dispute that the public and private transactions costs of implementing the Telecommunications Act of 1996 have been significant.

MANDATORY UNBUNDLING UNDER THE COMPETITOR-WELFARE STANDARD

Enough about the administration of deregulation. What about its substance? The centrepiece of the Telecommunications Act of 1996 was the opening of the local network. My second major point is this: following a consumer-welfare model would have made unbundling policy simpler and more socially beneficial.

Through its unbundling policies, the FCC affirmatively promoted preferred forms of market entry. Those modes of entry – and the business models predicated upon them – might have been immediately rejected in a truly deregulated marketplace rather than one that was subject to managed competition. It would not be credible to lay all the blame at Congress's feet by saying that the Telecommunications Act of 1996 compelled the FCC to follow an unbundling rule that ensured perverse economic consequences. Writing in his memoir in 2000, former FCC Chairman Reed Hundt said the following about the congressional compromises made to pass the Telecommunications Act of 1996:

> The compromises had produced a mountain of ambiguity that was generally tilted toward the local phone companies' advantage. But under principles of statutory construction, we had broad discretion in writing the implementing regulations. Indeed, like the modern engineers trying to straighten the Leaning Tower of Pisa, we could aspire to provide the new entrants to the local telephone markets a fairer chance to compete than they might find in any explicit provision of the law.[1]

Hundt's stratagem worked. By a 7–1 margin in *Verizon Communications Inc.* v. *FCC*,[2] the FCC's lawyers successfully convinced the Supreme Court in 2002 of the reasonableness of the agency's pricing rules for unbundled network elements (UNEs). Those rules are predicated on the novel concept of total element long-run incremental cost (TELRIC).[3] The TELRIC concept was so nuanced that the FCC devoted more than 600 pages to explaining it. Even if the FCC's TELRIC pricing model was not the *best* possible interpretation on economic grounds, it was deemed by the court to deserve deference on review under the *Chevron* doctrine in American administrative law.[4]

How much leeway did that imply? A great deal, for Justice David Souter wrote for the Court that the Telecommunications Act of 1996 created a 'novel ratesetting designed to give aspiring competitors every possible incentive to enter local retail telephone markets, short of confiscating the incumbents' property.'[5]

And what if those incentives led to a trillion dollars or more of wasted investment? That was not the Supreme Court's problem. With the exception of Justice Stephen Breyer, the court would defer to any method, even one never contemplated by Congress in the Telecommunications Act of 1996, that the FCC might devise for pricing UNEs: that is, as long as the court did not think that the method constituted a government taking of private property. And the court signalled in the same opinion that it had no appetite for deciding that constitutional question at any time in the foreseeable future.[6]

The court confirmed what the FCC's leadership had believed since 1996: that it had the wisdom to devise, and the authority to impose, the means to promote competition in local telephony. But those same officials and their successors were slow to acknowledge that the FCC correspondingly possessed the power to *distort* competition and investment in the telecommunications industry.

On the question of wasted investment, there is a puzzle. There is current excess capacity in the telecommunications industry despite FCC policies that created an incentive for underinvestment. The answer to this puzzle lies in the data. Eventually research by empirical economists may give us a definitive autopsy. It will be necessary to examine the level of investment in local network facilities (including cable television systems and wireless systems) versus the level of investment in Internet backbone facilities, undersea cables and other long-haul fibre-optic networks. For some investments, unrealistic predictions of demand may have more explanatory power than regulatory distortions.

As my co-author Jerry Hausman has argued, a powerful factor contributing to excess capacity in long-distance telecommunications was the unexpected degree of improvement in dense wave division multiplexing. At first, a given strand of fibre was split into two channels. The technology rapidly advanced to the point where a given strand of fibre now has over 100 channels, with the expectation going to over 1000. Thus, as companies installed new long-distance networks, technology improved so dramatically that capacity outpaced growth in demand, even with the Internet's rapid growth. The connection between this fact and the WorldCom bankruptcy will be made apparent later in my remarks.

It bears emphasis, however, that this excess capacity exists at the long-distance level, which is virtually unregulated in the United States. At the local level, relatively little new facilities investment by CLECs (Competitive Local Exchange Carrier) took place. Indeed, when Rhythms and Northpoint (the second and third largest CLECs offering DSL service) went bankrupt, their networks sold for under $50 million each. Thus we observed overinvestment in long-distance networks with no regulation, and underinvestment in regulated local networks, where the FCC (and state regulators) set prices for unbundled elements and wholesale services.

For the sake of argument, suppose that those policies were lawful but foolish. What should the FCC have done? Under Chairman Powell's leadership, the FCC in 2002 undertook a 'triennial review' of its policies on mandatory unbundling of local exchange networks. At that time, the agency continued to embrace the proposition that, in its words, 'access to UNEs would lead to initial acceleration of alternative facilities build-out because acquisition of sufficient customers and necessary market information would justify new construction'.[7] This is a testable hypothesis. After six years of implementing the Telecommunications Act of 1996, does empirical evidence support it? What would the FCC have to find empirically to continue to make this hypothesis the basis for its UNE rules? Empirical research by Robert Crandall of the Brookings Institution,[8] suggests that CLECs which built their own facilities were more likely to produce what the FCC calls 'sustainable competition'.[9] In New York and Texas, for example, where CLEC market share is higher than elsewhere, is there any empirical evidence that there was a greater rate of reliance on UNEs by CLECs? Answers to such questions are essential to knowing whether, as the FCC assumes, mandatory unbundling at regulated TELRIC-based prices achieves its intended purpose.

And what exactly is that purpose? Section 252(d)(2) of the Telecommunications Act requires an incumbent local exchange carrier to unbundle at a regulated price any network element which, if not offered on an unbundled basis at the regulated price, would 'impair' the CLEC's ability to compete.[10] The meaning of 'impairment' is critical. Not surprisingly, the definition was litigated in the Supreme Court after the FCC essentially said that any UNE that *can* be unbundled *must* be unbundled. The Supreme Court concluded that such a definition had no limiting principle, and it therefore remanded the rulemaking to the FCC.[11] The FCC then decided to use the phrase 'materially diminishes' to limit the scope of the statutory phrase 'impairs'.[12]

In May 2002, in *U.S. Telecom Association* v. *FCC*, the FCC's impairment rule was again struck down on judicial review, this time by the U.S. Court of Appeal for the District of Columbia Circuit in an opinion by Judge Stephen Williams.[13] At that time, the FCC was already in the midst of its triennial review of its unbundling rules. The FCC thus already had a proceeding under way in which to answer the following kinds of questions that would give economic content to the definition of 'impairment'. If FCC regulation succeeded in reducing the CLECs' level of 'impairment', what variable would we observe changing? Prices? Output? Investment? CLEC profit? Sales of complementary hardware and software? The FCC said that it wanted to review its UNE policies 'in light of [its] experience' since 1996.[14] Experience connotes empiricism and, unless the FCC clearly states its hypothesis concerning the predicted effects of its particular unbundling policies, such as the impairment test, it cannot know what changes to expect or the method by which to measure them.

The standard economic metric is consumer welfare, yet that is the one conspicuous variable that the FCC excluded from its laundry list of five factors that were supposed to unpack the phrase 'materially diminishes'.[15] I submit that no reasonable understanding of 'the public interest' can be reconciled with the FCC's exclusion of consumer welfare from the list of relevant considerations. A cynic might speculate that the reason for the omission is that consideration of consumer welfare would vitiate many of the FCC's conclusions on the essentiality of unbundling particular network elements. Consideration of consumer welfare would undo the competitor-welfare standard by which the FCC hoped to straighten the Leaning Tower of Pisa.

In this sense, the unbundling debate illustrates the potential circularity of regulation. 'Impairment' cannot be defined without reference to the price regulation to which UNEs are subject. Impairment is thus endogenously determined by UNE price regulation. Moreover impairment is endogenously affected by the allowed duration of the lease. Under existing TELRIC pricing, would a CLEC be impaired if it were required to lease a UNE for its useful life (more precisely, for the duration of its depreciable life for regulatory purposes), instead of being free to lease the UNE for a period that is terminable at will by the lessee and capped by regulators?

Furthermore what is the fundamental economic characteristic of 'impairment'? Increasingly the bottleneck of the telecommunications network is regarded as the trench in the street. The costliness of digging holes is a breathtakingly unpersuasive justification for mandating the unbundling of telecommunications networks, especially next-generation services. Would that as much attention had gone into the coordination of the actual trenching and sizing of conduit as went into estimating the forward-looking cost of an unbundled loop in a hypothetical network. A CLEC faces no barrier to entry with respect to the provision of a service if the ILEC (Incumbent Local Exchange Carrier) itself is overlaying existing facilities or if it is building new facilities or totally rehabilitating previous facilities. The ILEC faces the same sunk cost that a CLEC would. This analysis would seem to answer the FCC's central question in its triennial review: should the FCC 'modify or limit incumbents' unbundling obligations going forward so as to encourage incumbents and others to invest in new construction'?[16]

The FCC would clarify the meaning of 'impairment' if it assessed the magnitude of the real option conferred on the CLEC by mandatory unbundling of a particular network element at a TELRIC-based price.[17] The value of the real option held by the CLEC increases with three factors: uncertainty concerning technology, consumer demand and regulation, the duration of the lease, and the degree to which the leased assets are investments by the ILEC that are sunk rather than salvageable.

The real option view of mandatory unbundling meshes neatly with two of the five factors that the FCC had been using to determine the scope of unbundling; that is, before the D.C. Circuit's May 2002 decision in the *U.S. Telecom Association* case. The first factor is, in the FCC's words, 'whether the [unbundling] obligation will promote facilities-based competition, investment and innovation', and the second, again in the FCC's words, is 'whether the unbundling requirements will provide uniformity and predictability to new entrants and certainty in general'.[18] With respect to the second factor, a lack of uniformity and predictability will increase the standard deviation of returns for the ILEC, which increases the value of the real option that the ILEC is implicitly forced by the FCC to confer on CLECs. That increased value of the real option represents the value to the CLEC of waiting to see whether the ILEC's investments in new technologies pan out before the CLEC commits itself to making sunk investments in the acquisition of particular UNEs. The real option has the effect of discouraging ILEC investment. To the extent that innovation flows from investment, innovation is jeopardized by a rising value of the real option inherently conveyed to CLECs through mandatory unbundling.[19]

In contrast to such economic analysis, the FCC's definition of 'impair' as meaning 'materially diminishes' does nothing to reduce the regulatory risk that drives the value of the real option that the ILEC must give CLECs when the FCC mandates unbundling at TELRIC-based prices. A 'materiality' standard places enormous discretion in the hands of the regulator, which increases regulatory risk for those making decisions on investment in network infrastructure. That greater risk increases the value of the real option that the FCC forces the ILEC to confer on CLECs.

To its credit, the FCC in 2002 proposed what it called a 'more granular statutory analysis' of the unbundling requirements in section 251 of the Telecommunications Act. That recommendation is consistent with the proposal that Jerry Hausman and I made in our 1999 article in the *Yale Law Journal*.[20] We advocate an impairment standard that is product-specific, geographically specific and limited in duration. In essence a competitive analysis of each desired network element is required, with an antitrust-style examination of competition in the relevant product and geographic market over the relevant time horizon. This approach, incidentally, is consistent with the new regulatory framework that the European Union has adopted for the telecommunications; in that framework, competition law principles (of which consumer welfare maximization is the most elemental) are supposed to guide decisions about what and how to regulate on a sector-specific basis.

Under the Hausman–Sidak test, once the CLEC has demonstrated that the network element meets the basic requirements of the essential facilities doctrine, it will then need to show also that an ILEC could exercise market power in the provision of telecommunications services to end-users in the relevant geographic market by restricting access to the requested network element. Thus the regulator will mandate unbundling of a network element if, and only if, all of the following conditions exist:

1. it is technically feasible for the ILEC to provide the CLEC with unbundled access to the requested network element in the relevant geographic market;
2. the ILEC has denied the CLEC use of the network element at a regulated price computed on the basis of the regulator's estimate of the ILEC's total element long-run incremental cost;
3. it is impractical and unreasonable for the CLEC to duplicate the requested network element through any alternative source of supply;
4. the requested network element is controlled by an ILEC that is a monopolist in the supply of a telecommunications service to end-users that employs the network element in question in the relevant geographic market; and
5. the ILEC can exercise market power in the provision of telecommunications services to end-users in the relevant geographic market by restricting access to the requested network element.

In its practical application, this test would replace the FCC's current competitor-welfare standard with a consumer-welfare standard.

The Hausman–Sidak analysis also answers the FCC's request in its triennial review for an unbundling framework that incorporates what the Commission calls 'intermodal competition'.[21] The test would consider the effect of declining prices and growing subscribership for wireless as a factor bearing on the extent to which wireless–wireline displacement, rather than unbundling rules, have impaired CLECs.[22] The FCC's own statistics show that the number of wired access lines in the United States fell by two million between 2000 and 2001.[23] In August, *Forbes* magazine reported on the competitive implications of that fact,[24] and the *New York Times* reported that wireless was displacing wireline telephone access.[25] In September, the *Wall Street Journal* reported that AT&T Broadband and Cox Communication have signed up over 1.7 million local telephone customers and are adding 60000 every month.[26]

Competition occurs on the margin. So why does the FCC not acknowledge that cell phones now substitute for landlines for significant numbers of consumers? Even the Interstate Commerce Commission, the whipping boy of deregulators, managed to acknowledge intermodal competition between railroad, barges and pipelines in the 1980s, when it revised its policy on rate regulation for railroads serving captive shippers.[27]

Of course, intermodal competition between wireless and wireline telephony depends critically on the FCC's allocation of sufficient spectrum to accommodate the shift in demand. This dependency on government spectrum allocation is another example of the regulation-induced endogeneity of perceived market failure. Without enough spectrum allocated, the local loop looks like a bottleneck. That appearance of market failure is then considered evidence of the continued need for regulation. In the United States, we have never permitted the necessary counterfactual to come into existence, so as to assess without regulatory endogeneity whether the local loop really is a natural monopoly or an essential facility. If the FCC were to acknowledge the actual and potential displacement of wireline access by wireless, the exercise of mandating the unbundling of incumbent local exchange networks would sooner or later fade away.

TELECOMMUNICATIONS REGULATION AFTER WORLDCOM

WorldCom's accounting fraud poses a serious question for telecommunications regulators. Over the past 20 years, the principal economic insight in the regulation of network industries has been the asymmetric information between the regulator and the incumbent. The incumbent is typically cast as a dominant firm, if not an outright monopolist in law or fact. The concern over asymmetric information led to both incentive regulation and dominant-carrier regulation. Because the regulator's access to information was imperfect, the dominant carrier was subjected to greater obligations of disclosure, tariffing and reporting. The proposition that competitors were sophisticated veterans of antitrust and regulatory battles did not fit comfortably within this model.

On 26 September 2002, the former controller of WorldCom pleaded guilty to criminal fraud in connection with the company's accounting scandal and bankruptcy.[28] The same day, the *Wall Street Journal* reported that government reports unintentionally dignified WorldCom's incorrect claim that Internet traffic was doubling every 100 days.[29] The government thus contributed to the hype that caused tens, if not hundreds, of billions of dollars to be invested in long-distance fibre optic networks that go unused. Despite the intensity of the FCC's demands for information from the incumbents, the agency was blindsided by the WorldCom disaster.

The Securities and Exchange Commission (SEC) is not the only American regulator with a mandate to investigate WorldCom. The FCC has the authority and the responsibility to do so as well. Reasonable minds can differ over whether there is too much telecommunications regulation or too little, but, as long as we continue to regulate telecommunications, it is essential that companies give regulators truthful, complete and accurate information. Otherwise the FCC cannot make policies that reflect actual market conditions. For example, WorldCom and MCI have actively participated over the years in FCC proceedings determining whether AT&T should be released from price regulation or whether the Bell companies should be allowed to offer long-distance service. If false or unreliable information in such proceedings skews the FCC's development of regulations, the investment decisions and competitive strategies of telecommunications carriers also will be misdirected, all to the ultimate detriment of consumers.

The FCC is empowered to regulate communications by wire and by radio. Wireless communications requires a licence, and even the common carriage of voice and data over wired networks must get certified.[30] Some common carriers use wireless, and so they need both a certificate and a licence. In practical terms, the FCC's power to regulate comes from its power to deny certification or licensure.

By statute, wireless licensees must have 'character' as a basic qualification.[31] The FCC has written lengthy policy statements on the kind of conduct that constitutes a lack of good character.[32] Criminal behaviour is not required. Although character issues usually have involved radio or television broadcasters, the FCC has investigated wireless common carriers as well.[33] For example, the FCC refused to licence a company that concealed the fact that it started building towers for microwave transmission before the agency had approved their construction.[34]

The FCC has said that, 'where there has been a pattern of deliberate misrepresentation, revocation is the only appropriate remedy'.[35] The closest analogy to WorldCom may be a series of cases from the late 1980s involving RKO, an established broadcaster that was then part of a conglomerate corporation.[36] RKO lost or was forced to sell its radio and television stations at distressed prices because violations of law occurred in a completely different operating division having nothing to do with broadcasting. A lack of good character cost RKO hundreds of millions of dollars.

Measured in the billions of dollars, WorldCom's accounting fraud caused vastly more harm than RKO's conduct. So here is a modest proposal: to be true to its own precedent, the FCC should issue WorldCom a 'notice to show cause' why the agency should not revoke all of WorldCom's licences and certifications.

WorldCom's accounting fraud also destroys the company's credibility in proceedings before regulatory commissions and courts. WorldCom participates in litigation and regulatory dockets concerning local competition, long-distance entry by the Bell companies, US Trade Representative negotiations about interconnection pricing policies in other nations, and many other topics. Since 1996, WorldCom has argued to regulators that the cost of an unbundled loop is much less than incumbents say it is. Yet a central thrust of the SEC's investigation of WorldCom concerned its understatement of its own costs of local access.

If the FCC did strip WorldCom of its licences and certifications, the company would lose its value as a going concern and probably be forced into Chapter 7 liquidation. There is a temptation to give a bankrupt company a second chance, but, in WorldCom's case, a second chance holds little promise. Its brand name is probably worthless because of the taint of fraud, and its most capable managers have probably already jumped ship. The sequence of revelations of billion-dollar accounting adjustments increases the risk of massive successor liability for any potential buyer of WorldCom as a going concern. The vision of a viable, rehabilitated WorldCom is a mirage.

The FCC may be tempted to oppose WorldCom's liquidation in the name of preserving competition. That too would be a mistake. With so much excess capacity in long-distance networks, other carriers will eagerly court WorldCom's customers. Telephone solicitations at dinnertime are not likely to cease, and many large business customers may already have relationships with backup suppliers of telecommunications services. Moreover, since December 1999, the Bell companies have received regulatory approval to provide long-distance service in states containing about 45 per cent of the nation's access lines. More approvals are expected shortly. The Bells are well positioned to replace WorldCom as a competitor of AT&T and Sprint. Finally, as the FCC has recognized in other proceedings, the WorldCom network will still exist even after liquidation, should a completely new entrant want to buy all or part of the network and light its dark fibre.[37]

Chapter 11 carries another cost. Regulators would coddle a reorganized WorldCom, lest they fail by allowing it to fail a second time. The ramifications would be serious for innocent parties. Long-distance carriers experience economies of scale. Price must exceed marginal cost to recover fixed costs. If WorldCom emerges from bankruptcy having shed the fixed cost of its debt, it could underprice efficient competitors. Lack of capacity would not be a problem. Unlike WorldCom, its competitors have not been accused of accounting fraud, nor have they declared bankruptcy. If excess capacity must be taken off the market, it would be unjust and inefficient for it to be AT&T's or Sprint's because WorldCom's reorganization drove them under. Why should AT&T and Sprint shareholders suffer because of WorldCom's accounting fraud? And what would the FCC propose to do to keep the next bankrupt carrier afloat?

So it is decision time for the FCC. Since Congress passed the Telecommunications Act of 1996, the FCC has routinely questioned the accuracy of information supplied to it by incumbent local exchange carriers, whose networks it was trying to open to competition. Yet the FCC was oblivious to the largest accounting fraud in history, committed by a principal beneficiary of those very market-opening efforts. WorldCom's accounting fraud is tragic, as is the waste of enormous overcapacity in long-distance networks. But keeping WorldCom on life support would worsen the tragedy. The FCC should promptly determine whether WorldCom must surrender its licences and authorizations. If so, regulators should not interfere if WorldCom soon ceases to exist.

LESSONS LEARNED

There is a familiar saying in Washington: 'there is enough blame to go around'. The idea seems to be that individual culpability is inversely related to the size of the débâcle. When some government policy goes horribly awry in the United States, it is rarely the case, as it is in the United Kingdom, that a senior official promptly resigns. High-profile government positions in the United States are perceived to have only a professional upside.

While the US telecommunications industry lies enervated, the FCC is again occupied with the question of which network elements an ILEC must unbundle under legislation enacted six years ago. And, despite the WorldCom accounting fraud and bankruptcy, the Commission evidently misses the irony in its pronouncements about what an incumbent's forward-looking costs of operating a hypothetical telecommunications network would be.

What did six years of good intentions teach us? At least three things. First, the journey from regulation to a truly deregulated market is costly, and the alternative of managed competition is surely costlier. Second, a consumer-welfare approach to the mandatory unbundling of telecommunications networks would have been simpler, more intellectually coherent and more beneficial to society than the competitor-welfare standard that has permeated FCC policy from 1996 to 2002. Third, policy makers who cling to caricatures of incumbents and competitors risk missing the big picture.

Let me conclude by invoking the wisdom of Jim Quello, who served two decades as an FCC commissioner. He is widely credited with saying, 'What this industry needs is a whole new set of clichés.' It is a reminder of the failure of good intentions that audiences in 2002 groan at that quip instead of laughing. Let us hope that it does not take another six years for the joke to be funny once more.

NOTES

1. Reed E. Hundt, You Say You Want a Revolution: A Study of Information Age Politics 154 (2000).
2. *Verizon Communications Inc.* v. *FCC*, 122 S. Ct. 1646 (2002).
3. Implementation of the Local Competition Provisions in the Telecommunications Act of 1996, First Report and Order, 11 F.C.C.R. 15 499 (1996), *vacated in part sub nom*; *Iowa Utils. Bd.*

v. *FCC*, 120 F.3d 753 (8th Cir. 1997), *rev'd in part and aff'd in part sub nom*; *AT&T Corp.* v. *Iowa Utils. Bd.*, 119 S. Ct. 721 (1999).

4. See *Chevron U.S.A.* v. *Natural Resources Defense Council*, 467 U.S. 837, 842–5 (1984).
5. *Verizon*, 122 S. Ct. at 1661.
6. Ibid., at 1646.
7. In the Matter of Review of the Section 251 Unbundling Obligations of Incumbent Local Exchange Carriers Implementation of the Local Competition Provisions of the Telecommunications Act of 1996 Deployment of Wireline Services Offering Advanced Telecommunications Capability, Notice of Proposed Rulemaking, CC Dkt. Nos. 01-338, 96-98, 98-147, para. 23 n.69 (2002) (hereafter *UNE Triennial Review NPRM*).
8. See Robert W. Crandall, 'An Assessment of the Competitive Local Exchange Carriers Five Years After the Passage of the Telecommunications Act' (report prepared for SBC Communications, June 2001), available at http://www.criterioneconomics.com/documents/Crandall%20CLEC.pdf.
9. Ibid., para. 25.
10. 47 U.S.C. § 252(*d*)(2).
11. *AT&T Corp.* v. *Iowa Utils. Bd.*, 119 S. Ct. 721 (1999).
12. Implementation of the Local Competition Provisions of the Telecommunications Act of 1996, Third Report and Order and Fourth Further Notice of Proposed Rulemaking, 15 F.C.C.R. 3696 (1999).
13. *United States Telecom Ass'n* v. *FCC*, 290 F.3d 415 (D.C. Cir. 2002).
14. *UNE Triennial Review NPRM, supra*, note 7, para. 21.
15. Ibid., para. 4.
16. Ibid., para., 24.
17. See Jerry A. Hausman and J. Gregory Sidak, 'A Consumer-Welfare Approach to the Mandatory Unbundling of Telecommunications Networks', 109, *Yale Law Journal*, 417 (1999); Jerry Hausman, 'Valuing the Effect of Regulation on New Services in Telecommunications', *Brookings Papers on Econ. Activity: Microeconomics*, 1, 1997.
18. *UNE Triennial Review NPRM, supra*, note 7, para. 9.
19. This line of analysis is directly responsive to the FCC's request in its triennial review for comments on 'whether [the Commission] can balance the goals of sections 251 and 706 by encouraging broadband deployment through the promotion of local competition and investment in infrastructure' (ibid., para. 23).
20. Hausman and Sidak, *supra*, note 17.
21. *UNE Triennial Review NPRM, supra*, note 7, paras 27–8.
22. This analysis is relevant to 'the rapid introduction of competition in all markets', which is one of the five factors that the FCC had been using to judge impairment at the time of the *U.S. Telecom Association* decision (ibid., para. 21).
23. FCC, *Local Telephone Competition*, table 5 (various years).
24. Scott Wooley, 'Bad Connection', *Forbes*, 12 Aug. 2002, at 84.
25. Simon Romero, 'When the Cellphone Is the Home Phone', *New York Times*, 29 Aug. 2002, at E1, E7.
26. Peter Grant, 'More Consumers Answer Call of Cable for Phone Service', *Wall Street Journal*, 5 Sept. 2002, at B1, B4.
27. See, for example, *Burlington N.R.R.* v. *ICC*, 985 F.2d 589, 595-99 (D.C. Cir. 1993) (Williams, J.) (discussing ICC policy of rate regulation of railroads serving captive shipper).
28. 'WorldCom's Myers Pleads Guilty to Securities Fraud', *Wall Street Journal* online, 26 Sept. 2002.
29. Yochi J. Dreazen, 'Wildly Optimistic Data Drove Telecoms to Build Fiber Glut', *Wall Street Journal* online, 26 Sept. 2002.
30. 47 U.S.C. § 214.
31. 47 U.S.C. § 308(b).
32. In the Matter of Policy Regarding Character Qualifications in Broadcast Licensing, Amendment of Part 1, the Rules of Practice and Procedure, Relating to Written Responses to Commission Inquiries and the Making of Misrepresentations to the Commission by Applicants, Permittees

and Licensees, and the Reporting of Information Regarding Character Qualifications, 7 F.C.C Rcd. 6564 (1992).

33. In the Matter of Policy Regarding Character Qualifications in Broadcast Licensing; Amendment of Rules of Broadcast Practice and Procedure Relating to Written Responses to Commission Inquiries and the Making of Misrepresentations to the Commission by Permittees and Licensees, Gen. Dkt. No. 81-500; BC Dkt. No. 78-108, 1 F.C.C. Rcd. 421 (1986) ([c]ommon carriers are distinguished from broadcasters for purposes of character qualifications because no content regulation is involved and because such issues are adjudicated on a case-by-case basis without the guidance of a specific policy statement. As a result, reference is occasionally made in common carrier cases to broadcast policies and precedents as aids in resolving character issues). For an example of a recent revocation proceeding, see In the Matter of Application of Alee Cellular Communications, 17 F.C.C. Rcd. 3237 (2002).

34. *TeleSTAR, Inc.*, 3 F.C.C. Rcd. 2860 (1988).

35. *In re Revocation of the Licenses of Pass Word, Inc.*, 86 F.C.C. 2d 437, 449, para. 21 (1981).

36. *RKO Gen'l, Inc. (KHJ-Television)*, 3 F.C.C. Rcd. 5057 (1988).

37. Implementation of the Non-Accounting Safeguards of Sections 271 and 272 of the Communications Act of 1934, as Amended; and Regulatory Treatment of LEC Provision of Interexchange Services Originating in the LEC's Local Exchange Area, Notice of Proposed Rulemaking, CC Dkt. No. 96-149, 11 F.C.C. Rcd. 18,877, 18,943, para. 137 (1996).

CHAIRMAN'S COMMENTS

David Edmonds

Greg Sidak's chapter is a fascinating insight into the last six years in America. He discusses five years of good intentions; I am now coming towards my fifth year as the single regulator in the UK and I started with lots of good intentions based on consumer benefit. I profoundly believe that the primary purpose of regulation is to promote the interests of the consumer. As we move into the new world of Ofcom, and I might say I am delighted to have been appointed as a member of the board, I want to encourage, if I can, the board of that organization to adopt the same principle: what regulation is about is promoting the interests of the consumer. Now, in the world of TV and radio, the interests of the citizen are much more complex and this needs to be taken into account. But if you link consumers and citizens, then, as a regulator, you constantly need to focus on what you are trying to deliver for them.

In responding to the points made by Greg Sidak, I give some details of what has happened in the UK in my own sector, in terms, not of regulatory lawyers, because I do not think that is a good measure of activity in Oftel, but in terms of other resources. I have to admit that, in my five years of stewardship, I have managed to increase the costs of Oftel from £13.5 million a year to £20 million a year. My staff numbers are now running at about 230 compared to the 180 when I arrived and I make no apology for it. We were recently appraised by the Better Regulation Task Force which looked at the work of my organization and made a number of observations but no serious criticisms.

I believe that the telecommunications sector in the UK needs the current level of regulation because of the simple fact that it is dominated by a very powerful incumbent. At the heart of the telecommunications sector is a ubiquitous network owned by BT, an organization that still has the capacity, if it so wishes, to leverage a dominant position in one market into adjacent markets. I believe there are immense advantages to the incumbent, not just BT but perhaps some of the mobile telephone companies, in terms of brand, customer information, economies of scale and, in recent times, access to capital. Unless we have a regulatory regime that balances all of that with the consumer interest, we will find incumbents using their advantages to slow down regulatory action and impede competition. I have no doubt whatsoever that, for a period of years, BT did that in respect of unbundling the local loop. The regulator must have the resources, the skills and the finance to be able to intervene in areas where the evidence suggests that intervention is necessary in the interest of the consumer.

Greg Sidak talks about good intentions. Let me give you some examples where I think good intentions have resulted in good outputs. In the UK five years ago, we had no flat rate access to the Internet. Because of regulatory intervention, driven through by Oftel against the opposition of BT who claimed the network would fall over if we insisted on flat rate access, we introduced an unmetered wholesale product so other operators could compete against BT's own retail product. As a result, 4.5 million people in the UK are paying some of the lowest prices in the world for unmetered access to the Internet. It was a regulatory intervention that was focused and that was consumer-led.

I would also argue that our success in introducing broadband flows to a very large degree from actions by the regulator which drove local loop unbundling (LLU) into the UK market. Now LLU has not been a success, there have been about 1000 loops unbundled, but it has I am sure, provided the competitive stimulus and the threat to BT's own DSL (Digital Subscriber Line) offering to ensure that it rolled it out much more quickly than it would otherwise have done. So there is a second example of regulatory action requiring enormous effort, commitment and resource.

Third, though I cannot match the hundreds of pages that the FCC has recently published, Oftel did manage a 328-page publication last week in a Direction on partial private circuits (PPCs). Again, this is aimed at driving out benefits, both to competitors of BT and, in due course, final consumers, of much lower prices in terms of the provision of PPCs. The price cuts imposed on BT, subject to the consultation that is now going on, amount to between 30 and 50 per cent in terms of current charges. The enormous potential benefits flowing to the consumer, I would argue, hugely outweigh the extra resources resulting from regulatory intervention.

A fourth example is in the mobile market. Mobile termination charges were capped by a price control, set by me on advice from the Competition Commission four years ago. My proposals for an extension of the price controls for another four years are awaiting a Competition Commission decision. Conservative estimates suggest that £800 to £900 million remained in consumers' pockets thanks to that kind of regulatory action. So I am, as you will gather from this, an unrepentant regulator and, if I was to look back at the five years that I have spent in Oftel, I would say that rising intervention was made essential because of the need to meet the demands from other networks which do not have the capital and which do not have access to the BT network to get interconnection at prices that are fair, reasonable and non-discriminatory. I think all of that, paradoxically, does lead to more regulation rather than less regulation at a time when there is more competition than ever before. If you look at broadband as well as infrastructure competition between cable and ADSL (Asymmetrical Digital Subscriber Line), there are now some 40 suppliers picking up BT wholesale products. They are only in the market because of a regulatory framework that ensures that they have access on a fair and reasonable basis.

The first part of my response, therefore, is a strong belief that regulation at this stage in the evolution of the market towards competition will often have to be intrusive and may often be expensive. Nevertheless I recognize that a regulator should not intervene unless the benefits to consumers outweigh the overall costs of regulation.

Secondly, I will very briefly comment on Greg Sidak's remark about whether or not intermodal competition will lead to a diminution in regulation. He also referred to the European directives, which, I think, are clear, and a very positive step forward in regulation, encouraging greater reliance on competition law rather than *ex ante* regulation. The directives are clear about definitions of markets and identify those where *ex ante* rules are permitted. The level of market disaggregation is fairly detailed down as far as mobile call terminations. So I have the suspicion that, in the European model, while recognizing that intermodal competition may on occasion militate against the kind of intrusive regulation we are seeing at the moment, substantial withdrawal from regulation is a long way off. But I also think that greater reliance on evidence-based decision making will allow a tighter focus on areas where regulatory action can bring clear benefits.

Finally, I will comment on what Greg Sidak says about Worldcom and the whole question of company failure. It has been a major issue for us in the UK and, to be quite honest, at Oftel in the past we have paid little attention to the potential for company failure. We have been involved from time to time, as for example when a small company called Ionica went bust four years ago and when Atlantic went bust last year. But it was very apparent to us during last year that we did need to do some much harder thinking on this issue. We have been working with the Department of Trade and Industry (DTI) on whether or not we need a more coherent approach. My own view is probably not totally different from Greg's and I am not saying anything about his remarks in regard to Worldcom. I do not believe that regulators should mollycoddle operators and I do not believe that regulators should provide security blankets. I do believe, though that, at the end of the day, if you are a regulator and you are working in the kind of environment that we are in in the UK, and you are in the USA, if you see consumers being faced with the possible cessation of supply it is very difficult not to become involved. I do not think we have worked out the optimal way for that involvement to take place but I think it has raised a whole new set of issues which maybe I would not approach quite so clearly, and quite so committedly, as Greg Sidak has proposed.

2. Road networks: efficiency, externalities and consumer choice

David Starkie[*]

INTRODUCTION

In my 1999 Beesley lecture on airport regulation, I argued that there were a number of features about the airport industry that set it apart from the other utilities and this justified a difference of approach. This evening I wish to turn the coin over: road networks are treated differently from other network utilities, but this difference of approach has, in my view, been pushed too far. The distinguished American economist, Herbert Mohring, some time ago expressed the view that the external economies of transport considered to require special investment criteria have their exact counterpart in every other form of economic activity.[1] While sharing these sentiments, I will be emphasizing a different but related point: the need to introduce a market approach into road services by integrating pricing and investment decisions and by offering road users a choice of different road services at different prices.

Because of this, I concentrate on capacity-related issues and, consequently, I have little to say about the environmental impacts of road use. I touch upon road safety, but indirectly. I also concentrate upon the strategic network of motorways and trunk roads, the road industry equivalent of the high-voltage electricity transmission grid and the trunk gas network. This core network of motorways and trunk roads is in England the responsibility of the Highways Agency, whose budget for investing in and maintaining the network is set by the Treasury. In contrast, the urban network is the responsibility of local government, which funds road expenditure through the rate support grant system. The strategic network constitutes a minor part of the road network but it does, nevertheless, account for about one-third of total vehicle miles and is particularly important for the movement of freight. Although the inter-urban network is my focus, this will not be to the exclusion of other roads, because a number of points I wish to make have a general relevance.

The structure of the chapter is as follows. First, I review briefly recent developments in policies relating to the provision and pricing of road infrastructure. This is followed by a review of analytical studies undertaken in parallel with the policy developments. These analytical studies examine the pricing of road capacity either by treating the road network as a commercial entity with its own set of accounts or by focusing on efficient pricing and congestion-related charges. Both approaches provide a useful basis for considering in a later section a number of outstanding analytical issues including the costs of road supply. A number of less orthodox and, it is hoped, challenging proposals for increasing the capacity of the road network are then advanced. Finally the case is made for having an independent economic regulator for roads whose primary task would be to set and monitor charges for the use of different, specific parts of the network.

POLICY DEVELOPMENTS

Current roads policy is set out in the ten-year plan for transport, published in July 2000 with a reference date for commencement of the plan of April 2001. Its stated objective is to deliver a quicker, safer, more reliable transport system that respects the environment. To achieve this, the plan puts forward a number of aspirational targets, such as those relating to road accidents and congestion. Congestion, for example, is to be reduced, particularly on inter-urban trunk roads and in large urban areas. However, as Stephen Glaister (2002) has remarked, no explicit use is made of economic criteria to construct the plan. In spite of the mantra of integration, no attempt appears to be made to explain the allocation of resources between different transport sectors or to argue, except in very general terms, that the plan represents value for money.

Capital spending on strategic roads by the public sector is forecast at £13.6bn over the ten-year period (this is just over 20 per cent of proposed total public spending on transport). A further contribution for strategic roads of £2.6bn is expected to come from the private sector. Broadly speaking, this has the effect of returning expenditure levels to what they were in the early 1990s. Key features in the roads component of the plan include 100 new bypasses on trunk and local roads, 80 major trunk road schemes to improve safety and traffic flow at junctions, the widening of 360 miles of strategic road and the greater use of technology to keep road users informed.

To assist with decisions on road investment, use is being made of a new approach to project appraisal introduced following a review of the trunk road programme in 1997/8. This review was part of the newly elected government's integrated transport policy. The aim of the new form of appraisal is to give environmental factors more importance in the appraisal framework. A significant feature of the approach is the development of a simple summary of the key features of the road scheme, called an Appraisal Summary Table (AST), of which economic criteria are but a part.

Another strand of a more integrated approach is the consideration of a number of large road schemes in the context of multimodal studies carried out on a corridor or regional basis. These studies, first announced in 1999, are intended to consider the provision of more road capacity as one of a number of options. These options also include improving public transport to facilitate modal transfer and the introduction of network-wide tolls. Studies that have so far reported appear to suggest that public transport improvements would not contribute significantly to reducing congestion on the trunk road network, but that tolling would be an effective way of doing so.

Another notable policy development is the government proposal to modernize the taxation of the road haulage industry by introducing a form of lorry road user charging. This was announced in November 2000. A consultation paper on this proposal was released at the end of 2001 and a progress report earlier in 2002. Consideration is being given to charges varying according to the characteristics of the lorry, by time of day and by type of road, with a suggested implementation date of spring 2006.

ANALYTICAL STUDIES

A Commercial View of Roads

Undertaken in parallel with these developments in policy have been a number of research studies examining in greater depth current road taxation and proposals for pricing road use. One strand of these inquiries has further developed ideas for treating the road network as a commercial entity. The antecedents for this type of approach, sometimes referred to as 'cost recovery analysis', go back many years and an early example can be found in the 1968 *Road Track Costs* report, one of a series of white papers that underpinned the 1968 Transport Act. Although not the first to attempt such calculations, the report was notable in terms of the thoroughness of its approach and its introduction of economic principles into the analysis. It argued, for example (although not entirely convincingly), that by charging for capital expenditure as though it was a current item of expenditure, that is writing it off in one year, approximated a long-run marginal cost approach. The work formed the basis for the taxation of the road freight industry into the 1990s; the cost estimates were revised on an annual basis within a standard framework referred to as the Road Track Costs Methodology.

A not dissimilar approach was developed and refined in a series of papers in the late 1980s and 1990s by David Newbery.[2] The thrust of Newbery's work was to address the problem of providing and financing an adequate level of road provision. His approach viewed the road network as a public utility like water and electricity and he went on to suggest the establishment of a Public Roads Authority acting commercially, albeit within the public sector, with funding provided for by earmarking part of current road taxation as user charges. To distinguish between user charges and road taxes, the Authority would be vested with the capital value of the existing road infrastructure and on this it would earn an appropriate rate of return. If practical politics required initial user charges plus general revenue taxes to remain at existing levels, the initial value of the capital stock of roads and/or the required rate of return would be adjusted accordingly. To encourage the authority to invest and to forgo an interest in scarcity rents from a congested network, a price or revenue cap together with an independent regulator was seen as desirable, leaving the authority to adjust the balance of prices between different roads to correspond to relative congestion.

When advancing his argument, from time to time Newbery calculated the equivalent of a profit and loss account for the Road Authority. Similar calculations have recently been included in research commissioned by the DETR (Department of Environmental Transport and Regions) from the Institute for Transport Studies in Leeds (*Surface Transport Costs and Charges: Great*

Table 2.1   Comparison of 1998 road sector costs and revenues per veh./km

Cost or revenue category	Fully allocated cost (pence)	
	Low	High
Costs		
Cost of capital for infrastructure	0.78	1.34
Infrastructure operating costs and depreciation	0.75	0.97
Vehicle operating costs (PSV)	0.87	0.87
External accident costs	0.06	0.78
Air pollution	0.34	1.70
Noise	0.24	0.78
Climate change	0.15	0.62
VAT not paid	0.15	0.15
Sub-total of costs	3.34	7.20
Revenues		
Fares (PSV)	0.84	0.84
Vehicle Excise duty	1.10	1.10
Fuel Duty	4.42	4.42
VAT on fuel duty	0.77	0.77
Sub total of Revenues	7.14	7.14

Source: Department of the Environment, Transport and the Regions (2001).

Britain, 1998). The chief difference from the Newbery calculations was to introduce an alternative measure of the current stock of road assets based on the perpetual inventory method. Newbery based his capital stock values on an earlier government-derived figure to which he added the gross value of more recent road investment. Capital stock values from both the perpetual inventory method and Newbery were presented as alternatives in low and high estimates of fully allocated costs, using a 6 per cent discount rate. Also calculated were alternative high and low estimates of accident costs and environmental disbenefits. The basic output, expressed in vehicle kilometres for Great Britain in 1998, is shown in Table 2.1. It is interesting to note that there was a broad balance between average revenues and costs per vehicle kilometre in the high-cost case. In the low-cost case, revenues were twice the size of costs. Much of the difference between the low and high cost cases is accounted for by different assumptions regarding the value placed on environmental externalities; differences in the external costs of accidents and in the capital stock of roads were less important.

Efficient Pricing

A second significant strand of economic analysis has concerned the efficient pricing of road transport. The theory of pricing roads efficiently is long established, and reflects the fact that consumers of road transport services provide a good deal of the inputs required for their production (in the form of time and vehicular equipment). With a fixed stock of road capital, the quantity and quality of the inputs required from one consumer are dependent upon the quantities purchased by other consumers. The result of the interdependence is congestion: a fall in speeds (and thus increased inputs of time) as traffic volumes increase.

From time to time estimates of the total costs of congestion on Britain's roads have been produced. A recent and detailed calculation has been undertaken by consultants NERA, using a model which defines the cost of traffic congestion as equal to the difference between the so-called 'generalized costs' of travel (including travel time costs and vehicle operating costs) on the existing network at existing traffic levels and the travel costs incurred on the same network if traffic were able to move without impedance. The latter cost is usually based on observed speeds in light traffic conditions, subject to the constraints of the speed limits. The model has also been used to produce forward estimates of total congestion costs using the National Road Traffic Forecasts. Because congestion is an external cost (a cost imposed without compensating payments), in order to ensure that road output is efficient, the theory is that a toll or charge should be introduced at a level that reflects the costs of delay that the marginal road user imposes on other users of the road. The argument was refined by Alan Walters and others in the UK and by William Vickery in the USA in the early 1960s, when the first calculations of appropriate congestion tolls were made, but it was the 1964 report of the (Smeed) panel on road pricing, and its recommendation that direct pricing of congestion was the best method of rationing road space, that firmly placed the marginal cost pricing of roads on the UK policy agenda.

Recently the economic case for marginal cost pricing has been pursued with renewed vigour. The 2001 *Surface Transport Costs and Charges* report for the DETR carried out analysis using network models to estimate in some detail (by area, by road type and by vehicle type) the short-run marginal costs of road use. These estimates were based on current levels of traffic flow across the national network but, as the authors were at pains to point out, how the demand for the use of the network might respond to changes in user charges was not examined. Such responses would reduce the level of traffic and therefore lead to a reduction in the (initial) level of the congestion charges calculated in the study. In other words, the charges calculated were not optimal charges. However, a study published earlier in 2002, *Paying for Road Use*, and carried out on behalf of the Commission for Integrated Transport, has estimated the optimal level of congestion charge, given the existing stock of road capital. This study is a direct extension of the 2001 study for DETR and it uses the same network model but, importantly, incorporates estimates of how road traffic will respond to changes in user charges so that both imputed congestion charges and estimated traffic flows are closer to equilibrium levels. A caveat to be added, however, is that, in the model runs, although not in the subsequent policy prescriptions, the then existing levels of fuel taxes were assumed to remain unaltered. The significance of this for the level of optimal charge depends upon the view taken regarding the size of the environmental externalities to be covered by road taxes.

Selected outputs from the analysis are shown in Table 2.2. As might be expected, most of the measured benefits from congestion tolls set at equilibrium levels accrue in urban areas (80 per cent) but what is notable is how much of it accrues in the London conurbation; London in fact accounts for half the national benefits. Also notable is the size of the net benefit from tolling motorways; this exceeds by a large margin the total net benefit accounted for by introducing congestion pricing in all the provincial conurbations. Average weekday speeds on motorways are estimated to increase by just over 3 per cent, with a reduction in congestion of just over one-third. Across England as a whole the percentage reduction in congestion is calculated as 44 per cent with the net benefits from congestion charging totalling just over £2bn (at 1998 levels of flow and 2000 prices) before taking into account the costs of setting up and administering the charging system. The 44 per cent reduction in congestion is equivalent to a 7 per cent reduction in average journey time and five seconds per vehicle/kilometre saving in travel time.

Table 2.2   *Impact of congestion charging in England (7am to 7pm, Monday to Friday)*

	All England	All London	All conurbations	Motorways
Charge per car mile (pence)	4.2	26.6	5.6	3.5
Change in traffic levels (%)	–4.2	–13	–7.0	–2.6
Change in speeds (%)	+2.9	+13.5	+3.3	+3.2
Change in congestion (%)	–44.0	–56.0	–34.0	–36.0
Total time saving (million vehicle hours)	182.1	90.6	21.4	28.8
Annual revenue from congestion charges (£m)	5 666	1 838	882	1 140
Benefit of reduced travel time (£m)	1 875	915	228	332
Benefit of increased reliability	469	229	57	83
Loss to those 'tolled off' (£m)	313	127	50	52
Net benefit before collection costs (£m)	2 031	1 017	235	363

Source: Commission for Integrated Transport (2003), Table 6.1.

This analysis provides a valuable insight into a number of dimensions of the road problem. Of necessity a large number of assumptions were made and some of the data underpinning the analysis were not always robust; but the work does nevertheless mark an important advance. It is from this benchmark that I will now consider both issues requiring further investigation and a number of policy perspectives.

ISSUES ARISING

Costs of Supply

An important feature of the analysis contained in the *Paying for Road Use* report is that it calculates optimal congestion charges, given the capacity of the existing road network (and on this basis it estimates the total residual costs of congestion, after charging has been introduced, to be about £4bn). However, it is evident that parts of the network justify expansion at the toll levels computed in the report (and, at these expanded levels of capacity, the total residual costs of congestion will be less than £4bn, although probably still a significant amount).[3] Exactly how much expansion is justified once efficient prices are in place requires further analysis. What is needed is an integration of the demand and supply components; a comparison of marginal cost-based prices with the marginal costs of supply (or, more accurately, the incremental costs of supply) for different parts of the network.[4] The network-based analysis in the *Paying For Road Use* report provides a good indication of the former measure, but estimates for the incremental costs of supply are more difficult to come by.

The indications are that the incremental costs of supply can vary considerably across different parts of the network and can reach high levels for some links. The figures in Table 2.3 show some previously unpublished material on the costs of road construction submitted by the Department of Transport to the House of Commons Select Committee in 1995.

Table 2.3   Average costs of construction of one mile of lane capacity (1993 prices)[1]

		A	B	C
	Av. cost No of Lane		Lane	Col A/
	(£/mile) lanes cost		capacity	Col B
			(£/mile) (veh./hr)	(£hr/veh. mile)
Non-motorways				
Bypass, single carriageway	2.27	2 1.14	1 150	991
Bypass, dual carriageway	4.84	4 1.21	1 700	711
Dual carriageway				
Improvement from single				
motorways	2.21	2 1.11	1 700	647
New motorways (3-lane)	6.88	6 1.15	1 900	604
Widening	6.56	2 3.28	1 900	1 726

[1]   Includes costs of land, statutory undertakings, ancillaries and main works, but excludes preparation and supervision costs and VAT.

Taken at face value, these figures suggest economies of scale (costs per unit of capacity are less for dual carriageways than for single carriageway roads and are less for motorways than for dual carriageways). But economies of scale in the strict sense are not always a helpful concept in the utility industries. The more common situation faced is the expansion of an existing infrastructure and, in this context, the figures in Table 2.3 suggest that, when adding capacity to an existing motorway link in the road network, (long-run) incremental costs exceed (long-run) average costs. This is of particular significance, given that much of the programme of construction for the trunk road network is now focused on widening existing motorways. According to the figures in Table 2.3, the capacity provided by a vehicle lane is, on average, about three times as expensive to provide if done by adding to an existing motorway rather than by building a new motorway.

Widening costs are also highly variable. The Select Committee was informed that, if additional carriageways do not interfere with the existing road and junctions, the cost per lane mile could be similar to that for new motorways, but, if rebuilding of junctions is required, the cost could be around half as much again as the average figure quoted in Table 2.3. This variance is borne out by the National Audit Office in its 1993 report, *Progress on the Department of Transport's Motorway Widening Programme*, and by information supplied to me by the Highways Agency that suggested a variance for construction costs (providing that there were no major bridge widening schemes involved) of between £2.82m and £9.65m per lane-mile with an average of £6.03m. This average figure is broadly consistent with reports in the mid-1990s that the expected cost for widening the M6 between the Midlands and the Manchester conurbation was about £5m per lane-mile.

Taking this latter figure, we can make an estimate of what a vehicle would need to pay to cover the incremental costs of new capacity and then compare this estimate with estimates for typical congestion charges calculated in the *Paying for Road Use* report. Increasing the costs for widening of £5m per lane by, say, 20 per cent, to adjust to 2000 prices, using 6 per cent as the real cost of capital for a network utility and an annual average daily traffic flow (AADT) of 15 000 vehicles per lane (possibly a little above the maximum level of flow at which congestion begins) gives a capital charge of about 6.5p per vehicle mile. Once the annual costs for maintenance, policing and administration are added,[5] the overall incremental cost per vehicle mile works out at about 7.0p. This figure can then be compared with typical congestion charges that a vehicle would pay for undertaking a journey by motorway at the busiest times of the day, shown in Table 2.4.

Table 2.4   Typical motorway congestion charges

Route	Distance (miles)	Total charge (£)	Charge per mile (pence)
London–Rugby (M1)	80	3.40	4.25
Birmingham–Manchester (M6)	88	7.40	8.41
London–Oxford (M40)	55	4.50	8.18
Liverpool–Leeds (M62/M60)	75	5.70	7.60
Maidstone–Luton (M20/M25/M1)	73[*]	9.50	13.0

[*]   Statistic missing from published text, calculated by the author.

Source: *Commission for Integrated Transport (2002)*, report, page 35.

The incremental cost figure of 7p per mile is broadly similar to the congestion charge for the use of the M6, M40 and M62/M60. This suggests that, unless major bridge works or complicated junction alterations produce above-average costs, it would now be appropriate to widen these motorways even if efficient charges were levied. Widening of the motorway links between Maidstone and Luton would also be efficient; the price-cost margin is such that construction costs would have to be well in excess of the representative figure for it not to be worthwhile. However the case for widening the southern part of the M1 appears to be more doubtful.[6]

These, it could be argued, are back of the envelope calculations but I would suggest that, nevertheless, they give a broadly correct picture of the balance between incremental costs and the revenues to be expected from optimal congestion charges imposed at current levels of traffic flow. From them I would conclude the following.

First, there have been suggestions that it is probably not worthwhile tolling motorways because both levels of congestion and costs of construction do not vary much and therefore there is little to be gained from an efficiency point of view by doing so. The latest information appears to support the opposite conclusion. The variability of both measures is such that, providing the costs of setting-up and operating a charging system are modest, the introduction of tolls is most likely justified, especially if it is possible (using GPS technology) to extend tolling to a wider network of roads and, by doing so, reduce the problem of traffic diversion. Recent press reports that the Treasury has a preference for electronic-based charging of lorries using satellite technology are, if accurate, an indication that such technologies are now considered both feasible and cost-effective.

Second, if the perceived environmental impacts of road infrastructure are such that it is considered preferable to add capacity by widening existing trunk roads rather than building new motorways in open country, it seems most likely that providing more road capacity will cost increasingly more at the margin. In turn, this suggests that total revenues from marginal cost-based road user charges will exceed total expenditures; there is no reason, from an economic efficiency perspective, why the road account should have to balance and no reason why total revenue could not exceed total expenditure. It also means that efficient pricing would be compatible with a policy of cost recovery and it chips away at the generally accepted view that transport infrastructure is subject to economies of scale.

Third, more tentatively and, perhaps, more controversially, if optimal congestion tolls were applied to the network at existing levels of demand, a number of proposed motorway and trunk road widening schemes might fail to provide an adequate rate of return; it would not be efficient to build them at this point in time. But, because of the wide variability in both costs and revenues, it is difficult to say which schemes would, or would not, pass muster. The lack of (published) information on construction costs for specific schemes represents a serious gap in our current knowledge.

Measuring Outputs

The measures of congestion used in the preceding analysis start from the free-flow speed of traffic, the speed at which vehicles will choose to travel if traffic is light and vehicles do not impede each other. With an increasing traffic density, impedance increases and traffic speeds fall, the precise relationship depending particularly upon the type of road and the proportion of heavy vehicles. From observations, the traffic engineer has developed a number of generalized relationships between flows (expressed in terms of vehicles/hour/lane) and speeds for typical conditions. For example, at negligible levels of flow but with heavy vehicles accounting for 15 per cent of the total flow, the average *vehicle* on a three/four lane motorway is assumed to be travelling at slightly less than 70mph.

This assumption, based on the observed weighted mean vehicle speed, is particularly influenced by the speed of cars, which in 2000 had an observed mean speed of 70mph, the legal speed limit. But, of course, not all cars were travelling at exactly 70mph; the variance is relatively large and a majority of cars were travelling in excess of the speed limit, many well in excess of the speed limit. Moreover the latter proportion appears to be increasing (Table 2.5). The traffic engineer and the economist are therefore faced with a dilemma: how to account for behaviour which is illegal.

If, for example, we treat all vehicles travelling in excess of 70mph as though they were observing the speed limit, we get a lower free-flow speed. This in turn, would reduce the measure of congestion that emerged from the preceding analysis and it would reduce, too, the optimum level of congestion charge. By the same token, if the maximum legal speed limit was changed to, say, 65 or 75mph, this would also affect the economic analysis; the speed limit would have some effect on behaviour even though many vehicles exceed it.

Finally on this issue, it is to be noted that the speed–flow analysis assumes that the traffic flow is not interrupted by unexpected events such as accidents or roadworks. Consequently the analysis of congestion charges in the *Paying for Road Use* report also ignores the cost of congestion caused by such events. The report argues that, since the aim of congestion pricing is to deter those journeys from which the benefits are less than the congestion costs that they impose, the charges should be based on expected traffic flows and speeds. Nevertheless we should note that the congestion implications of an unexpected event increases when the network is operating at or near capacity. There is an economic argument for taking this into account when deciding upon the optimal timing for increases in capacity.

Table 2.5   Car speeds on motorways and dual carriageways, 1994 and 2000

	Average speed (mph)	Speed limit (mph)	Percentage over limit	More than 10mph over limit
Motorways				
1994	*68*	*70*	*47*	*14*
2000	70	70	55	17
Dual carriageways				
1994	*67*	*70*	*40*	*9*
2000	70	70	52	13

Source: Adapted from Department of Transport, 1994 and 2000 editions.

Investment Appraisal

If road congestion pricing was in place and the costs of expanding the network were known, the investment decision from an economic perspective would be reasonably straightforward: capacity should be added when the marginal cost-based price for road use exceeds the incremental costs of adding to the network. However, in the absence of road congestion pricing, investment appraisal has focused on the use of cost–benefit analysis and specifically the use of a computerized version known as COBA, developed over many years by Departments of Transport. The evaluation process projects forward traffic flows, calculates travel times, vehicle operating costs and accident rates with and without additional capacity and then calculates an economic value attached to these differences. The sum of these figures, suitably discounted, is then compared with (discounted) project costs to produce a rate of return or cost–benefit ratio. An assumption implicit in the approach is that prices for the use of the road network will remain at existing levels, these levels, of course, reflect average costs and not marginal (congestion) costs. Consequently rates of return will be high because traffic flows will be at suboptimally high levels so that the reduction of congestion will be that much greater:[7] all units of traffic with marginal social costs exceeding their travel benefits are included as beneficiaries in COBA.

This aspect apart, the results of the cost–benefit analyses are very dependent upon the values attached to travel time (because time savings dominate the stream of benefits) and the value of time remains a controversial subject decades after it was first introduced into the analysis (following, incidentally, seminal work on the subject by Michael Beesley). The values currently used for appraisal divide into two groups: values of time saved during the course of work journeys and a single value for all other time saved including commuting, leisure time, personal business time and so on. The former value is based on the gross wage rate plus additional labour costs, for different types of vehicle occupant (car driver, car passenger and so on). Current values used are based on 1998 wage rates. Non-working time values, on the other hand, are based on research carried out nearly 20 years ago and the values then agreed upon have been uprated to 1998 values in proportion to changes in average employee earnings during the intervening period. Perhaps not surprisingly, the rather dated nature of the research underpinning the values has been remarked upon, but in spite of the government having commissioned new research in the mid-1990s and more recently, this has yet to influence the values used.[8]

In addition to the government-commissioned research, the value of time issue has been a favourite subject for many other inquiries. This now considerable volume of work has illustrated how values are dependent on a large range of circumstances; on the different methodologies used and has shown that the results often have large statistical error terms. The initial government-commissioned review challenged received wisdom and in particular questioned the value of small savings in non-working time (research had indicated that savings of less than five minutes did not appear to have any value) and the practice of increasing the value of time through time *pro rata* with increases in income. This led the government to commission a review of the review. This questioned the validity of the analysis regarding the value of small time savings and, whilst agreeing that evidence pointed to income elasticities for non-business travel of less than unity, it suggested that further research was warranted.[9]

Possibly because of these differences of opinion regarding values of travel time, decisions about road schemes now appear to be based on values different from those included in the formal appraisals. For example, Nellthorp and Mackie (2000) noted that decision takers using the new AST approach (see p. 21) seemed to be downrating time-saving benefits, perhaps by a factor of two or three, relative to the conventional COBA values. They added: '[t]his could be either because the quantities of time savings were believed to be over-estimated, perhaps because of concerns about induced traffic or because the COBA values per minute were believed to be too high'. Distinguishing between different categories of non-working travel time and giving less weight to very small time savings might resolve the problem.[10]

OPTIONS FOR INCREASING CAPACITY

Utilizing Capacity More Efficiently

A great deal has been accomplished over the years using traffic management skills to increase the effective capacity of the road network. For urban roads, this initiative started in earnest during the 1960s when the then minister, Marples, drove forward schemes for box junctions, yellow lines and one-way schemes.[11] In recent years, as traffic densities have increased on motorways, more attention has been given to managing traffic on the strategic network. In order to make better use of available capacity, the Highways Agency is now moving away from focusing on asset management, with more emphasis being placed on its role as network operator. Increasing use of new technology is helping, for example, to improve the real time management of traffic.

One element in the equation is the disruption caused by roadworks to the normal flows of traffic. In spite of the Highways Agency skilfully planning and executing maintenance work (nearly all routine maintenance is carried out in the off-peak), inevitably with a heavily used network, roadworks continue to be a significant cause of congestion and, in the late 1990s, accounted for 10 per cent of congestion on the strategic network. In urban areas, such works also cause serious delays, although again this seems to be an area where there is a lack of data.

The measurement of congestion in the *Paying for Road Use* report opens up the possibility of more accurately measuring the cost consequences of roadworks. There are two aspects here. The first is the repair and maintenance of the highway itself and optimizing between the increased costs of building stronger pavements and undertaking repairs more rapidly (or at less inconvenient times) and the reductions in delay to road users. The second is the introduction of appropriate incentive mechanisms to encourage utilities to economize on the length of time they have access to the highway substructure for laying pipes and wires. Figures for the marginal cost of congestion suggest that, in many urban circumstances, to undertake utility works by reducing highway capacity costs a great deal indeed. The sensible approach is to charge the utilities for access, the opportunity cost, and a lane rental scheme to this effect is currently subject to trials in selected areas. Should the scheme be adopted more generally, an issue will be whether lane rents are set at economically efficient levels, taking into account local circumstances. However such an approach has the potential to make a major contribution to improving traffic flows in urban areas, perhaps proportionately equivalent to the prospective gains from introducing congestion pricing.

Another controversial issue is increasing road capacities by controlling vehicle speeds. The use of variable speed limits, such as those on the M25, are generally agreed to have made a significant contribution to effective capacities (and safety) by reducing the variance of speeds and lane utilization and, thereby, smoothing the flow of traffic. Their effectiveness, however, depends upon compliance. Thus far, levels of compliance appear reasonable on the M25 but, as the *Vehicle Speeds in Great Britain* reports indicate, normally the majority of motorists appear to pay little heed to maximum speed limits. Increased enforcement of existing limits using traditional policing methods is not really an option, if only because the police give speed enforcement low priority and are not willing to commit more resources to the task, given what they perceive as the high opportunity costs of doing so. Instead greater use is being made of technology, particularly speed cameras, to deter speeding in urban areas. It is doubtful, however, that this approach could have much success on motorways and trunk roads, unless the commitment of resources was very considerable. This is because exceeding the 70mph limit is endemic and to change behaviour will be very difficult without a very large number of prosecutions (which would probably be unacceptable politically). The circumstances suggest that *increasing* the maximum speed limit, together with stronger enforcement, might be feasible, but it is not at all clear that this would lead to the convergence of speeds and more balanced use of lanes necessary if network capacity is to be increased. (It is most likely to lead to an increase in accident rates.)

Another option, likely to have several beneficial effects, is to extend constraints on vehicle speeds by the universal, or extensive, use of electronic speed-limiters (the technology is similar to that incorporated in vehicle cruise control). Mechanical speed-limiters have been fitted to goods vehicles with a maximum weight in excess of 7.5 tonnes and to buses and coaches for some years. Applying them to other vehicles with, for example, a limit of 80mph will remove the tail of excessive speeding (17 per cent of cars on motorways and 13 per cent on dual carriageways exceed the current legal limit by more than 10mph) and lead to smoother flows of vehicles. In addition, it is likely there would be considerable reductions in greenhouse gas emissions and safety benefits.[12] In fact it is possible that the resulting reduction in accidents that would otherwise interrupt the traffic flow might be sufficient to offset the reduction in maximum speeds; *average* journey times might be affected little, if at all, by the speed constraint.

The case for extending speed-limiters to all business vehicles and, especially, light goods vehicles would seem to be particularly strong because reports indicate that drivers of such vehicles are more likely to exceed the speed limit.[13] One might be pushing at an opening door here if the road safety task force currently considering whether employers should be corporately liable in the event of negligence by their driver-employees recommends such a course of action. Nevertheless extending the application of speed-limiters is not without some costs and the cost–benefit analysis examining their phased introduction as the vehicle stock is renewed has yet to be done. But the multifarious nature of the benefits, including potential enhancement of road capacities, suggests that it is an option worthy of serious consideration.

Adding New Capacity

We have seen how congestion (or queuing time) is central to the argument for adding additional capacity to the network and how it is important in the economic evaluation of different projects. The value of time used in the COBA road appraisals is an average value of time, albeit an average depending upon the type of journey, the type of vehicle and so on. Nevertheless the result is that a unit of time saved is valued at a uniform rate, disregarding the fact that, in a stream of traffic of similar vehicles driven for a similar purpose, different drivers will vary in their valuation of their own time. Some journeys will be particularly urgent, some less so, whilst others will not be particularly time-constrained. The consequence is that drivers will attempt to drive at different speeds when they are able to, but if the road operates at high traffic densities this will not be possible. No matter how important it is for a particular group of drivers to save time, they will have to take their place in the traffic queue along with everyone else. In congested conditions the lowest common denominator prevails: there is no choice but to accept the prevailing low quality of service.

Equally, when consideration is given to adding capacity to the network, the tendency is to adopt a one-size-fits-all approach, to treat roads in effect as the travel equivalent of the National Health Service. The usual approach is a project design that adds relatively large tranches of capacity; a design capacity adequate to cater for traffic flows forecast for 15 years hence is common. What is missing is an approach to the problem that appreciates that different motorists using a road at a point in time will have different time values, even when the purpose of the journey is the same. Given these circumstances, when designing a scheme an alternative would be not only to consider different alignments for the road but also to consider adding varying amounts of capacity while using the price mechanism to control access to the added amount. A project adding only a limited amount to existing network capacity, but introducing a user charge to maintain its initial quality of service (for use by those with high values of time), might very well provide a better economic return than a traditional large-capacity product.[14] The shift in thinking should be towards offering road users a choice of quality/price options across the network.[15]

Perhaps in this respect an opportunity was missed when designing the Birmingham Northern Relief Road (BNRR), a toll concession that is to be operated by the private sector. Enabled by the 1991 New Roads and Streetworks Act, the BNRR has had a long gestation period. When this road is finally opened early in 2004 it will provide a priced alternative to the existing, non-tolled

M6 motorway where the latter threads its way through the West Midlands conurbation and, because the BNRR offers an alternative route subject to tolls, its opening will be of much interest. But as a private sector project its basic design characteristics appear to have changed little from the original public sector road proposal. It remains a dual three-lane motorway open to the usual types of traffic. A three-lane design is perhaps understandable when light and heavy vehicles share road space, but the alternative would have been to restrict the new road to light vehicles only and to have a dual two-lane configuration.[16]

The challenge is to extend the idea of priced options to the current roads programme. For example, it might be feasible when widening motorways to divide each extended carriageway into a 2+2 lane configuration, with half tolled and possibly restricted to light vehicles. Each pair of lanes could be divided by a hard shoulder and barrier, with the light vehicle lanes subject to electronic tolling and possibly a higher maximum speed limit. In the vicinity of junctions, to simplify entry and exit, the two pairs of lanes could merge to form a single four-lane carriageway, although in some cases the tolled pair might bypass relatively minor junctions. By using tolls to ration vehicle volumes, and thus maintain average speeds, and by eliminating the mixing of light and heavy vehicles, the consumer would be purchasing a higher-quality product. When added capacity, like the BNRR, complements rather than widens an existing route, there might also be an additional supply-cost advantage from introducing tolls. In circumstances where the incremental costs of adding capacity is high (and probably lumpy) it provides an opportunity to add smaller, albeit still lumpy, tranches of capacity while maintaining a high quality of service on what is added by varying the toll rate, by time of day (if necessary) and, more importantly, over time as demand in general increases.

Using tolls to maintain a high-level quality of service might also be a way of introducing selective additions to road capacity in urban areas (possibly as a supplement to road congestion pricing schemes). Again I would stress that the opportunity to use the price mechanism to ration the demand for the use of such additional capacity changes the design parameters. It allows for serious consideration of new roads of limited dimensions. A whole range of specifications become feasible, including narrow roads, grade-separated and for the exclusive use of light vehicles, and single lane (unidirectional) roads. Such small-scale roads could more easily make use of existing rights of way, particularly alongside or above railways that criss-cross the larger conurbations, thus keeping severance of the urban fabric to a minimum. In the late 1980s, a few specific projects of this type were drawn up under the concept title of Cruiseways©. One particular proposal, literally sharing rights of way with rail freight tracks (the latter used only as a railway at night when the road was shut), was subject to exploratory discussions with the executive of British Rail.

The general concept should also have more appeal in policy terms because it shifts the focus away from tolling an existing free-access network to which users have grown accustomed. Those objecting to tolls on new road capacity would have to argue on equity grounds and specifically that all users should have equal access to improvements in capacity and quality of service. But equity has a number of interpretations and it could be pointed out, with justification, that if values attached to queuing times differ between users then open access leading to congestion does not ensure equality of treatment.

CONCLUSIONS

Let me now turn to a few concluding thoughts that, to a degree, step outside the remit I set myself at the beginning of focusing on capacity issues and the interurban road network.

The main points made so far are, first, that there is a general lack of information on the costs of supply but, if road capacity is to be expanded by widening motorways, it is likely that unit costs at the margin are increasing. Consequently, optimal congestion tolls at existing levels of demand will probably indicate that it is not efficient to build a number of prospective schemes at the present time. I suspect that, in this regard, road infrastructure is not a special case; it is becoming increasingly evident that rail infrastructure also has similar cost characteristics. The CAA has also indicated that large airports too are an increasing cost industry, all of which leads me to the conclusion that, in the UK, there are probably many instances where transport services are sold at too cheap a price.

Second, the better use of existing capacity might focus on economizing on the length of time that road capacity is curtailed by roadworks, particularly those works undertaken by the utitily industries, and by trying to reduce speed differentials on high-speed roads, possibly by fitting all vehicles with electronic speed limiters. There are relatively few good data on the costs that roadworks impose on road users, but it is quite possible that an efficiently specified lane rental approach might improve urban traffic flows to an extent similar to that to be achieved from congestion pricing.

Third, it is suggested that there is a case for thinking again about the design parameters of roads and for considering integration of the price mechanism in the design process. Specifically, the suggestion is to consider the construction of smaller parallel or complementary roads of limited capacity, but with service qualities maintained in the face of increasing demand by the use of tolls. The general effect of the latter would be to offer road users a choice of varying quality/price options.

In conclusion, I would suggest that the time is fast approaching when we may need to have in place an economic regulator for roads. A regulator has been viewed as essential for a privatized road network and desirable if the network is commercialized under a public roads authority. But there is also a case for having an independent economic regulator regardless of privatization or commercialization of the road network. His or her remit would be to promote the efficient pricing and provision of road services by calculating appropriate lane rentals for occasions when public utility industries dig up the road, and efficient charges for the use of different parts of the road network, including urban networks (with calculations based on the long-run incremental costs of supply as well as short-run costs of congestion). Such an approach would increase the transparency of the rental and charge-setting process and reduce the incentives that governmental road providers might have to substitute politically determined pricing of the kind that bedevilled many of the utility industries before their privatization.

One is mindful here of a need to assuage the residual fears of the motoring public and their representatives that road pricing is likely to become just another layer of taxation. In this context, credit is due to the Treasury for the stance it has taken on proposals to reform the taxation of the road haulage industry. Its consultation document, *Modernising the Taxation of the Haulage Industry*, which includes proposals for advanced technology, distance-based charging, pledges that charges will be offset through reductions in other taxes levied on lorry ownership and use. Such developments are important if one is to build upon the apparently increasing acceptance of road pricing ideas, albeit an acceptance with the *quid pro quo* that charging revenues are reinvested in transport. The Institute of Directors, the RAC Foundation and the Freight Transport Association have all given their conditional support. It is to be hoped that the government will now seize what might, with hindsight, prove to be a defining moment in UK transport policy.

NOTES

* I would particularly like to thank Colin Robinson for inviting me to give the lecture on which this chapter is based and for comments on an earlier draft. I would also like to thank David Thompson, Stephen Glaister, Tom Worsley, Peter Mackie, John Dodgson, Richard Willson, Peter White, Richard Lewin, Stephen Littlechild and Nick Fenton and David Simmons for their assistance. The usual disclaimers apply.
1. Mohring (1976).
2. For example, see Newbery (2000) in which references will be found to his earlier published work.
3. The levels of total congestion costs reported from time to time in the media appear to invite the conclusion that the optimal level of congestion is zero and that all congestion is detrimental to economic growth. Note that the NERA analysis referred to earlier estimated that the total costs of congestion given *existing* road charges/taxes was about £7bn (for 1998), which suggests

that the costs of suboptimal charges at existing road capacity levels is about £3bn (£7bn less £4bn).

4. See Keeler and Small (1977) for an application of such an approach in California, and Starrs and Starkie (1986) for an application in South Australia.
5. Derived from tables 7.8 and 7.9 in *Surface Transport Costs and Charges: GB 1998*.
6. The congestion charges in Table 2.4 do not take into account taxes on fuel, which in 1998 for motorways was about 5p per vehicle mile (net of VAT which might be considered a general revenue tax). The *Paying for Road Use* study assumed that, with the introduction of congestion charges, the fiscal impact would be neutral, so that the monies raised from congestion charges would result in lower fuel taxes. This reduction, and its effect on traffic flows and congestion taxes, was not included in the published modelling results. After this reduction, traffic flows and congestion taxes would be a little higher than shown. After reducing the 5p per mile figure to allow for a fuel tax rebate, the remaining tax on road fuel would be of similar magnitude to the environmental and accident cost externalities forecast in the 'high cost' scenario in the *Surface Transport Costs and Charges* report. This remaining tax might, therefore, be considered a charge covering the environmental/accident costs. Alternatively, if one takes the report's 'low cost' scenario, remaining fuel taxes exceed estimated environmental/accident costs, so that an additional penny or two could be added to the imputed charges per mile shown in Table 2.4, but doing so would not alter the basic conclusions arrived at.
7. There are some circumstances when this is not the case, but the value of an investment when the existing network is not subject to congestion pricing will generally be greater than if the existing network is tolled. See, for example, Williams *et al.* (2001).
8. The exception is research on the units of account to be used for expressing the results of the economic appraisals.
9. On this issue, see Mackie *et al.* (2001), Gunn and Sheldon (2001) and Wardman (1998).
10. One additional element to consider in the context of a revised framework is the economic benefits of more certain travel times. Travel time uncertainty has a cost distinct from the mean time taken and, in so far as road investment improves the reliability of the network, this should be taken into account. However, it is possible, as was noted 30 years ago (Starkie, 1971) that, by not explicitly including this factor in value of travel time research, appraisal values of time may have become distorted.
11. The extent to which one-way schemes added to network capacity was controversial.
12. For a good treatment of optimal speed limits with an emphasis on safety, see Plowden and Hillman (1996).
13. RAC reports on motoring, various years.
14. With existing designs, the final increments of capacity are being added at relatively high cost to cater for relatively low-valued marginal demand.
15. That welfare gains from adding new capacity with tolls can exceed gains from adding more toll-free capacity is illustrated in Starkie (1986), which also reviews the theoretical basis for money-time options in road capacity. See also Glazer and Niskanen (2000).
16. Excluding heavy vehicles might also eliminate some diseconomies of scope. The additional cost of providing for heavy vehicles is the consequence not only of the additional lanes that might be judged necessary, but also of increases in pavement thickness. The thicker pavement required for heavy vehicles usually extends across the whole of the carriageway and not just to the additional capacity (lane(s) required to provide for heavier vehicles. On this point, see Small *et al.* (1989).

REFERENCES

Commission for Integrated Transport (2002), *Paying for Road Use: Technical Report*.
Department of the Environment, Transport and the Regions (2001), *Surface Transport Costs and Charges: GB 1998*.

Department of Transport (varous years), *Vehicle Speeds in Great Britain: Statistical Bulletin*, Annual Series.

Glaister, S. (2002), 'UK Transport Policy 1997–2001', *Oxford Review of Economic Policy*, **18** (2), 154–86.

Glazer, A. and E. Niskanen (2000), 'Which Consumers Benefit from Congestion Tolls?', *Journal of Transport Economics and Policy*, **34** (1), 43–53.

Gunn, H. and R. Sheldon (2001), 'The Value of Time', *Transport Economist*, **28** (1), 18–24.

Keeler, T. and K. Small (1977), 'Optimal Peak-Load Pricing, Investment, and Service Levels on Urban Expressways', *Journal of Political Economy*, **85**, 1–25.

Mackie, P. *et al.* (2001), 'Three Controversies in the Valuation of Travel Time Savings' (mimeo).

Mohring, H. (1976), *Transportation Economics*, Cambridge, MA: Ballinger.

Nellthorp, J. and P. Mackie (2000), 'The UK Roads Review – A hedonic model of decision making', *Transport Policy*, **7**,127–38.

Newbery, D. (2000), 'Road Pricing and Road Financing', in J. Preston, H. Lawton Smith and D. Starkie (eds), *Integrated Transport Policy: Implications for Regulations and Competition*, Aldershot: Ashgate.

Plowden, S. and M. Hillman (1996), *Speed Control and Transport Policy*, London: Policy Studies Institute.

Small, K., C. Winston and C. Evans (1989). *Road Work: A New Highway Pricing and Investment Policy*, Washington, DC: Brookings Institution.

Starkie, D. (1971), 'Modal Split and the Value of Time: A note on "idle-time"', *Journal of Transport Economics and Policy*, **5** (2), 216–22.

Starkie, D. (1986), 'Efficient and Politic Congestion Tolls', *Transportation Research*, **20A** (2), 169–73.

Starrs, M. and D. Starkie (1986), 'An Integrated Road Pricing and Investment Model: A South Australian Application', *Australian Road Research*, **16**, 1–9.

Treasury (2001), *Modernising the Taxation of the Haulage Industry: a Consultation Document*.

Wardman, M. (1998), 'The Value of Travel Time: A Review of British Evidence', *Journal of Transport Economics and Policy*, **32** (3), 285–316.

Williams, H. D. Van Vliet, C. Parathira and K. Kim (2001), 'Highway Investment Benefits under Alternative Pricing Regimes', *Journal of Transport Economics and Policy*, **35** (2), 257–84.

CHAIRMAN'S COMMENTS

Leonard Waverman

This is an excellent paper that addresses a number of issues in a very important and somewhat neglected sector. Another title for the paper could have been 'What is the optimal level of congestion?' When we discuss the optimal degree of safety we want to have that environment of safety where the marginal accident costs just equal the maximum prevention costs. What David Starkie does in this paper is to show how important it is to look at both the demand and the supply sides of the equation for congestion, to determine the optimal level of congestion. We have to consider the costs of increasing supply, relative to what are the consumer welfare losses for congestion pricing which work on the demand side. And David has given us some ideas, some back-of-the-envelope calculations, especially on the supply side. What are the costs of adding capacity to the road network; are they relative to optimal congestion costs? He discusses the problems with the various studies and ends up showing that we know even less on the supply side than we do on the demand side. Clearly we need better numbers. Let us consider what should be in the calculations, which are some of the issues he addressed.

For example on the demand side, which David spends some time looking at, I did my own back-of-the-envelope calculation. Think about the case he analyses where one report said we should not include the benefits of saving five minutes for non-business trips and then that was overruled, so as to include those benefits. I said to myself why are they fighting over five minutes? Well, if there are 15000 trips per day, per lane, then 15000 times five minutes is a lot of hours – 1250, to be exact. And if there is some pressure on capacity, let us say it is 200 days a year, and we value time at £10 an hour, it turns out that five minutes a day per vehicle is worth, in terms of benefits, £2.5 million. Now if you look at the supply costs, as David has in his paper, in most cases you would want to spend that kind of money because the cost of supplying roads is less than £2.5 million, which is the benefits of five minutes per trip saved. And so five minutes turns out to be an important number in these kinds of calculations. This shows how important are questions such as the valuation of time, and whether we should include non-wage driving. The more we value time and the time of all the drivers who are on the road at that busy peak hour, who are hurt by a few minutes when an extra car enters the road, then the more is supply valued. This means that an additional increment to capacity saves a lot for society because it reduces this valuable cost of congestion. And so it is really important to get the demand side right.

I would agree with David Starkie that we do not know where this magic cut-off of five minutes came from. Maybe there are psychological studies which suggest that, if you are not going to work, then saving five minutes is irrelevant. If you are driving on holiday it really does not amount to much and so you could disregard small amounts of time lost. I would like to know where these studies come from. David goes even further and asks whether we should in fact ignore non-wage driving. What if we drop everything but business trips from the calculation? Well, then we are going to get little additions to the network because most people on the road, most of the time, are in fact serving no economic function in the sense of adding to national accounts. If we do not value them, we really do not want road additions.

However time lost is time lost! Those of us even on leisure time are making choices at the margin between leisure and labour. There is an opportunity cost of leisure and so the value of leisure lost cannot be zero. What the correct number is I am not sure about, but I would think it is closer to the wage than it is to zero, because it is an opportunity cost concept. And so I think it should be included.

But I am an economist, so let me give you the two-armed economist answer: it should be included, but on the other hand, if you included all, it is like adding non financial losses, such as pain and suffering, to insurance claims. If we allow people to claim for pain and suffering, we get over-insurance and we get misallocations of resources, some argue. In the same way, if we add these non-pecuniary trips into the equation, we likely get too many highways. I remember when I was living in California and they built the BART system – Bay Area Rapid Transit Line. For a trip by car, which would normally take one hour and ten minutes, BART would take 17 minutes, and all the studies showed the number of people who would shift to this new system. But people did not shift. They went back and asked people why they were staying on congested roads instead of taking this lovely public transit, and people said, 'We love congested roads.' This was pre-mobile phones: 'nobody calls me', 'I can listen to my kind of music'. And so in fact it turned out that people actually positively valued being stuck in traffic.

So we have to worry about all these issues on the demand side. If we are going to look at both the demand and the supply sides we want to make sure it is not apples and oranges but that we have all the right things in both. And on the supply side of course we have to add the environmental costs as well, which David alluded to but did not address. These are crucial numbers to additions, to supply cost calculations as well.

I think that the fact that many of these potential cost 'adders' are not in national accounts is a red herring. Think of public good investments like parks and all kinds of leisure activities which are not in national accounts. If we said there is no value to non-wage elements then we would have no parks. It cannot be that national accounts are the basis for making investments in public goods.

Other issues which should be more carefully analysed are, for example, David's discussion of lowering congestion by lowering speed limits to the lower variability of speed. I thought of a Ferrari at 180km per hour: how is it increasing congestion if it is going that fast? But then it is really the variance, the differential speeds in queuing, that affects the variability of traffic and that affects the average speed. When I drive it is not the fast guys I worry about, it is the slow guys. So my suggestion is reverse speed governors: nobody can go below 80. That might have a problem of course as well, so I am not too sure about his speed governor idea, either.

Another consideration to analyse could be the exclusive lane or the pool concept as in the USA. I do not know what the cost–benefit analyses of those are. The only example I can think of here is that terrible two-mile lane that goes from Heathrow towards London. I cannot imagine the cost–benefit analysis that shows that is of value to society: to have a lane exclusively from the airport for black cabs and buses. I am sure those black cabs are taking mainly tourists. I do not know what that adds to our economy and I do not know why there could not be a toll on that – £50 for anybody who wants to use it. It would be a very simple toll mechanism where there is only one entrance point to it. I understand the prime minister was caught in the non-exclusive part of it and managed to get driven in the taxi line, but not in a taxi. And in non-rush hour why that is still exclusively for taxis and buses is unknown as well.

Finally David ended by talking a little about the regulator. A regulator in a deregulation environment has kind of a bad odour to it. Maybe we could call it something else. Having someone else but with some authority to put all these numbers together and hire David as a consultant would be very valuable.

3. The Enterprise Act: pluses and minuses for competition policy

George Yarrow

INTRODUCTION

Following a long period of review and relative inaction, two 'legislative buses' have now turned up in what, for this type of exercise, is an unusually brief period of time. First came the Competition Act in 1998, which brought UK competition law into much closer alignment with EC law. Now we have the Enterprise Act (EA) which, at least at first sight, appears to be more influenced by antitrust on the other side of the Atlantic.

The headline-grabbing aspects of the new Act are the criminalization of certain types of cartel activity and, to a lesser extent, the 'depoliticization' both of merger control and of those aspects of the old regime that were retained when the Competition Act was introduced. For the rest, it might be argued that the Act is little more than a tidying up exercise.

Arguably the economic content of the Act, at least in terms of its practical impact, is minimal. The public interest criteria of the Fair Trading Act (FTA) are, in relation to mergers, replaced by a substantial lessening of competition (SLC) test, and the notion of complex monopoly is eased out, to be replaced by market investigations of situations where, for one reason or another, there is cause to believe that competition might not be as effective as it could potentially be. It is not immediately clear, however, that, in practice, these changes will make a significant difference to the way in which policy currently operates.

On the other hand, the economic assessments relied upon in competition policy and the processes that govern the application of competition law are not fully separable activities: they interact, and together they determine the all-important outcomes. On this basis, it would be inappropriate to consider the 'economic' aspects of the Act in isolation from the wider context. In what follows, therefore, I devote attention to some of the 'process' issues, as well as covering the more obvious economic points relevant to an evaluation of the Act.

MERGER CONTROL

Let me start with two aspects of the EA that are concerned with merger control: the substantial lessening of competition test and the 'depoliticization' of the merger control process.

The SLC Test

The old 'public interest' test of the FTA has few remaining devotees, and I do not dissent from the general view that its demise, and its replacement by a test focused on the anticipated competitive effects of a merger, is a positive step (the first plus for the EA).

It can, of course, be questioned whether this step amounts to very much in practice, given that the Office of Fair Trading (OFT) and the Competition Commission (CC) have for many years now interpreted the public interest test in ways that have placed the predominant emphasis on effects on competition. At a minimum, however, the new legislation puts a floor under these past developments in enforcement practice, and it thereby hampers any possible, future backsliding. It is also helpful to have the priorities set out so clearly in primary legislation, since authorities do frequently (and rightly) refer back to their statutory duties. Clear and straightforward responsibilities should aid the decision-making process in multi-member authorities such as the CC.

Consumer Welfare and Efficiency Gains

An alternative replacement for the public interest test would have been one based upon consumer welfare, and such an approach has its advocates. In this context, it is sometimes argued that the SLC test and a consumer welfare test are, in effect, the same thing, so that it does not matter a great deal how the test is framed.

I have dealt with this issue in a previous Beesley lecture and will not revisit the arguments tonight. Suffice to say that, although it is to be expected that there should be a strong correlation between the decisions implied by the two tests (on the proposition that competition is generally good for consumers), there are also cases where the tests can lead to different decisions. More importantly, framing the test in terms of consumer welfare would, in my view, increase the likelihood that, in practice, rather more weight would be given to short-term consumer effects in assessments. Effects of mergers are more difficult to measure the further out into the future they stretch, and there can be a tendency towards 'measurement bias'. That is, those things which are easier to quantify are given more weight.

A focus on competition helps to offset this bias, since it rests on a presumption that any substantial lessening of competition will likely lead to (unquantified) consumer harm assessed over the longer term, even in cases where it might appear that a merger could lead to some temporary reductions in prices or to other, immediate, consumer benefits. In the absence of the presumption as to the longer-term effects of competition, the danger would be that mergers policy might become excessively interested in short-term price effects (that is, become more 'regulatory' in its approach).

These points are closely linked to the issue of 'efficiency defences' in merger cases. Under the EA, consideration of efficiency gains is largely to be handled via consideration of their effects on competition, not as a separate exercise on a par with the competition assessment itself. Thus, for example, if prospective efficiency improvements will have the effect of increasing competitive pressures in the market, that will be counted as a positive point in the wider SLC assessment.

There remains, however, the possibility that there could be anticipated efficiency gains, which are expected to be partly shared with consumers, in circumstances in which it is also expected that competition will reduce in intensity as a result of the proposed merger. How, if at all, should such considerations be weighed in the balance? Experience teaches us that any such prospective gains have a tendency to be greatly overstated. This may be the result of the familiar 'appraisal optimism' that tends to develop when the information provider has an interest in a positive evaluation of a project or transaction, or it may be the result of a less innocent, more conscious attempt to influence the policy decision. Either way, it is often associated with a tendency to ascribe anticipated future efficiency gains to merger, irrespective of whether or not they can, in fact, be directly or 'causally' linked to the transaction.[1]

In contrast to those who would favour a consumer welfare test for mergers, there are some who would favour elimination of explicit references to consumer welfare or to efficiency considerations in the framing of mergers policy. One of the arguments here is that the cases in which an SLC test is likely to deviate from a consumer welfare test are so infrequent that they are best ignored so as, for example, to avoid 'special provisions' that might, in the event, be inappropriately applied and/or exploited.

I have considerable sympathy with this view, although I do not think that it is a foolproof fix for the enforcement problem. It is true that any 'gateway' created in legislation is potentially open to misuse. So, however, is the notion of an SLC itself, which inevitably lacks precise definition, is problematic to quantify exactly, and requires the application of judgment. Thus enforcement agencies could also create special cases via the ways in which they judge whether or not, in particular circumstances, a substantial lessening of competition can be expected to occur. In the end, the competent authorities have significant discretion and, in my view, it is better to recognize this explicitly, by setting out when and how customer benefits or efficiency considerations can be brought into play, rather than risking 'adjustments' in the SLC assessments themselves, which might be made to accommodate exceptional circumstances but that might then have adverse, 'knock-on' effects in more standard cases.

Overall I think that the EA has struck a reasonable balance in addressing the relevant issues. The OFT will not be required to refer a merger if, notwithstanding its view that there will be an SLC, it is also of the view that consumer benefits would outweigh the anti-competitive effects. Similarly the CC will be able to take consumer benefits into account to some extent at the remedies stage. In both cases, however, it appears clear that a high burden of proof will have to be satisfied for these considerations to have an effect on outcomes. There is, therefore, some flexibility/discretion to deal with 'special cases', combined with some protection (albeit, in my view, still not enough protection – see below on appeals) against the misuse of this flexibility/discretion.

SLC and Collective Dominance

The SLC test is based on practice that has developed in the USA, Australia and elsewhere, but not in the EC. Is this a plus or a minus? The answer depends partly, but only partly, on whether or not there is perceived to be a significant difference between the two criteria (SLC/collective dominance). Views differ on this, but my own position is that there *is* a significant difference between the two. What I think has happened is that the European Commission has sought to interpret collective dominance in ways that bring it closer to the SLC test. However, the notion of collective dominance was introduced for the purposes of Article 82, which are by no means the same as the purposes of merger control.

Article 82 is concerned with market situations in which competition is already limited to a significant degree, and one of its chief preoccupations is to prevent *further reductions* in competition. Whilst merger control is likewise concerned with reductions in competition, the starting point is somewhat different: pre-merger, there is not necessarily a situation of dominance. It could, of course, be maintained that merger references should only be made where there is pre-existing dominance, which would bring the two frameworks into line.

The counter-argument is that this would unduly restrict the scope of mergers policy. Thus, whilst accepting the proposition that there is nothing necessarily wrong with a dominant position *per se* (the basis of Article 82 and Chapter II of the Competition Act (CA)), there are nevertheless sound reasons for wanting to place constraints on certain ways in which a dominant position may be achieved. More generally still, there are reasons for wanting to constrain the way in which significant/substantial accumulations of market power occur, even if neither the 'before' nor the 'after' position satisfies normal tests for dominance.

To illustrate, dominance (or significant/substantial market power) achieved by means of innovation is generally considered acceptable because of the benefits generated along the way. There may be some restriction of competition as a result of successful, major innovations, at least for a period, but it would clearly be wrong, as a general matter, to subject innovative activity to detailed oversight by the OFT on the ground that it could potentially lead to an SLC. In contrast, when dominance or market power is created by merger, there is no *direct* product market benefit: all the immediate action is in capital markets. Market conduct may change later, but this does not alter the fact that the *means* by which a dominant position is achieved itself confers no product market benefits.

In many ways, therefore, merger control is more naturally linked to Article 81 than to Article 82. It is concerned with economic conduct (for example, in the case of Article 81 or Chapter I of the CA, horizontal price fixing[2]) that, irrespective of the structure of the relevant market, does not appear to yield economic benefits in and of itself, and which also might be expected, with an appreciable frequency, to reduce competition.

The attempt by the European Commission to 'develop' the concept of collective dominance so as to address merger control issues has had a number of adverse effects, including the following:

- a muddying of the waters in relation to the distinctions between Articles 81 and 82, increasing uncertainties in the application of competition law;
- scarce enforcement resources have been absorbed by the inevitable legal challenges;
- outcomes may have harmed the reputation of, and reduced confidence in, the enforcement authority.

The UK has, therefore, done well to avoid these problems by introducing a test (SLC) that is specific to merger cases but that is more similar to the tests associated with Article 81/Chapter I (restrictions of competition) than to the tests associated with Article 82/Chapter II (dominance, abuse). Other things equal, lack of alignment with EC policy is obviously a minus for the approach – but, crucially, other things are not equal. Any desire for harmonization does not, I think, provide justification for settling on an increasingly problematic alternative. In any event, it can be noted that: (a) alignment with the EC approach is certainly no worse, and arguably significantly better, under the EA regime than under its predecessor, and (b) the EC Merger Regulation is currently under review, and there must at least be a possibility that the European test will shift to SLC. To the extent that the UK decision helps in any way to influence things towards such an outcome, that would be a further plus.

Process and Institutional Issues

The principal reforms to the processes of merger control introduced by the EA are as follows:

- the Secretary of State will play no role in the process, save that she/he can create exceptional public interest gateways which allow for the consideration of wider (than SLC) effects in certain cases (such as issues of national security or newspaper mergers);
- the OFT, not the Secretary of State, will have responsibility for making references to the CC;
- the CC will make decisions on whether or not to allow a merger to proceed, and on what terms (that is, relevant remedies), not the Secretary of State;
- appeals to review the decisions of the OFT and CC can be made to a new Competition Appeal Tribunal (CAT), independent of the OFT and CC.

In short, the OFT and CC will move from being advisory bodies to becoming decision-making bodies.

Again the immediate practical import of these changes can be expected to be limited. It has been many years since politicians have been inclined to override the advice of the competition authorities with any significant frequency, and the legislative changes therefore largely have the effect of bringing the formal framework of policy into line with recent practice.

The principal value in the changes therefore probably lies in increasing the barriers to intervention that would face any future minister who might be inclined to take competition policy back to the past. As recent, renewed political interest in regulated sectors shows, stability of objectives is not a characteristic that political processes can be relied upon to supply, so the benefits of the EA in this regard are by no means trivial.

After this long run of pluses, I now come to the first minus. The EA continues to hold to the traditional UK position that the relevant decisions, having been made by an administrative body, should not be subject to judicial oversight *on their substantive merits*. Appeals will operate according to the principles of judicial review, and will therefore be concerned chiefly with procedures followed, rather than with the substance of the economic assessments. Irrational or manifestly wrong reasoning can be rejected by the CAT, but these are low hurdles for the enforcement authorities to clear.

In the context of merger control, this reluctance to give weight to a 'second opinion' may not be a major fault in the wider scheme of things. Only a small fraction of merger proposals are blocked, appeals take time, and delay may impose substantial costs of its own. There are, however, two issues of principle at stake, which are of more general importance. First, particularly given that there is no simple measuring rod for the 'degree of competition', economic assessments frequently involve complex judgments about which there can be scope for reasonable disagreement. To one observer of a particular market, a rise in concentration might signal weakening competition in a market; to another the same change in market structure might signal intensifying competitive pressures. Underlying these judgments may be different perspectives on what is actually meant by a 'lessening of competition' and on what is to be counted as a 'substantial' effect. Given this, the question is: should an expert, administrative body be afforded the protection of substantive immunity when deciding on these issues?

Secondly, when dealing with matters of remedies, the authorities are not simply saying yes or no to the proposals of others. The development and evaluation of at least some forms of remedies is a proactive process that is *regulatory* in nature. Alternative options are 'generated' and assessed against a given (and not necessarily unambiguous) purpose. This may be *regulation for competition*, but it is regulation nonetheless, and it is not hugely different from the activities of some of the sectoral regulators. Again it can be asked: should such activity be allowed to proceed, possibly according to processes that differ from those elsewhere in government (Regulatory Impact Assessments have been heavily promoted in other areas of government activity, for example) and without the checks and balances afforded by rights of appeal on the merits of decisions?

Whilst the UK has been willing to follow the USA and Australia in adopting the SLC test, and had earlier followed the EC when introducing the Competition Act, on questions of appeals we have been much more insular. This alone does not make the UK position wrong, but successful public policies tend to be copied by others and the fact that the UK approach to these matters has not been widely adopted elsewhere should give pause for thought. I take up this issue again below, in a context where it may have more serious implications than it does in merger policy.

MARKET INVESTIGATIONS

When the CA was introduced the government had the option of simply dropping the scale and complex monopoly provisions of the FTA, thereby bringing UK domestic competition law more closely into line with EC law. I was among those in favour of such an approach but, in the event, is was an option that was rejected.

The EA has now addressed the FTA 'left-overs', not by complete disposal but rather by replacement in the form of a system of 'market investigations'. The purpose is to allow for investigations in situations where the OFT suspects that some feature or combination of features of a market prevents, restricts or distorts competition, but where the perceived competition problems cannot adequately be addressed by application of either the Competition Act or EC law.

The procedure in such cases is that

- the OFT (or a sectoral regulator) reviews the market,
- if potential competition problems are discovered, a reference may be made to the CC,
- the CC carries out a detailed investigation of the market, of up to two years in length, and,
- where the CC identifies competition problems, it can, on the basis of its findings, determine remedial actions.

The first point to note about this system is that the powers afforded to the authorities are very broad in scope. Investigations are not limited by a specific feature of a market (for example the existence of price fixing, or of dominance, or of a concentrated market structure, or the fact that a market lies in a particular, regulated sector). Similarly the scope for remedies is broad, although there are obvious constraints in cases where significant legislative activity would be required to implement the intentions of the CC.

Second, as in relation to remedies in merger cases, I think it is appropriate to describe the relevant activities as *regulatory* in nature. Thus the CC will be able to take steps to remedy not only any perceived adverse effects on competition identified but also any perceived detrimental effects on consumers.

These points can be illustrated by reference to the recent CC investigation of small business banking. I am not here concerned with the merits of the CC's findings and recommendations in this case. Rather, what is of interest is that, first, there is nothing in the EA that would have had a great impact on the way in which that case was conducted. That is, it is perfectly possible to envisage a market investigation reference from the OFT that would have led to a similar investigation and a similar outcome.

Second, whatever the overall merits of the CC's recommendation to constrain business banking tariff structures, it was not a measure that can easily be justified in terms of helping to promote competition.[3] As a number of commentators have argued in relation to the small business banking case, and also more generally, *prima facie* it is to be expected that forcing a reduction in prices will tend to reduce competitive pressures in a market, for example by reducing incentives for entry and expansion, and by reducing options to develop competitive advantage via differentiation in tariff structures. That is, in substituting regulation for competition, the latter is, to at least some degree (which will vary with the case), 'crowded out'.

As I understand it, the rationale for the measure was that price competition was currently weak; that such competition could not be expected to develop very quickly, even taking account of the implementation of other measures recommended by the CC; and that, in the interim and for a specified period, the major banks should be required to reduce charges to small business customers. Now go back 20 years and recall the debate on telecoms pricing around the time of the privatization of British Telecom (BT), particularly the arguments of Michael Beesley and Stephen Littlechild. The market had been partially liberalized (Mercury had been licenced); competition could be expected to develop; it would nevertheless take some time for the impact of that competition to be keenly felt by BT; and, in the interim, there was a case for providing consumers with some degree of protection on prices. Thus was born RPI-X, and my point is simply that the CC recommendation in small business banking is out of the same stable.

Let me carry the comparison further. Regulatory bodies now wishing to change the licence conditions governing price controls (or indeed any licence conditions) will typically conduct a detailed review and propose what they believe are appropriate changes. If those changes are not accepted by the regulated companies, there is, in effect, a right of appeal to the CC, which considers the arguments *on their merits*. The appeal is not to the courts, but it is an opportunity to get a second opinion nevertheless. In contrast, there is no such mechanism available in the case of market investigations. If the companies affected by CC determinations consider that the remedies are too onerous, there is nowhere to turn for a second opinion.

In defence of the new arrangements, it can be argued that the market investigations will at least go through a two-stage process: the issues will be considered by both the OFT and the CC. This is, however, only true up to a point. The OFT responsibility is to make references, not to remedy adverse effects on competition and consumer detriments. Responsibility for the *regulatory* analysis (remedies) falls only to the CC. This can again be compared with licence change in regulated sectors, where the analysis of the remedial action can occur twice (once by the regulatory authority and again by the CC in the absence of acceptance by the relevant company).

To my mind, therefore, the EA creates a new regulatory engine, with potentially wide scope (any market might be referred), less than clear objectives (how are effects on competition and effects on consumers to be weighed in the balance when determining measures to be taken?) and not subject to an effective appeals process (although the scope of judicial review may, gradually, be expanded to fill some of the gap). The irony is that, in matters regulatory, the nearest equivalent we have to competition is a substantive appeal process in which alternative analyses of the effects of proposed remedies can be tested against each other. The EA has failed to embrace such 'competition in assessment' and, in my view, this is a big minus (by virtue of being a missed opportunity, not because the EA has necessarily made matters worse). The arrangements are unlike those in the USA, Australia or Europe, and I do not expect them to be widely copied. I would also hope that a future government will address these matters at some future time.

CRIMINALIZATION

Detailed analysis of the provisions of the EA concerning the criminalization of certain types of cartel behaviour is probably a matter chiefly for lawyers; or at least that is how it appears to an economist taking a first look at the labyrinthine sections of the legislation dealing with the issue. I cannot avoid the matter entirely, however, because there are some general issues that raise fairly immediate economic points:

- Punishment for violations of the law is just one type of incentive system. It might be asked: can the proposed approach be expected to be an effective and efficient incentive/deterrence mechanism?
- All enforcement mechanisms absorb scarce resources. Given the objectives of the OFT, will the new arrangements lead to an efficient allocation of those resources?
- Criminalization is a US import. Does it fit with the rest of the UK system?

These questions are closely related to each other and, as will become clear, I have no very definite answers to them. My position on criminalization is one of agnosticism.

Incentives and Deterrence

Incentives not to offend certainly depend upon the severity of the punishment once caught. In this respect, criminalization should increase the deterrence effect, helping to improve compliance with competition law, *ceteris paribus*.

Again, however, other things are not necessarily equal. Incentives also depend upon the probability of detection (some argue that this is the more important factor), and it cannot just be assumed that this will be unaffected by the EA. Successful cartel hunting depends to a significant degree on defections by cartel members, and incentives to defect are affected by the punishment mechanism. Questions abound at this point. To what extent might the implications of criminalization for the burden of proof (see below, on enforcement resources) be expected to influence incentives to defect? Will more severe punishment lead to tighter, better organized conspiracies? Will the 'right people' (that is, those most responsible for cartelization) be caught and punished? How sensitive are incentives to the particularities of leniency programmes?

Standing back a little from these issues, the popular notion that throwing offenders into jail will have a major deterrent effect seems sometimes to come perilously close to popular sentiment on matters such as capital punishment, and crime more generally. It is probably good politics, but the economics is less certain.

That said, I think it is right that there should be some movement towards individual punishment. Limited liability companies were not created to protect individuals against the risks of being caught engaging in knowingly illegal behaviour. Offenders may currently suffer as a result of CA fines to the extent that their own rewards are geared to company financial performance,[4] but the vagaries of intra-company incentive schemes may mean that this is not a very strong effect. The brunt of financial penalties under the CA is borne by shareholders,[5] and while it may be held that it is shareholders who are ultimately responsible – they appoint the managers – the realities of separation of ownership and control suggest that it is unrealistic to expect such an indirect incentive mechanism (hit shareholders who will then punish managers) to work very effectively.

Criminalization, however, is not the only way of increasing the level of individual punishment: raising civil penalties is an obvious alternative. Offending individuals could be fined or made financially liable, they can be disqualified from acting as directors of companies, and so on. It is not clear to me that the various alternatives to criminalization were fully explored before the relevant decisions were taken, leaving at least a suspicion that political showmanship may have had an undue influence on the outcome.

Enforcement Resources

In general, the higher the penalty the higher it is appropriate to set the burden of proof, because the cost of wrongly convicting the innocent is greater. It is to be expected, therefore, that, as a result of criminalization, there will be some increase in the costs of securing an outcome in the relevant cartel cases: extra resources will be absorbed in the collection and analysis of evidence, and in any subsequent prosecution. The extra resources absorbed include those expended on cases that do not come to fruition, as well as on cases that do. Cartel cases can also be expected to take longer, and there may be costs of delay over and above the immediate outlays directly caused by extended time frames.

There is potential here for a misallocation of enforcement resources. Excessive time and effort might be devoted to a very small number of high-profile, criminal prosecutions, at the expense of less glamorous, more humdrum cases.

Prospects are not brightened by incentive systems in government: agencies and departments are increasingly adept at the public relations (spin?) required to grab media attention, not least to increase their own standing in the government hierarchy, and individual careers can be made on a single high-profile case.

There is, of course, nothing inevitable about such negative eventualities: it will depend upon how the OFT handles its new powers, and we wait to see how it turns out. Perhaps the only piece of advice that I would offer to the Office at this stage is that, in operating the new system, it should strive to ensure that the rate of detection of cartels does not fall.

Does it Fit?

As already stated, criminalization is a US import and is something of a 'bolt-on' to the CA system, which is itself largely an import from the EC. In general, I am in favour of American imports and my chief concern is that, in following this road, the level of import may be too low rather than too high. This is linked to the apparently strong British aversion to judicial supervision (which is second nature across the Atlantic) and a correspondingly strong British inclination to rely on weakly supervised, expert administrative processes that are frequently characterized by relatively muted dialogue/interchange on complex issues (see above). Put in a more elevated way, the European approach tends to rely more heavily on investigative processes, whereas the Americans rely more heavily on adversarial processes. The broad question is: how well will criminalization sit alongside our investigative, administrative system?

More specifically, one of the issues for the UK will be how criminal investigations are to be dovetailed with existing anti-cartel activity under the CA. Will the pursuit of criminal investigations hinder and delay other anti-cartel activities, for example for fear that a criminal prosecution might be prejudiced by those other activities? At a minimum, working with the Serious Fraud Office will create new tasks for the OFT, and it will be a challenge to ensure that such work does not detract from other important tasks.

A related point is that criminalization leads to a requirement that the relevant offences be carefully defined *ex ante*. The focus is, therefore, on the precise form of the behaviour/conduct, rather than on its economic effects. This creates the possibility that conduct of type A may be a criminal offence, conduct of type B may not be a criminal offence, yet, of the two, type B conduct might have significantly greater adverse effects on competition and on consumers.

It is ironic that one of the central arguments for reforming the old restrictive practices legislation, by replacing it with Chapter I of the CA, was that the Restrictive Practices Act embodied a *form-based* approach which was easily manipulated. That is, good legal advice could help find means to achieve equivalent economic effects that did not fall foul of the legislation. The CA approach was seen by many commentators as superior because it concentrated on the thing that really mattered, namely the effect of conduct in terms of the harm done to competition or to consumers.

Yet here we are, four years later, witnessing a significant return to a form-based approach. It is not, of course, a complete reversal (the new legislation is incremental, and it does not substitute directly for the CA) and there are arguments that the form-based approach is appropriate for certain types of behaviour (which should be illegal *per se* irrespective of their actual economic effects). I would, however, suggest that a check for consistency in policy is in order. Are the new proposals vulnerable to any of the more substantive criticisms made, in earlier periods, of the pre-CA restrictive practices legislation? Will, in practice, a form-based approach (more legal, less economic) come to predominate in non-criminal cases? Could we, therefore, end up moving along a path that might, to an outside observer, look just a teeny bit like a circle? Or will the fact that restrictive agreements are not illegal *per se* under Article 81 (or Chapter I of the CA), coupled with EC modernization reforms in relation to the notification of agreements, significantly undermine the prospects for criminal convictions (because the defendants can claim that they honestly thought they were entering into agreement that satisfied the criteria of Article 81(3))?

CONCLUSIONS

On balance, and notwithstanding doubts on some of its features, my view is that the EA represents continued, albeit limited, progress towards better designed competition policy. In particular, the general philosophy of basing policy on institutions that are largely free of detailed, day-to-day political supervision, and that operate with clear, hierarchical (for example competition effects first, consumer effects second) and limited objectives seems to be exactly right. The EA provisions in relation to merger control are the closest fit to this general philosophy. It is an approach that has worked well in the regulated sectors of the economy, although I cannot pass by this comment without saying that it is a pity that government policy towards the regulated sectors seems now to be tending in the reverse direction.

My reservations about the EA are threefold. First, there is a continuing reluctance in Britain to replace (retreating) political supervision of competition law enforcement with judicial supervision of the *substance* of enforcement decisions. Given the complexity of the issues, and not least difficulties surrounding the meaning to be attached to the notion of competition itself, I think that this is a distinct weakness. It is not so much that the EA has made matters worse in this area, rather that a legislative opportunity to make a major advance has been missed.

Second, I believe that market investigations should be viewed as a form of regulation, not as a form of competition policy (at least in the antitrust sense). Given this, it would be preferable to model the institutions and procedures more closely on those of regulators, and to separate them from other aspects of competition policy so as to achieve greater focus in what are, at bottom, different tasks. The provisions for market investigations also appear not to be well directed to the problems whose resolution would yield the greatest payoffs. Restrictions and distortions of competitive processes very frequently occur because some other aspect of public policy is not conducted in ways that achieve government objectives with minimum (feasible) effects on competition. Several examples spring to mind in just one policy area with which I am painfully familiar, the impact of environmental and of health and safety regulation in the energy sector. Billions of pounds can be wasted by regulation that, without in any way better achieving its own objectives, unnecessarily distorts markets. Might it not be a good idea for Derek Morris and his colleagues to be directly asked to address this type of issue? No one else in government seems to be doing so in the methodical and detailed way that is required, and that is characteristic of the best work of the CC.

Third, the framework of competition policy in the UK continues to be lacking in overall coherence. The CA reflects the EC administrative system; criminalization comes from the USA, where adversarial, court-based proceedings play a much more central role; market investigations perpetuate the UK idiosyncrasy of complex monopoly provisions in another guise. Appeals mechanisms are patchy in their operation: there is full appeal on the substance of a case to the CAT for Chapter I and Chapter II cases (and substantive 'appeals' to the CC on licence changes in regulated sectors), but there is only the more limited scope of judicial review in relation to mergers, market investigations and enforcement of licence conditions in regulated sectors (some of which enforcement is very close to CA enforcement).

By way of a final conclusion, my own preference would be for a somewhat different system along the following lines:

- CA arrangements as now;
- merger decisions handled by the OFT, with rights of appeal on procedures and substance to the CAT;
- the CC as an advisory 'Regulatory Commission' focused on 'policy failure', particularly regulation that unnecessarily distorts competition, but which could encompass sins of omission as well as sins of commission;
- the CAT to handle appeals on those decisions of sectoral regulators that affect competition (such as certain forms of licence enforcement, as well as licence change);

- penalties for cartel behaviour imposed on individuals as well as on companies, but (and this much more tentatively) which are civil, rather than criminal, in nature.

NOTES

1. The relevant comparison is, of course, between expected, *future* efficiency gains in the absence of the merger and expected, future gains if the merger goes ahead. The latter may be substantial, but may not necessarily be higher than the former. Indeed, if the merger would reduce competition, one of the effects will likely be to reduce pressures to achieve efficiency gains in the future, in which case efficiency *losses* might properly be attributable to the merger, even though actual efficiency is expected to improve over time.
2. Vertical agreements differ because the economic effects of coordination of *complementary* activities can, in general, be expected to be very different from the economic effects of coordination of *substitutable* activities.
3. This is not to say that constraints on tariff structures can never be justified in terms of promoting competition. For example, depending on circumstances, limiting the allowable degree of price discrimination can sometimes have a pro-competitive effect. The CC recommendation was, however, not targeted specifically at discrimination. The aim seems rather to have been to reduce *average* prices.
4. There are also reputational losses to consider.
5. It is often argued that fines can be passed through to consumers, who thereby suffer doubly from the offence (higher prices as a result of the cartel and higher prices as a result of the fine). In most market circumstances, however, a one-off fixed cost, such as a fine, can be expected to be absorbed by shareholders.

CHAIRMAN'S COMMENTS

Sir Derek Morris

Introduction

With Professor Yarrow being a leading economist in the competition policy arena, and my own background being in economics, and with the Competition Commission (CC) having recently published draft economic guidance on the application of the proposed new competition-based tests in the Enterprise Bill, I had rather contemplated an orgy of competition economics. But, perhaps not surprisingly, George Yarrow's paper is mainly about legal process because, it must be admitted, there is little economics in the Bill itself. I will resist, therefore, the temptation, on this occasion at least, to go off into the economic issues which actually determine 95 per cent of the substance of CC inquiries and instead respond to some of the very interesting points which have been raised.

Process

With regard to a number of the process issues raised, I should first stress that the new regime, the legal framework for the procedures to be adopted and the institutional arrangements are all matters for the government. The CC is not a policy-making body, but must carry out whatever duties are assigned to it, and no more than that. It is therefore in a personal capacity, though as someone who has of course observed the whole debate leading up to the bill, that I say that I am not persuaded that the bill raises procedural problems of the sort described.

The question of whether the right of appeal to the Competition Appeal Tribunal (CAT) should be a full rehearing or judicial review has been discussed at every stage of consultation and debate on the bill. The case for judicial review is that there will have already been a first-stage appraisal by the Office of Fair Trading (OFT), then a determinative second stage investigation by a completely separate institution, namely the CC, which neither can choose which cases to hear, nor has any previous association with the case which might be thought to predispose it in any particular direction. A full rehearing would just substitute another set of judgments for the previous second-stage set. These may or may not be a better judgment. To put the matter this way is in no sense to comment on the quality of the Appeal Tribunal: one could not hope for a more able, expert body or president. The point, rather, is to do with the nature of the problems involved and decisions to be made, which are quintessentially *ex ante* forward-looking judgments about, for example, the effects in the future of a merger. The courts have rightly eschewed what Mr Justice Lightman referred to as engaging in 'prophecies'. That should be left to the second stage determinative body.

What parties want to know, and have a right to expect is: were the judgments made fair and reasonable in the light of the evidence; was a proper process followed which, consistent with reaching a judgment in the time available and with the resources available, allowed the parties the opportunity to present evidence, be heard and be informed of arguments on which the CC sought to rely; did the CC meet but not exceed its legal duties; and were any remedies proportionate to the harm identified? If all these characteristics of a finding apply, which is what judicial review ensures, then the notion that the whole issue must nevertheless be considered a third time and decided a second time has, in my view, little merit.

This proposition immediately raises two questions which I will seek to answer. First, if this is correct, why is there provision for a full rehearing in relation to decisions by the OFT under the 1998 Competition Act? In a sense, this helps to make my point. The 1998 Act very largely operates on an *ex post* basis, that is, certain things are prohibited and the question facing the authorities is whether one or more parties did or did not breach a prohibition. That is, in principle, susceptible of a right answer. One body (the OFT) will have made a decision on that, and I can quite see that, where it has found illegal activity, and imposed fines, a full appeal is reasonable. This is precisely what the CAT was set up to do. But that is a quite different set of circumstances from those that will apply to market and merger inquiries and I do not believe that there is a 'read across'.

Second, why, if this is correct, does the issue keep coming up, even though it is to all intents and purposes now settled? Here I want to go behind the process to what I believe is a major issue of public policy, though rarely seen in these terms. It is, I think, quite understandable that large companies (which tend to be those most likely to face a merger or market inquiry) and their legal advisers would want to establish as many opportunities as possible to avoid a decision by the competition authorities which is adverse to their interests. A full rehearing by the CAT would give three such opportunities, and then the scope for judicial review of the CAT would create a fourth. But this raises a fundamental question of whether that is the right balance as between their interests and those of consumers or other, often much smaller, companies who are likely to experience the adverse consequences if there is an inadequate level of competition in the economy. The whole point of competition policy is to disperse protected positions and to maintain or create intense competitive pressure on companies when they are not subject to it, or where they would avoid it through merger. It is designed to ensure a more level playing field for efficient smaller or newer players and also ensure that the benefits of this feed through to consumers.

The smaller players are rarely heard in the debate. It is noteworthy that there are here present, out of an audience of perhaps 200 or more, no representatives of small or medium-sized businesses and two who have roles in representing consumers (the Chairman of the NCC and, the Director-General of Fair Trading), though there are also a small number from government departments who might come under this heading. So the regular audiences which debate this point may well want ever more checks and balances. But while all the various hoops are being gone through, consumers, if there are competition problems, may well be disadvantaged, and their position is no less legitimate than the one more usually heard.

The inference I draw from this is that, provided the proposed processes are compatible with the ECHR (European Court of Human Rights) (and legal advice indicates that two independent stages of assessment plus judicial review is certainly that), it is a public policy judgment, not a legal matter as to the proper extent of such procedural checks and balances. This is then for the government of the day, and the bill reflects its views. The CC can have no view, but must apply whatever regime is laid down by Parliament. But my personal concern lies quite the other way. It is that a series of changes in or associated with the bill, each of which may be commendable will, nonetheless, in combination make the constraints on action too tight.

The new regime will see detailed guidance being available, case management and tight timetables, provisional findings being published and judicial review to an expert body. Each, as I say, is commendable and I genuinely welcome them. But the CC will, I believe, be almost unique in the world in having to carry out its inquiry functions within such constraints and to such deadlines. The combination of getting evidence, analysing it, holding hearings with all interested parties, familiarizing them with all the main arguments and dealing with the usually voluminous responses, coming to decisions consistent with both the evidence and the guidelines, providing provisional findings and assessing the no doubt equally voluminous responses, establishing determinate, practical, appropriate and proportionate remedies and justifying all of this publicly in detail, with every step subject to judicial review, all in the course, for a normal merger, of four months could be viewed as stacking the process heavily against intervention. Many here may applaud that, but it is not clear that it is in the best interests of promoting a fully competitive economy. No doubt it would all be a lot easier if, like the courts, which face many of the some constraints, the CC could take as long as it needs, but giving the competition authorities much longer is problematic and not at all what business would want.

So I see no legal issue here. Rather there is a public policy issue as to the right balance to be achieved as between the interests of different parties. The settlement presented in the bill is, in my view, far from being pitched too much against the interests of the main parties who are likely to come before the Commission.

Regulation and Banking

I next turn to the argument that the CC's role under the Enterprise Bill is essentially regulatory (though I recognize that this is a grossly simplified summary of a very interesting section in George Yarrow's chapter). I am bound to say, however, that I do not see it that way myself. Clearly if one were to define 'regulatory' as any type of action by a public body then, tautologically, the CC is a regulating body, but this statement then has little if any policy content. A much more meaningful, and indeed very important, distinction is between actions or decisions that, by requiring continuing conformity with specified regulations, directly regulate company activity, and those that may have equally or more far-reaching effects but create no continuing regulation and require no lasting conformity with such rules. A price control is a clear example of the first; prohibition of a merger or divestment of some activities are equally clear examples of the latter. In between lie actions, for example requiring provision of more information, which have elements of regulation but whose main impact is to create more competitive conditions.

On the basis of this, I think quite natural, understanding of the concept of regulation, the CC has for many years preferred and, as its draft guidance makes clear, will in future prefer remedies that are pro-competitive and deregulatory, and which work with the grain and not against the grain of the market. In practice this means a preference for prohibition (in merger cases), divestment, informational remedies or behavioural undertakings which help to free markets, for example on access issues. Consistent with this, the new regime envisages an explicit role for the CC to identify regulatory restrictions which, whatever their prudential role, appear too costly in terms of restrictions on competition, and to make recommendations. The government is committed to responding publicly in 90 days.

In this context it is worth pointing out that regulatory remedies in the sense I have described feature in only five of the last 50 cases where the CC has come to an adverse finding. The role of such remedies is essentially where there is no better, more pro-competitive alternative. In fact, I have a suspicion that any perception of the CC as unduly regulating really reflects its interest rate remedy in the recent SME (small and medium-sized enterprises) banking inquiry, where George Yarrow and I sat across the table from each other and debated, in the most reasonable and convivial manner I hasten to add, just such issues.

So let me say a word about this. Like George Yarrow I will not seek to rehearse the case or debate the substance. Indeed I cannot go beyond merely emphasizing certain points in the published report. As it made clear, the CC first considered pro-competitive remedies, in particular structural ones requiring some degree of divestment. For reasons spelt out in the report they were variously either not appropriate to the detriments found, not practical or not proportionate. We then moved on to a range of pro-competitive behavioural remedies related to such matters as facilitating switching of accounts, provision of various types of information and so on.

We then, like any responsible competition authority, had to answer the question whether those measures would, in our view, be sufficient in any reasonable time scale. The answer to that question, on the evidence presented to us and the merits of the case, was that they would not be sufficient. At that point it would have been quite unacceptable to say that we must never ever use a regulatory remedy, and simply allow a significant part of the detriment to SMEs to continue. And so we added one specific regulatory measure, aimed at precisely the source of the overcharging we had identified, but giving the banks complete flexibility to opt for alternatives which, for example, they had already developed in relation to personal customers. It was an interim measure to be reviewed in the light of progress. The impact was considerably less than the persistent excess profits identified, so that there was no question of this creating a barrier to new entrants provided they were no less efficient (the alternative proposition that seems to underlie at least some objections to the interest rate measure, namely that any level of excessive prices and profits is justified because less would reduce incentives to entry, is clearly false). Equally compelling, if more competition does evolve the measure will have been redundant, which is fine; if not, it will have been essential to remove at least some of the disadvantage experienced by SMEs as a result of inadequate competition.

I very much hope that, in three years' time, no problems will remain. If they do, and further action is necessary, I very much hope, in the circumstances of the day, that purely structural or behavioural remedies will suffice. But if neither is the case, it would be a clear failure of public policy to rule out recourse to further regulatory action just because it is regulatory. The key point of all this that I want to emphasize is that this rather exceptional remedy reflects the facts of the case, not some subterranean proclivity of the CC, still less a sign of a fundamentally regulatory as opposed to competitive regime.

Will such remedies remain rare? I cannot say. The CC's draft preferences are clear in our guidance now out for consultation. Subject to that it will depend entirely on what cases and what sorts of problems are referred to us. All that I would rule out is a situation where structural remedies cannot be pursued because they are impractical or disproportionate; behavioural ones are not strong enough; but regulatory ones are deemed off-limits.

Criminalization

On the topic of criminalization of conduct under the 1998 Competition Act, I was not entirely sure where George ended up. This, I should immediately say, is not a criticism, as his approach was rather to voice some understandable concerns about the new approach, rather than simplistically conclude that it was just good or bad. In the same spirit I have the following observations.

First, as he pointed out, criminalization is not the only individual-based incentive or penalty available. In fact, disqualification as a director is a lesser, but still very significant, penalty included in the new regime, reserving imprisonment for only the most severe infringements. Second, incentives in this context are of course about actively stopping breaches of the prohibition, and a critical part of that incentive structure is, in my view, the leniency programme. The huge incentive on members of a cartel to be first to the OFT is an equally huge incentive not to be in a cartel which exposes you to the threat that someone else will break ranks. To put this another way, without the leniency programme, the probability that the OFT might discover your cartel could be quite small, undermining the fact that the personal penalty if you are caught could be very severe. What the leniency programme may be thought of as doing is massively increasing the subjective probability that you will be found out. This coupled with the severe personal penalty could make for a very effective regime. If the result is a few high-profile cartel cases to highlight the dangers and a leniency programme that highlights the risk of being found out, then that could be a very cost-effective and low-resource way of reducing the number of cartels.

In passing I should add that there is, as George Yarrow pointed out, a potential issue as to how such criminal cases will sit alongside the Competition Act case which relates to the same cartel. I would not belittle this point (it clearly needs considerable thought) but, in the light of the debate on this to date, it does not seem to be insurmountable. There may *ex ante* be no single answer, as it may well depend on the individual circumstances, which element is pursued and, if both, in which order; but I cannot see that the benefits of having provision for both types of penalty – fines on companies and disqualification or imprisonment for individuals – is in any way undermined by this.

So I think criminalization is an idea whose time has come in the UK. Public perception of cartel activity has, I think, changed, just as it did through time in relation to insider dealing. Like cartels, this moved from being the way of the world, to rather distasteful, to illegal. Moreover recent accounting scandals have led many more people to accept that some business conduct is 'criminal' in its everyday sense and should be treated as such. Cartels are now in the same territory. Will criminalization be effective? I can only quote James Griffin, Assistant Attorney-General at the US Department of Justice responsible for enforcement of the antitrust regime, who said that cartel members frequently asked for a larger fine and no prison sentence, but not once in his time at the DoJ did anyone ask for a smaller fine and a longer sentence.

Conclusion

George Yarrow characterized UK competitive policy as like a jackdaw, stealing Chapters I and II of the 1998 Competition Act from Europe, the Substantial Lessening of Competition test and criminalization from the USA and, one might add, including a purely home-grown market inquiries provision derived from the monopoly provisions of the 1973 Fair Trading Act. I think that is probably right. Where we may disagree is whether that is a bad thing. No system is perfect. Absorbing what appears to be the best of the rest is probably not an unsound benchmark for action in any walk of life, and certainly not if the alternatives are to copy just one other system, warts and all, or completely plough one's own furrow.

I would, for example, suggest that the proposed UK regime and all the changes associated with it will provide a more robust merger regime than that in Europe in terms of both analyses and procedure, but without the immensely time and resource-consuming procedures based on the courts in the USA. In similar vein there is every prospect that US-style criminalization will make the UK's domestic version of Articles 81 and 82 more, rather than less, effective. And market inquiries fill what many consider to be a gap in both regimes.

So, sadly, I never got to the economics, to some interesting and sometimes quite tricky issues: what different types of competition exist and should be recognized in the regime; is the so-called 'efficiency defence' in mergers valid; how to assess non-collusive but nonetheless coordinated or uncompetitive behaviour in oligopolies; how can competition be weighed up against consumer benefits where they are not synonymous; what is the role of profitability in a merger or market inquiry and how should it be measured; is SLC preferable to collective dominance as a competition-based test and, if so, why; is the so-called 'portfolio theory effect' valid; do economists adopt unrealistic benchmarks for what competition is or how it occurs? And so on.

I refer to these not just because my own background is an economic one. There is a danger of economists 'nodding through' all manner of concepts to do with competition because those concepts are boringly familiar to them, while lawyers understandably focus on the legislative structure and procedural matters, so that no real debate surfaces on the economics until it is, in a sense, too late. I hope that the issuing of the CC's draft guidance for consultation will avoid this, and look forward to reviewing the responses to it.

4. Ofcom and light touch regulation

Martin Cave

The Communication Bill, published in November 2002, imposes duties on Ofcom to review regulatory burdens:

> (1) Ofcom shall keep the carrying out of their functions under review with a view to securing that regulation by Ofcom does not involve –
> (a)   the imposition of burdens which are unnecessary; or
> (b)   the maintenance of burdens which become unnecessary.
> (2) Ofcom shall, from time to time, publish a statement setting out how they propose during the period for which the statement is made to secure that regulation by Ofcom does not involve the imposition or maintenance of unnecessary burdens. (Clause 6)

In the draft bill, this state of affairs was described as 'light touch regulation', but the Joint Parliamentary Scrutiny Committee found this formulation inappropriate. In my view, the phrasing is largely a matter of taste, provided that the underlying notion is accepted that regulatory intervention should be restricted to cases where it yields a positive return *vis-à-vis* the relevant fall-back – reliance on competition law.

The key question, therefore, is how light can light be? A question of this kind cannot be answered in the abstract, but is addressed here, in four dimensions. The first three relate to telecommunications, pay-TV and public service broadcasting. In practice they deal with the regulation of three firms, BT, BSkyB and the BBC. The fourth dimension, however, is more speculative, since it concerns the new *modus operandi* for the allocation of spectrum, a significant input for each of the three firms or organizations noted above.

Each of the three firms or organizations to be considered is operating largely in isolation from the others' markets, despite a limited amount of cooperation between the BBC and Sky in Freeview, and between BT and BSkyB, to counteract the 'double play' of the cable companies in providing telephony and entertainment. Thus BT, BSkyB and the BBC largely remain in their own silos. They share among them, however, the common characteristic that the collapse of the TMT bubble has had a major effect on their competitive positions. Three years ago BT was competing with alternative carriers which had good access to the capital markets. Many of them are now bankrupt or weakened, although their physical assets survive. The multitude of operators queuing up to unbundle BT's local loops has also evaporated. BSkyB has clearly gained in financial strength *vis-à-vis* the cable companies, and has seen off the threat of ITV Digital. The BBC has benefited from a generous licence fee settlement in a period where its advertiser-supported competitors have experienced substantial, and possibly enduring, declines in real income. There is little doubt that this environment has had a major influence on the nature of the competitive constraints imposed upon the largest firms in the electronic communications industry, depriving Ofcom of early opportunities to relax regulation.

REGULATING BT

Several months before Ofcom was due to come into operation, the world of European communications regulation was turned upside down by the coming into effect in July 2003 of the new electronic communications services directives.[1] Although this will have a smaller effect in the UK than elsewhere, because OFTEL has for many years past been attempting to rebase its regulatory interventions on the principles of competition law, the new arrangements will impose additional disciplines and restrictions.

At one level, the new regime is a major step down the transition path from monopoly to normal competition, governed exclusively by generic competition law.[2] Its provisions are applied across the range of 'electronic communications services', ignoring pre-convergence distinctions. It represents an ingenious attempt to corral the NRAs (national regulatory authorities) down the path of normalization, allowing them, however, to proceed at their own speed (but within the uniform framework necessary for the internal market). Since the end state is one governed by competition law, the current rather arbitrary and piecemeal approach will give way to something consistent with that law. However competition law is to be applied (in certain markets) not in a responsive *ex post* fashion, but in a pre-emptive *ex ante* form.

According to the underlying logic, a list of markets where *ex ante* regulation is permissible is first established, the markets being defined according to normal competition law principles. These relevant markets are analysed with the aim of identifying dominance or significant market power (SMP) – the terms are used interchangeably – on a forward-looking basis. Where dominance is found, the choice of an appropriate remedy can be made from a specified list, or an additional remedy can be introduced with the European Commission's approval.[3]

The Commission is issuing a recommendation on the definition of relevant markets, defined broadly in the manner of competition policy. Member states can also add or subtract markets, using specified (and quite complex) procedures.[4] The markets for *ex ante* regulation are chosen according to the cumulative criteria of (a) persistent barriers to entry, (b) dynamic aspects (referring to the elimination of barriers or to the existence of adequate competition behind them), (c) the comparative efficiency of *ex ante* versus *ex post* regulation. The relevant markets are largely wholesale, and broadly match areas where OFTEL currently intervenes. This reflects an underlying hypothesis that, provided access can be guaranteed to wholesale or network markets, retail markets, where entry is easier, can be deregulated.

Under the new arrangements, intervention can occur in relevant markets only where *dominance* (single, joint or vertically leveraged) is found. Article 14 of the Framework Directive contains a prohibition on intervention in markets that are effectively competitive, implicitly defining markets where dominance is absent as effectively competitive. The effect of this is to create a series of market-by-market 'sunset clauses' which come into operation as the scope of effective competition expands. This is a change of fundamental deregulatory significance, and a major step along the route towards convergence with competition law.

Under the directives, NRAs will have the power to impose *remedies or obligations* on firms found to enjoy significant market power in a relevant market. In the case of wholesale access or interconnection markets, the obligations are, in ascending order of rigour: transparency, non-discrimination, separate accounting, mandatory access and cost-oriented pricing. The NRAs will act within a framework of duties set out in Article 8 of the Framework Directive.[5] The measures they take shall be proportionate to the policy objectives identified. This can be construed as meaning that the intervention is appropriate, no more than is necessary and, by implication, satisfies a cost–benefit test, in the sense that the expected benefits from the intervention exceed the expected costs. Article 8 additionally specifies policy objectives, which determine the weights appropriate for use in the cost–benefit analysis. For example, Article 8(2) requires NRAs to promote competition for electronic communications networks and services by maximizing users' choice and value for money, eliminating distortions or restrictions to competition and encouraging efficient investment in infrastructure.

The scope for choosing remedies will be largely at Ofcom's discretion. Most of the remedies will be applied to network or wholesale markets within the context of concerns about the vertical leveraging of market power. This is explicitly stated in the recommendation and is implicit in the Commission's list of markets, which are predominantly wholesale rather than retail markets. Price caps can be employed for retail markets, but (as noted above) lightness of touch may imply withdrawal from retail price control.

This process is illustrated, in a cautious fashion, by OFTEL's recent decision on the control of BT's retail prices, which came into effect in August 2002.[6] In 1997, retail price control was focused upon residential subscribers, excluding those with the largest bills. In 2002, OFTEL chose to turn the price control into a constant nominal price regime, subject to BT's agreement to provide a new wholesale line rental product, which would encourage consumer switching. If the product is taken up by service providers, the retail price cap will switch to a constant real price (RPI-0) 'safeguard' control.

The process described above illustrates the potential for exit from retail regulation. A new wholesale product comes into existence which has the potential to make retail price control redundant. A mechanism is maintained in case the new competitive pressures fail to work. BT has the potential to benefit, as do its competitors, as do consumers. This is a kind of higher-level incentive regulation, in which the various parties are given an incentive to avoid regulation entirely.

It is difficult, however, to achieve the same effect further up the supply chain. Here the conflict between the vertically integrated controller of a dominant network and its downstream competitors is much more stark. Regulation, or its relaxation, is virtually a zero sum gain for BT and its competitors. It is helpful to examine what options are in relation to access to BT's network facilities available under the directives.

The Access Directive contains two such remedies.[7] In essence, one mandates access while the other mandates access at cost-oriented prices. The two remedies are as follows:

> Article 12 of the Access Directive: *Obligations meet reasonable requests for access to, and use of specific network facilities. An NRA may impose obligations on operators to grant access to specific facilities or services, including in situations when the denial of access would hinder the emergence of a competitive retail market, or would not be in the end user's interests.*

This represents an obligation to be implemented in circumstances similar to, but significantly broader than, those in which the essential facilities doctrine is applied under competition law. The extension of the test lies in the replacement of the precondition under competition law for mandatory access, that the asset is essential and cannot be replicated, by a much broader condition that NRAs can mandate access in circumstances where its denial 'would hinder the emergence of a sustainable competitive market at the retail level, or would not be in the end-user's interest'. There is a risk that the last phrase in particular might open the door for extensive regulatory intervention.

The obligation is silent about the pricing of such access, except to the extent that it prohibits 'unreasonable terms and conditions' having a similar effect to denial of access. The range of pricing principles may therefore encompass 'retail minus'.[8]

> Article 13 of the Access Directive: *Price control and cost accounting obligations. This deals with situations where a potential lack of competition means that the operator*

concerned might be capable of sustaining prices at an excessive level, or applying a price squeeze, to the detriment of end users. National regulators should take into account the investment made by the operator and the risks involved.

The circumstances identified as appropriate for the application of this rule are 'situations where a market analysis indicates that a potential lack of effective competition means that the operator concerned might be capable of sustaining prices at an excessively high level, or applying a price squeeze to the detriment of end users'. There is, however, a major distinction between these two cases. In the case of excessive pricing, the question is whether SMP is being exploited directly through an excessive price and the natural remedy is cost-oriented pricing. In the case of a margin squeeze, the hypothesis is that the operator with SMP is foreclosing competition in a vertically related area by setting a margin that fails to cover costs. Cost-oriented pricing for interconnection or access to customers should only be considered when dealing with an operator with SMP which is both persistent and incapable of being dealt with by other remedies. A classic case for its application might therefore be access to the local loop, either for call termination or for the purposes of leasing unbundled loops – provided that one operator enjoys a monopoly or position of dominance in the relevant geographical area. Even here the impact on incentives for infrastructure investment by competitors must be taken into account.

OFTEL has already issued guidelines on imposing access obligations under the new regime.[9] These discuss the circumstances in which different pricing remedies might be applied. Key points are (para 3.24):

> in markets with SMP and little prospect of competition developing, it is generally appropriate to set cost-based prices;
> in markets with SMP but where market power is diminishing, it may be sufficient to rely on the imposition of a general non-discrimination obligation implemented principle or by directing that prices should be set at 'retail minus'. This ensures that an operator with SMP cannot impose a margin squeeze on its competitors;
> where new services are being introduced, even by an SMP operator with substantial market share, cost-based regulation should normally be avoided. Price control could deter investment and discourage innovative market offerings.

On the other hand, where the innovative product in question is a wholesale product, OFTEL considers that competitors should have access to it. This is based on the view that, provided that the wholesale pricing regime is, for example, retail minus, the incentives to invest and innovate will still be there (para A4.5–6).

These proposals look fairly sensible: cost-oriented prices are set only for durable bottlenecks; other dominant wholesale positions are dealt with via an obligation to supply and a non-discrimination requirement. However there is no mistaking the regulatory burden that is imposed. Ofcom will be continually arbitrating among the categories of cost-plus, retail minus and no mandatory access. Moreover, it is – sadly – not the case that, once the regulator has decided to determine a cost-based price, or to investigate discrimination, the exercise is simple and straightforward.[10]

In the first place, many wholesale services are produced under conditions of increasing returns to scale, so that simple average cost pricing does not, in practice, place the vertically integrated retail affiliate and its competitor on equivalent terms: the former will be responding to marginal cost, the latter to a price equal to the (higher) average cost. This can be resolved in some cases through capacity charging, but it is complicated.

Second, many wholesale services have complex cost drivers, so that the process of establishing cost-based prices is controversial. Third, price is only one dimension of enforcement of non-discrimination. Other patterns of discriminatory access include delay, quality degradation and failure to provide equality of access to information: the breakdown of supposed 'Chinese walls' which separate wholesale and retail in the integrated firm.

These problems are illustrated only too clearly by OFTEL's recent history of regulatory interventions, or decisions not to intervene. The sad history of local loop unbundling is the most obvious case: 40 or so consultations, statements and determinations issued by OFTEL over a three-year period, and scarcely more than 1000 unbundled loops. This leaves a distinct impression that BT has got away with it. The second example is complaints involving the relationship between the retail and the wholesale price, and the availability, first of BT's Internet access products and latterly its broadband products. These lengthy disputes have taken place against a highly charged policy atmosphere, which has complicated matters further.

What is the way forward with such access disputes? The cleanest way of dealing with them is via vertical separation: the LoopCo or NetCo options about which BT's competitors are so enthusiastic.[11] But the alleged analogy between the successful separation between gas pipeline and gas retailing activities and the separation of the loop, usually mustered in support of the break-up of BT, is not persuasive. The local loop is not a natural monopoly. The boundary between the loop and the core network in telecommunications is such a moveable feast that a break-up would jeopardize network innovation. There is also the little matter of how, legally, it would be achieved. Fortunately, neither governments nor regulators have the power to enforce separation without good reasons and a lot of due process. Nor is it straightforward under the new regime to make a company separate 'voluntarily' through overzealous regulatory action.

Without vertical separation, what does the future hold? Given that the interests of BT and of its competitors are irreconcilable in relation to vertical issues, unless Ofcom interprets a light touch as quitting the battlefield, a medium term future of continuing intervention is unavoidable. It can be mitigated by better and speedier processes, which the new regime requires. It may also be possible further to limit interventions in marginal cases, especially where innovation is involved. But the only obvious salvation is the alternative network providers whose arrival has recently been delayed by the recession, even though it might, possibly, be speeded up by liberalization of spectrum. On this footing, the medium-term future seems to hold, unavoidably, the prospect of considerable regulatory grappling between Ofcom and BT.

REGULATING BSKYB

BSkyB has, virtually single-handedly, achieved an historic transformation of broadcasting in the UK over the past 15 years. It did so by a willingness to make immense risky investments in a new platform and in the acquisition and packaging of content, decisions which turned out to be spectacularly right. Nor did the story end with analogue. The transfer of the subscriber base to digital and its subsequent massive expansion represented a second successful, and by no means risk-free, phase. The collapse of ITV Digital and its replacement by a non-pay service, Freeview, has removed an obstacle in BSkyB's path. The financial weakness of NTL and TeleWest also places BSkyB in an extremely strong position in the medium term.

I shall discuss two respects in which Ofcom is likely to interact with the pay broadcasting system, and particularly with BSkyB. These are through the use of competition powers in relation to the various content markets associated with pay television and through the regulation of conditional access systems and associated services. Content is, by construction, excluded from the scope of the new European regulatory arrangements outlined above. The principal relevant legislation is therefore the Competition Act 1998. Following passage of the Communications Act in 2003, however, it will fall to Ofcom to implement the earlier Act.

Concerns that BSkyB might be in a position to abuse its power in a variety of pay-TV-related markets have been current since the mid-1990s, when the company in essence changed from being a loss-making start-up to a dominant cash-generating player. The Office of Fair Trading conducted an investigation into BSkyB's position in the wholesale market for programmes in the mid-1990s.[12] This was followed by an unsuccessful attempt to attack arrangements for the collective sale of Premier League rights to BSkyB and the BBC under the now defunct Restrictive Trade Practices Act. The Office of Fair Trading has recently completed an investigation under the Competition Act 1998.

The scope of that investigation is shown in the OFT press notice which announced that the OFT proposed to make a decision that BSkyB had behaved anti-competitively, infringing UK competition law.[13] The conduct impugned was described as follows:

> BSkyB's margin between the wholesale price it charges distributors and the retail price paid by its own subscribers may not be wide enough to allow a normal profit to be made by a third party distributor of its premium channels, even if it is as efficient as BSkyB in distributing;
> the discounts BSkyB gives distributors when they take packages of premium channels may be set at a level that prevents rival premium channel providers from entering the market;
> the discounts that BSkyB offers to distributors on one version of its rate card for its premium sports and film channels (i.e., the 'Pay-to-Basic' version) may prevent rival premium channel providers from entering the market and may distort distributors' marketing decisions.

The list above shows that themes similar to those examined in the earlier OFT review were resurfacing, and it is therefore possible to say something about the complexity of the issues at stake.

The first course of conduct – an alleged margin squeeze between wholesale programme prices, where the OFT found that BSkyB has a dominant position, and retail charges, where there are competing suppliers – falls in well-worked competition law ground; as noted above, similar allegations have been made in relation to BT. However, if the conceptual framework of a margin squeeze analysis is fairly well established, its implementation in practice, except in the case of simple commodities, is extremely difficult. Problems arise in separating the costs of delivering wholesale and delivering retail services. Suppose, for example, that the same transponder that delivers programmes to households at retail also supplies cable head-ends at wholesale. It may also be argued that some marketing costs are generic to all pay-TV platforms (that is, wholesale), while others are promoting a single retail service (Sky).

The other conduct referred to in the press notice relates to discounts at the wholesale level. The fundamental competition policy issue here is that discounts for packages (by comparison with paying the sum of the prices of the individual services sold separately) are a form of bundling. Such bundling can be an efficient method of rent extraction, or it can be a means of foreclosing entry into the market. The numerical example below relates to retail pay-TV markets, but reads back to wholesale markets as well.[14]

Suppose there are three equal size groups of pay-TV subscribers, and two channels A (sports) and B (movies). The reservation prices of type A subscribers for the two services are 6,6; those of type B are 10,2 and those of type C 2,10. Note the important negative correlation of preferences between B and C, on which a lot depends. I suppose that the marginal cost of supplying a subscriber with either channel is zero.

Without bundling, the best the operator can do is to charge six per channel and sell one channel to types B and C, and two channels to type A. With bundling, however, the operator could profitably adopt either a pure bundling strategy, a sole offering of both channels for 12, selling to all subscribers; or a mixed bundling strategy, in which one channel can be purchased for 10 and two for 12. What the bundling has done (and here the negative correlation of tastes is of fundamental importance) is to flatten (in this case make horizontal) the demand curve for the two channels combined.[15] There is therefore no exclusion through price, and the operator captures all the consumer surplus. This may generate a competition problem if the pricing is excessive, but if the fixed costs of providing the service are high, the total revenue might be only just enough to cover it, leaving an outcome which is both efficient and which avoids excessive profits.

Bundling has a darker side, however, as a means of sustaining or creating market power. Complementarity in demand creates opportunities for an operator capable of providing a range of services to use bundling to foreclose entry by a competitor which faces difficulties in supplying the whole range. Such a competitor may have to incur extra entry costs by acquiring expertise in an unfamiliar area. Alternatively it may have to form an alliance with another firm which already has that expertise. If the inputs (such as programming rights) which are necessary to make a challenge across the board come up in a staggered rather than a synchronized form, entry may impose extra costs.

This leaves open the possibility that, post entry, the previous incumbent might no longer find the bundling strategy profitable. This might arise because, faced with a single service competitor, the incumbent was forced to unbundle its service and compete on a channel-by-channel basis. If it can be shown that this would happen, pre-entry conduct would not be relevant to predicting the exclusionary effect.

The purpose of the above discussion has been to illustrate the difficulty of applying competition law to a business which is vertically integrated, has a complex cost structure (as illustrated below, in the discussion of conditional access systems) and equally complex complementarity and network effects on the demand side. Blatant infringements can be identified and punished easily. More complex cases are much more difficult to resolve.

In December 2002, the OFT announced its conclusion that BSkyB was not in breach of competition law; it was dominant in markets for the wholesale supply of certain premium sports and film channels; evidence of a margin squeeze was on the borderline and there were insufficient grounds for finding that BSkyB has abused a dominant position in respect of the mixed bundling of its channels.[16] In many ways, this outcome is not surprising. One would not expect a sophisticated firm like BSkyB to breach competition legislation in a blatant way. Equally one would expect a profit-maximizing firm with market power to push up into the territory on the borderline between abusive and non-abusive behaviour. Attention may now refocus on structural remedies upstream, as the European Commission is undertaking an investigation of the collective selling of football rights by the UK Premier League.[17]

I now turn to a regulatory matter affecting pay-TV: the provision of conditional access and related services. These are covered by the new directives. The Commission's recommendation on relevant markets identifies one market as suitable for *ex ante* regulation: broadcasting transmission services and distribution in so far as they provide the means to deliver broadcast content to end users.

The situation with respect to the wholesale market for ancillary technical broadcasting services (including conditional access services) is complex because digital conditional access systems are subject to *ex ante* regulation under the Advanced Television Services Directive. In the UK it is OFTEL which implements that directive. Under the new arrangements, member states have the choice either of sticking to the old regime, under which all digital conditional access services are regulated, or of applying the new regime which, for *ex ante* regulation to be applied, requires the finding of dominance. In the latter case, a separate market might exist for each platform, thus replicating the current arrangements.

Because cable systems in the UK are closed networks, the issue of mandatory access to their facilities does not arise. It does, however, arise in relation to the facilities made available by SSSL, a wholly-owned subsidiary of BSkyB, which provides conditional access and related services to BSkyB (covering channels such as Sky News and Sky Sport and non-Sky channels included as part of Sky packages) and to other customers such as the free-to-air broadcasters.

The directive requires that prices for conditional access services be fair, reasonable and non-discriminatory. The problem, however, is how to interpret these words. One interpretation which OFTEL has firmly rejected is an ingenious implementation of the efficient component pricing rule. According to the latter, the user of a service should pay the incremental costs which it imposes, plus an opportunity cost equal to the loss of downstream profit incurred by the supplier of the service, based on the margins which it loses on business which competitors take from it. If significant 'business stealing' of this kind occurs, this figure may be large. If it has no impact, the opportunity cost is zero. If, however, the advent of the new service brings more downstream business to the access provider (because it makes the package more desirable) then the opportunity cost is negative and price should be less than incremental costs.

Instead OFTEL's approach starts with incremental costs and then permits mark-ups based upon a variety of demand-side considerations.[18] In fact, the cost structure of conditional access systems is rather complex. The fundamental components of costs are the set-up costs required to install the system and operating costs necessary to maintain it. The fixed costs include development or purchase of the intellectual property rights upon which the CAS operates, and the purchase of capital equipment necessary to encrypt the signals and provide the other services. Operating costs include the maintenance and operation of the systems and the replacement of the smart cards upon which security relies. Some of these costs are driven by the number of subscribers, some by the number of channels available to each subscriber, while others are independent of either. An additional possible cost is the subsidy to set-top boxes necessary to bring subscribers onto the platform. Also some general advertising expenditure may be directed at the provision of digital satellite services in general. The upshot is that incremental or attributable costs represent a relatively small proportion of total costs. The allocation of the mark-up is therefore critical.

In its May 2002 statement, augmented by subsequent guidelines,[19] OFTEL announced its decision to maintain the then current system under which it did not set *ex ante* prices for services but instead enunciated a number of principles which it would use to establish whether the requirements of fair, reasonable and non-discriminatory pricing had been achieved. Negotiations would then take place in the shadow of these principles with the safety net of a complaint to OFTEL in case they fail. In summary, in OFTEL's view, 'fair and reasonable charges ... should take account of the willingness to pay of the access seeker ... OFTEL would expect to see close linkage to willingness to pay for conditional access services and expected retail revenues from selling subscription services... It is unlikely to be fair and reasonable for subscription funded retail packages of significantly different retail price to the end user to be charged a similar price for conditional access. Public service broadcasters should expect to make a reasonable contribution to the cost of provision of conditional access services which are common to all purchasers of those services' (para. S9-11).

It is clear that a considerable range of negotiated agreements could satisfy these principles. Access prices are therefore likely to be subject to continuing controversy, despite OFTEL's rejection of a complaint by ITV that it was being overcharged for conditional access.[20]

REGULATING THE BBC

There has been much debate about how much control Ofcom should have over the BBC. Here I am concerned, not with the regulation of the BBC's public service broadcasting content, but with decisions about how far the corporation should extend its activities and their competitive consequences. The key issue for the government is how best to achieve its own objectives of developing the BBC's capacity as a public service broadcaster and promoting a competitive broadcasting sector.[21]

It is helpful, first, to address the question of whether a public broadcaster such as the BBC is likely to have the motive to behave in an anti-competitive way. At first sight, it may seem that an organization not subject to the profit motive may lack the incentive to behave in a way which distorts competition, but might instead act as a countervailing force to anti-competitive conduct by other firms. But if the public firm's objective is not to maximize profit but output, it is likely to behave more aggressively than an otherwise equivalent investor-owned firm in excluding its competitors from markets or weakening their ability to compete. Such a firm may be prepared to expend resources to eliminate or weaken a competitor, without the expectation of long-run positive returns. If, moreover, the expansion of activities is subsequently validated through a higher licence fee, the incentives to expand are even stronger.

The most important provisions of the regulatory regime, which will apply to the BBC, are defined outside the Communications Bill in a new agreement between the BBC and the secretary of state for culture, media and sport. But the draft Agreement is as silent on the meaning of public service broadcasting (PSB) as the draft bill itself. The absence of a satisfactory definition is a clear impediment to the development of a fully justified view of the appropriate arena for use of the licence fee. Although the definition of PSB is ultimately a political decision of government, some safeguards are practicable and desirable, particularly relating to the expansion of the BBC's activity into new areas.

The approvals process for new BBC public services was revisited as part of the 1999 licence fee settlement and two major changes were made. Previously consent for a new service could be granted by the secretary of state immediately following approval by the BBC Board of Governors. Under the revised arrangements, the proposals are subject to public consultation, and there is an obligation on the BBC to persuade the secretary of state that the proposed service would not have a significantly adverse impact on the market. The latter constraint is the reason that the secretary of state withheld consent on two occasions for BBC 3, when approval was given to other new digital TV and digital radio services. Consents granted by the secretary of state are based largely on general principles covering what the service will include. They are typically very broad in scope and allow the BBC considerable flexibility to introduce revisions and enhancements under the umbrella of the consent, bypassing the formal consultation process. For example, the BBC has recently introduced an Internet search engine as part of the public service BBC Online. Although this 'new' service may be covered by the existing consent, it is unlikely to have been considered when the consent for BBC Online was granted in 1997.

Educational publishers and IT suppliers are taking action against the BBC's launch of an extensive Internet-based curriculum support service, aimed at teachers and pupils, using £150 million of licence funds, which was given approval (subject to conditions) by the government in early 2003. While the

BBC is arguing that its digital curriculum service will only cover a subset of subjects, the publishers allege that this will cost the UK publishing market £400 million and force a number of the BBC's rivals out of the market, reducing competition in an educationally and economically important sector.

To deal with these issues it is desirable that:

- the government specify in more detail the criteria to be applied in determining whether the BBC should be allowed to undertake an activity;
- the BBC's Agreement be constructed in a way which gives a firmer steer in relation to the range of BBC activities for the full duration of the Agreement; in other words, it should be more forward-looking and less subject to amendment in the course of its life;
- the existing practice of giving umbrella authorizations be abandoned;
- in the case of a material change in the scope of the BBC's licence fee-financed activities, Ofcom prepare for the secretary of state a report indicating the likely impact on existing and potential competitive suppliers of the BBC's entry into a field of activity.

Turning to the linkage between the BBC's commercial and its PSB activities, there are several areas that create tensions. In exploitation of intellectual property, BBC Worldwide may receive preferential treatment in the licencing of BBC programmes for overseas exploitation. In relation to production facilities, concerns arise about the BBC's relationship with its subsidiaries, which supply it with production facilities (such as studios, outside broadcasting units, IT support and playout services). By incorporating commercial subsidiaries, the BBC can change the structure of the market. For example, the incorporation of BBC Broadcast has created a firm with significant presence in the markets for playout, access services and creative services.

The trailing of commercial products on air is a valuable means of advertising to audiences the availability of magazines, books, videos and other products that support particular programmes. Although the BBC does not sell its airtime for advertising, it does make airtime available for the promotion of commercial products, according to undertakings given to the OFT in 1990. Finally, there is the public service/commercial split of fixed production costs. Where the BBC is sharing costs between public service and commercial channels, the issue of cost allocation is an important one, as inappropriate allocation could amount to a subsidy of the commercial service.

Issues of this type have been raised in a speech by the Director General of Fair Trading (DGFT) who remarked that 'the increasing tendency of the BBC to launch services or markets beyond its traditional public service remit ... could raise difficult competition issues'.[22] The Bill makes it clear that Ofcom will play a role in policing the boundary between the BBC's public service and commercial activities. It will need to build up the expertise to do so.

SPECTRUM

This final section deals with an aspect of activity which Ofcom should find more innovative and invigorating. The Communications Bill, as well as giving Ofcom responsibility for frequency management (subject to a degree of ministerial direction), creates the opportunity for the development of secondary trading in spectrum. This has been provided for under European law since the new regulatory arrangements came into force in July 2003.

Secondary spectrum markets were a major component of the independent review of spectrum which was published in March 2002, to which the government has responded.[23] This was scarcely an original or an unexpected proposal. The UK government, like governments elsewhere, had experimented with primary offerings of spectrum through auctions, but in a very restricted format: in the UK at least, the lots were prespecified; the licences could not be applied to a use other than that specified; they could not be traded within the terms of licence; in the case of the third generation website auction, an undertaking was given that no additional spectrum would be released or licenced to provide the same services for a specified number of years.

Many people now believe that these restrictions contributed to the unexpectedly high price for the third generation website licences and, arguably, to the unexpectedly low price of the broadband wireless licences subsequently auctioned. In the former case, the exclusivity of the licences was seen as a means of generating or maintaining rents. In the latter case, the restriction of the licence to a particular untried purpose may have discouraged bidders. Clearly both of these dangers would be mitigated by a combination of reducing restrictions on use and permitting secondary trading.

The Radiocommunications Agency (RA) recently completed a consultation on spectrum trading.[24] It identified four modes of spectrum trading. Under mode 1, there is a change of ownership only; under mode 2, there is a change of ownership accompanied by some partition or aggregation of the spectrum, but the use of the spectrum remains unchanged; under mode 4 there is a change of ownership and change of use; while under mode 3 ownership changes, and the spectrum is reconfigured.

The consultation document sought comments on a possible sequencing of spectrum trading. The agency put forward the possibility that, in the first wave, change of ownership (mode 1) would apply to all licence sectors and licence classes, while mode 2 (including reconfiguration) or mode 3 in some cases (including reconfiguration and change of use) would apply to the following licence sectors: public wireless networks, broadband fixed wireless access, private business systems and terrestrial fixed links. An exception would be made for 3G licences, where the government is currently minded not to introduce trading until three years after the first substantive launch of a service in the UK. A second phase could incorporate trading in spectrum for broadcasting, programme making and special events, and for aeronautical and maritime purposes. For the purposes of the consultation, it was suggested that some forms of trading might be implemented by the end of 2004, the second wave following on thereafter.

This timetable is acceptable, but should not be delayed. Much work has to be done in defining the rights associated with particular licences. The key issues are how to set the duration of licences, an interesting policy issue requiring a balance between efficiency and the possible generation of windfall gains for existing licensees, and the much more technically complex question of how to define interference rights and responsibilities, especially in a context in which what is licenced is not, as at present, apparatus in a particular location for a particular use, but access to spectrum over a particular area for a number of possible uses.

If the UK manages to meet the target of spectrum trading by 2004, it should still have a significant lead over most other countries in the development of the new technologies which might be unleashed by liberalizing spectrum markets. While it is true that, in prime spectrum ranges, international obligations will continue to impose major restrictions, there should be more scope for innovation in higher frequencies.

There are also important developments overseas. In the United States, a Spectrum Policy Task Force has produced a report to the Federal Communications Commission (FCC), proposing a combination of market-based and open-access approaches, with limited use of the now dominant 'command and control' approach.[25] Simultaneously, a paper by FCC staff members proposed a mechanism for a rapid transition to market allocation of spectrum, by creating incentives to participate in the market process.[26]

Ofcom should consider utilizing some of these new ideas. One such is the emergence of band managers which acquire spectrum through an auction process (provided that the auction does not confer market power) and then distribute it to 'retail' customers. More generally, thought has to be given to the way to ensure that spectrum markets are thick enough and liquid enough to permit effective trading.

CONCLUSIONS

When Trotsky was appointed Commissar for Foreign Affairs of the first Soviet Government in 1918, he said: 'I shall just issue a few revolutionary proclamations and shut up shop.'[27] That did not happen. Nor, in my opinion, will the equivalent strategy work for Ofcom. I have identified by illustration a number of areas of economic regulation where some kind of intervention is likely or inevitable. Because of the strong position in their respective marketplace of BT, BSkyB and the BBC, the account has focused on these three companies. In summary:

- there are reasonable prospects for deregulating BT's retail activities, but it seems certain that *ex ante* regulatory oversight of some of its network or wholesale activities would be a feature of life in the medium term. There is no obvious alternative to imposing access obligations and policing margin squeezes. Apart from the important issue of the speed and organization of intervention, the key margin of lightness of touch may be the type of access pricing imposed;
- BSkyB is in as strong a position as ever in a number of pay broadcast markets. Greater regulatory certainty in the pricing of conditional access service is desirable, but it is right that alleged content market abuses should be dealt with through competition law;
- the licence fee system places the BBC in a highly advantageous position, and it is important that that should not avoidably distort competition elsewhere. Various measures have been suggested which Ofcom could take to reduce this danger.

Finally, I have identified a new frontier where Ofcom's initiative could open up markets and liberate the country's productive potential.

It is ironic that, having initially endorsed light touch regulation, I have forecast continuing complex regulatory interventions in relation to BT and BSkyB, and proposed two extensions to Ofcom's work, in relation to the BBC and to spectrum trading. The principal saving grace is that all these interventions are increasingly falling within a single intellectual framework, that of competition law, and that the days of *ad hoc* intervention are numbered. This does not make it easy, but at least it is (or should be) consistent.

NOTES

1. These directives will be transposed in the forthcoming Communications Act. Note that content markets are excluded from these provisions.
2. For a brief review, see M. Cave, 'Economic Aspects of the New Regulatory Regime for Electronic Communication Services' at http://users.wbs.warwick.ac.uk/cmur/publications/discussion_paper02mec859nottracked.pdf
3. Market definition and analysis are elaborated in, respectively, a recommendation and a guideline. A recommendation on remedies was in preparation in early 2003.
4. 'Commission Recommendation on Relevant Product and Service Markets within the electronic communications sector susceptible to *ex ante* regulation in accordance with Directive 2002/21/EC of the European Parliament and of the Council on a common regulatory framework for electronic communications services and networks.'

5. Directive 2002/21/EC.
6. 'Protecting consumers by promoting competition', OFTEL's conclusions, 20 June 2002.
7. Directive 2002/19/EC.
8. Under this pricing rule, the access seeker pays a price for access equal to the price of the relevant retail service, minus the retailing costs saved by the access provider.
9. 'Imposing Access Obligations under the New EU Directives', OFTEL, September 2002.
10. The points are elaborated in more detail in M. Cave, 'Can Regulators Get Smart about Discrimination?' at http://users.wbs.warwick.ac.uk/cmur/publications/discussion_papers. htm
11. See M. Cave, 'Is LoopCo the answer?', *INFO*, **4**, 2002, 25–31.
12. 'The Director General's Review of BskyB's Position in the Wholesale Pay TV Market', Office of Fair Trading, December 1996.
13. OFT Press Notice, 17 December 2001.
14. I have borrowed this example from Dr R. Inderst of the LSE.
15. Some recent work on demand for cable television in the United States had shown that the demand curve is flatter (the price elasticity of demand is higher) for larger bundles of channels than for smaller bundles. See G. Crawford, 'The Discriminatory Incentives to Bundle: Case of Cable Television', University of Arizona, 2001.
16. 'BSkyB: the outcome of the OFT's Competition Act Investigation', December 2002; see also note 17.
17. 'Commission opens proceedings into joint selling of media rights to the English Premier League', Press Release IP/02/1951, European Commission, 20 December 2002.
18. 'Statement on the Pricing of Conditional Access Services and Related Services', OFTEL, May 2002.
19. 'Terms of Supply of Conditional Access: OFTEL Guidelines', October 2002.
20. 'OFTEL confirms conditional access policy, OFTEL publishes decision on ITV complaint', Press Release, 22 October 2002.
21. This section draws on M. Cave, R. Collins and P. Crowther, 'Taming the BBC', at http://users. wbs.warwick.ac.uk/cmur/publications/discussion_papers.htm January 2003.
22. John Vickers, 'Competition Policy and Broadcasting', a speech at the IEA Conference on the Future of Broadcasting, 14 June 2002.
23. 'Government Response to the Independent Review of Radio Spectrum Management', DTI, 15 October 2002.
24. 'Implementing Spectrum Trading – a Consultation Document', Radiocommunications Agency, July 2002.
25. 'Spectrum Policy Task Force Report' (ET Docket No. 02-135), FCC, November 2002.
26. Evan Kwerel and John Williams, 'A Proposal for a Rapid Transition to Market Allocation of Spectrum', OPP Working paper 38, FCC, November 2002.
27. I. Deutscher, *The Prophet Armed*, New York: Oxford University Press, p. 331.

CHAIRMAN'S COMMENTS

Irwin Stelzer

I have four points to make on Martin Cave's chapter. Let me preface this by revealing an interest. I do consulting for News International and at one time, but no longer, consulted for Sky. As for the BBC, I watch it, trying to identify the America that it reports.

The first point goes to procedure. My experience of regulation is that procedure matters a great deal, and that all is not well in the world of procedures in Britain. You do not have an Administrative Procedures Act, creating the danger that regulators will inadvertently become the tools of competitors who, upset by moves by their competitors, can use complaints to the regulators as a cost-increasing way of coping when they cannot cope in the market.

Second, I would be inclined to give more weight even than Martin does to the difficulties associated with regulating vertically integrated entities that have market power at one horizontal level. He did make this point when he talked about the problems confronting Lord Currie: highly complex discrimination and costing proceedings. I have been in a lot of those. To call them highly complex is really to understate their difficulty, and I cannot help wondering about these endless battles over cost allocation between segments of the business, and this endless war over access terms, which are not just about price, they are multidimensional terms that are very difficult for a non-incumbent to surmount. These problems are so daunting that we should give greater weight to structural changes, to vertical disintegration, simplifying the life of the regulator, and avoiding a lot of these problems.

Third, and in a way a similar point as far as the BBC goes, drawing the boundary between public service and commercial activities is rather a hellish chore. I once had a wonderful debate about this with Gavyn Davis, who had written a sensible report on this subject. I am driven to the conclusion that a really rigid vertical separation would be appropriate given the political realities in which the BBC operates. The BBC is rather like the Irish referenda on the euro: when the BBC does not get what it wants, it invites the politicians to come back and try again. Sooner or later it gets what it wants.

Finally, I think it is worth re-examining the question that Martin raised when he talked about these entities as separate. I am not overwhelmed by convergence predictions, but I think the notion that there is little overlap between BSkyB and BBC is overdone in the sense that they both do compete for product and they both do compete for audiences; I have never been convinced that pay-TV is a separate market. The econometric studies I have seen suggest quite the opposite. This makes regulation much more complicated for Ofcom because it is going to have to realize that these are interacting entities with areas of cooperation and areas of competition on the supply side, and areas of competition on the demand side. That is going to make for a difficult life for regulators.

The fifth of my four points is that people matter. We like to think we are governments of laws, not men. Actually we are really governments of people. Good regulators can make a difference: look at the competition we have managed to introduce into the electricity service since Callum McCarthy got there. Stupid regulators can really cause harm.

5. What to do about the railways?

Chris Nash[*]

---

1   INTRODUCTION

A recent Italian prime minister is supposed to have said: 'There are two kinds of madman; those who think they are Napoleon and those who think they know how to run the railways.' The future of the railways in Britain has recently become clearer, and in some respects I think a sensible way forward has been found. But few would deny that problems remain, and that 'what to do about the railways' remains a very serious issue.

Part of the problem is that, to my mind, railways have many unique characteristics, which means that policies which may work well for other network industries become highly problematic when applied to this industry. This was not always recognized at the time of privatization and has helped lead to one set of acute problems at the present time: those of achieving a sensible timetable and an efficient use of capacity. A second key issue remains the scale of increases in costs, and particularly those of major projects, in recent years. A third one, very much linked to the first two, is that of determining what services it is sensible for a railway to provide and at what prices. A fourth one is giving the correct incentives to train-operating companies to provide such services. Finally, there have been the problems surrounding long-term investment. This identification of issues relies partly on my own knowledge of the industry, but also rests heavily on those identified in the recent Mercer report (Mercer, 2002) which brings together the conclusions of an extensive set of interviews with those in the industry. The report sees the key problems as a failure to maintain and renew the network adequately, poor long-term investment planning and strategy, suboptimal utilization of capacity and an onerous and bureaucratic safety regime. The first and last of these are among the causes of the escalation

[*] I am grateful to Jeremy Drew (Drew Management Consultants) for comments on an earlier draft of this paper; also to Simon Coulthard (Railtrack) for the Transpennine capacity allocation example, to John Thomas (Office of the Rail Regulator) for commenting on factual matters and to Dan Johnson (ITS) for the preparation of other tables and graphs. All errors and opinions expressed however, are solely my responsibility.

of costs, but the Mercer report also identified a need for clearer value for money tradeoffs and the need to improve incentives to operators as key issues.

We will consider each of these issues in turn, but first it is worth mentioning one issue which will not be discussed beyond this introduction, and that is the fundamental structure of the industry. This is not to say that I am convinced that the current structure is ideal. Indeed I do think that the sectorized railway of the 1980s achieved major advances and might well have left us much better placed today if those reforms had been allowed to continue. Figure 5.1 shows what was achieved in terms of traffic, admittedly in a time of economic boom, and Figure 5.2 the near halving of government support which was simultaneously achieved, starting from levels considerably less than those pertaining now. But I do not think it would be at all sensible to try to recreate that railway now; the costs would be too great. Moreover, in principle, the structure in which passenger services are franchised out, freight services are fully privatized and infrastructure separated from operations seems to me to be the best way of introducing the forces of competition into the industry. That it has had some success is apparent from Figures 5.1 and 5.2; while much of the growth of passenger traffic may be attributed to external factors such as the state of the economy and road congestion, and the declining impact on rail of further growth in car ownership, as well as fares regulation, these factors do not explain to the same extent the growth in freight. The revival of rail freight traffic, with its

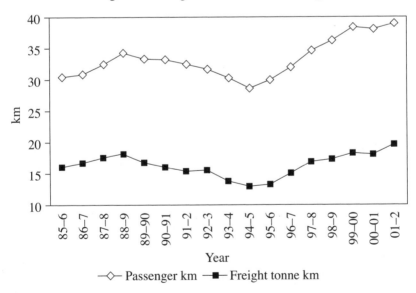

Source: SRA, National Rail Trends, 2001–2, quarter 1.

Figure 5.1   Rail traffic on the British rail network

associated growth of rail market share across a whole range of commodities (Table 5.1), is associated with new investment and a greater priority given to freight services in the new structure, and must be considered a major success of privatization. Moreover, until the introduction of Direct Rail Support in 2001/2 as a result of the problems of Railtrack, support to the industry had been coming steadily down (Figure 5.2).

At the same time it can hardly be denied that major problems have arisen with the new structure of the industry. My view is that the problems that have arisen are more to do with the detail of how it was done than with the basic structure upon which privatization was based. In other words, the problems are very much ones of regulation, although, as will be seen, much more ones falling within the province of the Strategic Rail Authority than that of the rail regulator himself.

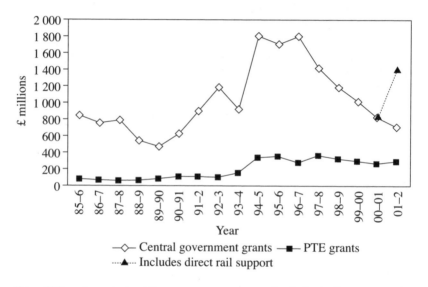

Note: PTE grants are grants paid by passenger transport executives for local rail passenger services in the main conurbations, excluding London.

Source: SRA, National Rail Trends, 2001–2, quarter 3.

Figure 5.2   Government support to the rail industry

2   TIMETABLING AND THE USE OF CAPACITY

The usual approach to reform in network industries is to conclude that it is the infrastructure that is the natural monopoly, whilst it is possible for a variety of operators to use it to compete for the final market. Thus it is necessary to separate the infrastructure from service provision and to regulate the infrastructure provider to avoid abuse of monopoly power and to ensure open and non-discriminatory access to alternative service providers. The latter is particularly an issue if the infrastructure manager is also a service provider, so there is an argument for forbidding this. Regulators usually seek to ensure that prices reflect long-run marginal costs and that infrastructure managers actually provide the necessary capacity. Provided that there are no economies of scale in infrastructure provision, this ensures that the infrastructure manager makes a reasonable return; if there are economies of scale then some sort of mark-ups on long-run marginal cost will be required, but as long as demand is not too sensitive to price this will not be a major distortion. Open access to service providers is expected to lead to sufficient competition for regulation not to be required in that part of the market, or only to be required on a temporary basis as competition builds up.

Table 5.1   Rail share of road–rail total freight, Great Britain, by commodity (per cent)

Year	A	B	C	D	E	F	Other	Total
1975	2.9	76.0	35.7	26.3	13.9	13.9	11.8	19.0
1980	1.9	71.4	34.8	20.7	13.5	11.8	10.7	16.4
1985	2.0	49.4	31.7	21.5	13.0	8.1	10.1	13.4
1990	1.3	54.3	30.0	20.8	12.8	5.8	4.7	10.9
1995	1.2	57.1	24.0	18.4	9.4	5.3	4.4	8.5
1996	1.1	60.3	21.8	22.0	8.7	6.1	4.4	8.5
1997	1.5	62.0	23.7	21.3	8.9	5.0	4.7	9.1
1998	2.2	69.2	25.7	23.5	10.4	5.2	6.7	10.2
1999	2.2	68.6	25.4	25.7	10.4	4.3	8.0	10.9
2000	2.1	76.2	20.0	25.2	12.2	4.8	7.5	10.7
2001	2.5	74.7	19.4	31.0	10.9	4.5	6.4	11.6

Notes:
A: Food, drink, agriculture.
B: Coal.
C: Oil and petroleum.
D: Metal.
E: Construction etc.
F: Chemical.

Source: Fowkes and Nash (2002).

The first big problem that the British government faced in applying this approach to the railways was that the characteristics of rail infrastructure do not fit this model in a number of ways. Firstly, rail infrastructure is subject to major economies of scale, indivisibilities and time lags in adjustment of capacity. In the words of the Department of Transport (DTp, 1993) para. 3.2:

> Work carried out by British Rail and the government's advisers, Coopers and Lybrand, has confirmed that the majority of rail infrastructure costs are common, that is, they cannot be uniquely attributed to any particular operator or even class of operator. The majority of costs also tend to be fixed, at least in the short to medium term.

The department went on to say, in para 3.3:

> If Railtrack were to charge all operators a proportion of common and fixed costs through a standard tariff ... it would drive off the railways traffic which was in a position to pay for its avoidable costs.... The strong market position of some industries makes it possible to sustain such an approach to charging. But on the railway that could lead to traffic loss and increases in charges for remaining operators.

Thus it would be necessary either to subsidize Railtrack or to adopt a much more differentiated charging system according to what the market could bear. The then government was convinced that it was better to allow flexibility of charges, and for all government subsidies to be channelled through train operators, who would then have a purely commercial relationship with Railtrack (para. 1.3): 'Where subsidy of the operation of railways is appropriate on social grounds, it is more efficiently directed at particular services and paid to the operator rather than to the provider of the infrastructure.'

The idea was that the government would only have a relationship with the service provider, and the service provider would then buy in its use of infrastructure on a commercial basis. This may work in sectors where infrastructure is readily expanded at a roughly constant marginal cost, for then the only concern to the government is the marginal cost of infrastructure provision, and that will be reflected in the price quoted by the service provider. For railways, the cost of infrastructure capacity expansion varies enormously with the precise details of what is required, and it is impossible to take sensible decisions about service levels to incorporate in franchise agreements without looking carefully at their implications for the infrastructure.

At the same time, the problem of allocating capacity is much more complex for railways than for most network industries. Rail customers require the linking of a specific origin to a specific destination at a specific point in time. Of the other network industries only telecommunications shares this characteristic, but there capacity expansion is not usually a problem, and therefore congestion and the need to ration capacity are much less of an issue.

In a free market, presumably Railtrack would seek to charge each train-operating company according to what they were willing to pay, and to design a timetable which yielded Railtrack the maximum revenue. Probably they would enter into some long-term contracts which gave specific rights which might prevent short-run maximization of revenue, but which reduced risks for both parties. Designing a timetable which achieved these aims would not by any means be an easy task, but at least it would be clear what they were trying to achieve.

In practice, the market is not free. In effect it has two regulators with different responsibilities. One form of regulation of passenger services is through the franchising process. At the time of privatization, it was clear that the complete withdrawal of government support from rail passenger services would have led to closure of a large part of the network, and indeed even the allocation of capacity according to what the market would bear would lead to a decline in local and commuter services in the regions with capacity being reallocated to inter-city services. The government was not prepared to see this, at least in the short term. There is good reason to suppose that a purely market-based determination of rail services will not be optimal – rail services provide benefits to users which cannot always be recouped as revenue, and they provide non-user benefits by diverting passengers from more congested and more environmentally polluting modes. But political pressures led to a situation where, even when there was a good case for replacing trains with buses, the government did not wish to see this happen. Thus the government determined in favour of a franchising system, with fairly tightly defined public service requirements specifying minimum levels of service in terms of frequency, speed and time of day. Slots on the infrastructure were reserved for these services. The franchises also controlled some fares, namely season tickets on commuter services, and ordinary or 'saver' fares (the standard walk-on leisure ticket) elsewhere, while, under pressure from MPs of all parties, provisions to require all passenger service providers to participate in through and interchangeable ticketing and provision of impartial information were incorporated into their licences in order to preserve so-called 'network benefits'. (For a thorough description of the various regulatory controls on rail passenger service providers, see OPRAF, 1996).

In awarding the franchises the government granted the franchisees access rights which exhausted a substantial part of the infrastructure capacity; the precise timing of trains, and the allocation of remaining rights, were in the hands of Railtrack, but subject to decision criteria which required them to take account of a wide range of social as well as commercial considerations, and to regulatory control to ensure that these were respected.

Regulation of access prices and conditions, and the allocation of capacity, became the responsibility of the rail regulator. He first consulted on infrastructure charges in the document Office of the Rail Regulator (1994a). In terms of the structure of track access charges, it was concluded that freight and open-access operators should pay a negotiated charge, at least covering their avoidable costs and making as large a contribution as possible to fixed and common costs. Franchised operators should pay a variable charge equal to the cost implications of running additional trains, and a fixed charge equal to their other avoidable costs plus a share of fixed costs not covered by freight and open-access operators. While there was complete open access for freight, open-access passenger operation was limited to origin–destination pairs not already served by through services and other services that had negligible impact on franchisees. This was to make it easier to let franchises at the lowest possible levels of subsidy; if there was a risk of new entry on the most profitable parts of the franchise the subsidy needed to keep the remainder running would be increased.

This was seen as a temporary arrangement; after the initial period of franchising, moderation of competition (which greatly restricted open-access entry) would be removed, and Railtrack would have no obligation to meet the needs of franchisees before giving capacity to other operators. The implications of this for the cost of franchised passenger services were to have been a risk on the franchising director's budget.

The services that were actually provided thus became the results of the strong constraints imposed by the passenger service requirements of the franchise agreements, the access rights possessed by the franchised train operators, the commercial desires of the train operators and the availability of capacity. Where agreement on the use of capacity could not be achieved, the parties concerned had the right of appeal to the regulator, who would resolve the issue according to a set of decision criteria (Table 5.2). It was stated that none of these criteria would take precedence over any other, leading to what appears to an outsider to be an extremely unclear and difficult process, and one that did not ensure that slots went to services of the highest social value.

The result of this set of constraints is that it appears to be very difficult to negotiate timetable changes, or to adapt services to changing demands. There is no easy mechanism for transferring slots from low-value uses to high. A mechanism does exist for Railtrack to buy back slots for which it has a more valuable use, but it is understood that this mechanism is almost unused, and it is not possible in the case of slots required to meet franchise conditions without the agreement of the Strategic Rail Authority (SRA). Transfer of a slot from, for instance, a low-value short passenger train to a higher-value freight train will involve the SRA, Office of the Rail Regulator (ORR), Railtrack, at least two operators and perhaps also a passenger transport executive (PTE). Given that the two trains will move at different speeds, in practice, the transfer may require retimetabling affecting all operators on the route. This problem has of course become acute in the light of the growth in both passenger and freight traffic seen in Figures 5.1 and 5.2. Moreover it may be sensible to leave some slots free in the interests of reliability but there is currently no real mechanism for achieving this.

Table 5.2   ORR decision criteria

A. Sharing the capacity, and securing the development of, the network in the most efficient and economical manner in the interests of all users of railway services having regard to safety, environment and proper maintenance, improvement and enlargement of the network
B. Contract compliance
C. Reliability
D. Maintenance and renewal of the network
E. Connections
F. Service pattern
G. Spread of services
H. Flexibility
I. Efficient rolling stock utilization
J. New entry
K. Stability
L. Commercial interests of Railtrack

Source: Railtrack Track Access Conditions, 15 February 2002.

As well as the key problem of the allocation of capacity, there are big problems in achieving well integrated timetables in a system with many different train operators. The biggest absurdity is the number of cases where services operated between the same points by different operators produce a combination of duplication of services a few minutes apart and then big gaps – a common problem when timetables are not coordinated. Certainly the timetables present nothing like the simplicity and regularity of the clockface Swiss Taktfahrplan, even on routes where services operate at more or less regular intervals (Railway Reform Group, 2000).

As an example of the problem of capacity we may quote the Transpennine route between Leeds and Manchester Piccadilly. The principal operator on this route is currently Arriva Trains Northern, who aspire to operate a regular interval express service every 15 minutes between Leeds and Manchester. Most of the trains are only two to three cars long, so the issue is attractiveness of the service rather than capacity for passengers. There is major conflict with stopping passenger services operated by North West trains and with freight trains. In the current timetable it is possible to accommodate four express passenger services, a stopping passenger service and a two-hourly freight, but only by departing from a strict regular interval service for the express passenger service, and by the freight train waiting for nearly an hour in the passing loop at Marsden (Figure 5.3). To provide the express passenger operator with a 15 minute regular-interval service, on the present infrastructure, would mean removal of both freight and stopping passenger services from this route (Figure 5.4). On the other hand provision for an expansion of freight traffic would require more bunching of the express passenger trains (Figure 5.5), as well as removal of the stopping services or their delay in a passing loop while fast trains pass. The issue of which is the best solution will be discussed further in section 4, and the issue of providing incentives for train-operating companies to seek such solutions in section 5. In the meantime, we merely note the complexity of such issues, involving for instance in this case at least three different train-operating companies, Railtrack, the Strategic Rail Authority, two Passenger Transport Executives and, potentially at least, the regulator. We also note that it is difficult to justify major investment in expanding capacity on a route where many trains are only two or three cars long.

What is the solution to the problem of the allocation of capacity? It is clear that there is only one body which can provide clear leadership in terms of formulating a strategy for the current and future timetable in the light of the social costs and benefits of different types of service, and that is the Strategic

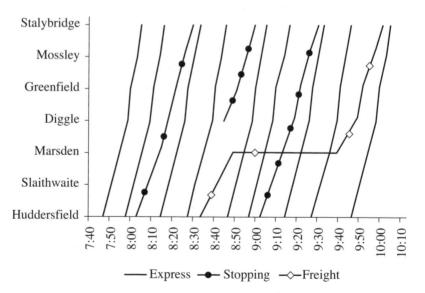

Source: Summer 2002 working timetable.

Figure 5.3   Actual allocation of track capacity between Huddersfield and Stalybridge in busiest two-hour period

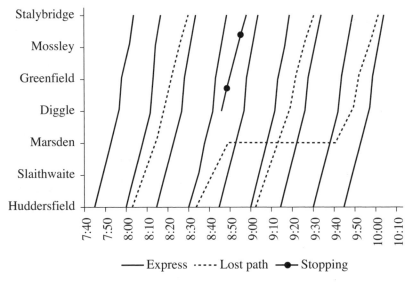

Source: Nash et al. (2002).

*Figure 5.4   Allocation of capacity required to deliver transpennine express
services at 15-minute intervals*

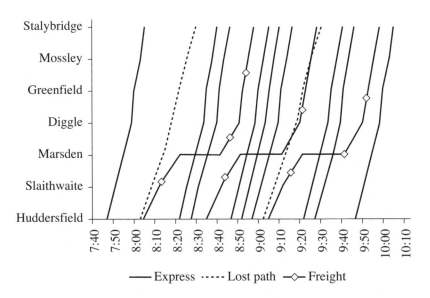

*Figure 5.5   Theoretical reallocation of track capacity to additional freight
services between Huddersfield and Stalybridge*

Rail Authority. The SRA determines the Passenger Service Requirements and has an overview of all services – passenger and freight. It is therefore encouraging that it appears to be taking a much more forceful approach to these issues, but it may be that it needs to take the lead in specifying the timetable to a much greater extent than to date.

At the limit, this might extend to the SRA completely specifying the timetable for all passenger services, with the role of the train operating company (TOC) being reduced to that of a contractor running what was prescribed. There will clearly be objections to this on the basis that the SRA is replacing the knowledge of the TOC as to what its passengers want with bureaucratic decisions from a more remote body. It is clear that some at least of the TOCs have made valuable innovations which might never have come if they had not had considerable freedom to develop their services in accordance with their own knowledge and research. Striking a balance between providing the TOCs with sufficient freedom to develop their services and yet integrating the results into a sensible overall timetable is one of many challenges facing the SRA.

3   INCREASES IN COST

A second major problem at the present time is increases in the cost of maintaining, renewing and enhancing the infrastructure. Roger Ford, of Modern Railways, used to talk of a Ford factor of two; namely that schemes today typically cost twice as much as they did under British Rail. But he is now quoting examples where the current estimate is anything up to ten times what was estimated a few years ago. Clearly that is leading to a situation where there is a strong risk that the proposed maintenance and upgrading of the system will not take place, and rightly so – all expenditure on railways, as in any sector, needs to be justified on the basis that the benefits exceed the costs.

It is very hard for an outsider to understand cost increases on this scale. But there appear to be at least four distinct reasons for them. The first is the obvious one of transactions costs. Involvement of so many different parties involves substantial costs of negotiating agreements, drawing up contracts and monitoring and enforcing them. However there are other major factors at work. Clearly reducing these may involve structural change, for instance by taking more maintenance work in-house, but it may also involve different approaches to contracts, based more on partnership and rewards for overall performance than on the detailed tracking of the causes of every individual failure.

A second reason is that, under the arrangements regarding possessions, train-operating companies have to be compensated for loss of revenue their services suffer while the scheme is under way. These sums of money may be very considerable. In the case of the Leeds First scheme in Leeds, for instance, the sum involved was around £100mn (*Modern Railways*, August 2002). These costs are inflated by an increased requirement to close all lines on a route even if not all are being worked on. Clearly this loss of revenue is a real cost of a scheme to an integrated railway as well. But in the past it was never quoted as part of the capital cost of the scheme or given the prominence it now attracts.

A third reason is safety spending. The railways have been required to spend substantial amounts on enhancing safety standards, for instance by the widespread installation of the Train Protection and Warning System, which prevents trains from passing signals at danger, although it is only fully effective at speeds below 70mph. This is costing around £10mn per life saved, by contrast to the figure of £1.24mn used in appraising road investments with implications for safety. There is a risk of even more extravagant expenditure on the European Train Control System (Railway Safety, 2002). It has been shown that if the Hidden enquiry recommendations on this were implemented in full, very large expenditure would be involved as well as substantial loss of capacity for a saving of perhaps one life per annum. The irony of these expenditures is that, if they lead to a situation where railway capacity is reduced and enhancement is deemed too expensive, diverting traffic to road, they will undoubtedly worsen the safety of the transport system as a whole rather than improving it (CFIT, 2002a). Compliance with legislation on access for the disabled is also a major cause of inflated costs and it must be asked whether this is always the most efficient way of meeting these needs.

Fourthly, and on the basis of hearsay rather than hard evidence, there is the question of attitudes to risk. It is not surprising that private sector contractors require a risk premium to undertake rail investments; it has long been recognized that the private sector will take a more cautious approach to risk than should the public sector. But in the light of escalating costs of projects and safety problems, as with Hatfield, it seems clear that the private sector is now adding substantial risk premia to all projects involving rail infrastructure. This revises questions about the wisdom of all risk transfer; for instance, it may be very expensive to transfer revenue risk on major projects given the degree to which long-term revenue is determined by factors outside control of the industry.

The result of all these forces is that rail investment is now becoming so expensive that it is increasingly difficult to justify it. Increasingly it is being said that road investment is both cheaper and more effective in dealing with transport problems. Unless urgent action is taken to control these escalating costs, there is a real danger that rail will price itself out of the market, but it is not clear what that action should be.

At the time of privatization, like many commentators, I foresaw big problems in the totally new and untried area of the relationship between TOCs and Railtrack. By contrast I thought contracting out of track maintenance and renewal was a familiar and well tried approach to driving down costs. However it appears that working on the track, particularly while trains are running, imposes problems that are different from those experienced in other industries where contracting out of maintenance work is the norm, and even in the USA railroads do not typically choose to contract out this part of their maintenance work. In its early years Railtrack did not have or acquire sufficient knowledge of the state of its assets to be able to monitor what its contractors needed to do as against what they were actually doing, and the widespread use of subcontractors by the primary contractor has made the monitoring of performance and safety standards even more difficult.

In getting costs under control it will clearly again be SRA who, together with Network Rail and ORR, has to take the lead. It may also be that they will have to take more of the risk in rail projects to get back to a situation where projects may be undertaken at reasonable cost. Whether it makes sense ultimately for Network Rail to undertake more track work in house is less clear, but it does appear that the relationship between Railtrack and its contractors, and between the engineering contractors and their subcontractors, has been one of the most troublesome areas of the new structure of the rail industry. Action is now being taken to greatly reduce the amount of subcontracting in this field (in fact, all track maintenance is now being taken in house by Network Rail).

How to escape from the situation where the railway is obliged to undertake vastly expensive safety expenditure, completely distorting its costs relative to road, is another major problem. As the Mercer report states, there appears to be no body charged with the task of balancing safety with cost. In retrospect, perhaps the transfer of responsibility for rail safety to the HSE (Health and Safety Executive), a body with no responsibility for roads, was counterproductive. Research (Jones-Lee, 2000) fails to find any evidence that people are willing to pay more to reduce rail than road fatalities. It would make more sense if the Department for Transport were responsible for rail safety as well as road, and could apply consistent criteria across the two modes.

4   WHAT SERVICES SHOULD BE PROVIDED?

There are very good economic reasons for not leaving the decisions on what rail services to provide to be purely commercial ones. If it were the case that the commercial sector was subject to constant returns to scale, imposed negligible externalities and operated in a competitive market, then of course market forces would achieve efficient pricing and socially optimal investment in that sector, and there would be no problem. But that is rarely the case in transport and particularly not so for rail systems. Rail systems are subject to major economies of traffic density (Caves *et al.*, 1987), particularly regarding the infrastructure and for passenger services in terms of the improvement to service levels that follows as traffic grows. Firstly, rail infrastructure is subject to major economies of scale and indivisibilities such that the marginal cost of additional use of the infrastructure will typically not cover average cost even in the long run, when the level of infrastructure is well adjusted to demand. Secondly, increased traffic density leads to further economies of scale, either in the form of marginal train operating costs being below average if the additional traffic is accommodated by raising load factors or train length, or in the form of benefits to existing users if train frequencies are improved (the so-called Mohring effect). Of course at any point in time the system may be subject to specific bottlenecks that are very expensive to overcome, but this does not change the fact that on average railways are subject to major economies of scale.

It is often objected that these forms of economies of scale exist throughout industry and that if subsidies were provided for these reasons then it would be necessary to subsidize everything. This is a misunderstanding. In most sectors, economies of scale may exist at the level of the individual plant, but customers are serviced from a string of plants at different locations, and the supply chain can be adapted to optimize economies of scale. What makes that untrue for transport infrastructure or services is that infrastructure or services at one location can only serve the market at that location; they cannot service a global market. Of course this does apply to other distribution activities, such as retailing, and may well provide *a priori* justification for subsidizing the village shop. But it is not true of the economy as a whole.

Another counterargument as to why these effects do not require a non-commercial approach to transport provision is that, to the extent that rail companies are able to practise price discrimination and capture the benefits to users of additional traffic, the need to earn a surplus above marginal cost may not be a problem in terms of economic efficiency. Indeed if perfect discrimination may be applied then it is only worth maintaining services that can cover total costs in this way (Joy, 1971). This is more likely to apply for freight traffic, provided that there is no regulation preventing negotiation to obtain the best price for each traffic flow, than for passenger, where naturally such negotiations are impossible. Since privatization, freight operating companies have no longer been able to practise price discrimination in this way as a result of open access, which leads to surpluses being competed away. To a certain extent Railtrack was initially able to maintain such discrimination in the freight market, although it is no longer able to do so, as will be explained below. It is also possible to practise a degree of price discrimination, particularly in the longer distance passenger market, where quite complicated fares structures exist in order to segment markets according to their price elasticity of demand. However such discrimination is far from perfect, particularly in shorter distance markets where complicated fares structures and use of advance purchase tickets are not feasible.

Where it is assumed that economies of scale may be matched by perfect price discrimination, the policy conclusion is that externalities should be charged for, but that both pricing and investment decisions may be left to purely commercial criteria, provided that charges for the use of the competing mode are appropriately set. For any sector where it is deemed not reasonable to make this assumption, there is a case for government intervention in both pricing and investment decisions.

The above argument would hold even if there were no problems with the pricing of other modes, but this is far from the case. A recent study (Sansom *et al.*, 2001) has shown that road users typically pay far less than the marginal social cost of their journey, even when minimal values are attached to environmental costs (Table 5.3). In the case of heavy goods vehicles this is partly because of the failure to charge appropriately for the damage they cause the roads. It should be noted that this study was using data from 1998; the big cut in vehicle excise duty on goods vehicles following the year 2000 fuel price protests will have worsened the situation. But for all road users a major consideration is the levels of congestion in and around urban areas, even on motorways and trunk roads (Table 5.4). The same study showed that rail passengers also typically pay somewhat less than marginal costs (the exception is in the London area, where on average passengers pay slightly more than marginal cost, although in the peak they undoubtedly pay less) (Table 5.5), but that rail freight users pay slightly more than marginal cost (Table 5.6).

Clearly the best way of tackling this gross underpricing of the competing mode is at source. There is good evidence that congestion pricing in the major

Table 5.3   Marginal cost and revenue analysis, by type of vehicle and time of day

Categories	Costs Infrastructure operating cost & depreciation	Vehicle operating cost (PSV)	Congestion	Mohring effect (PSV)	External accident costs	Air pollution
Car, peak	0.05		13.22		0.78	0.18
Car, off-peak	0.05		7.01		0.80	0.18
LDV, peak	0.06		13.99		0.52	0.76
LDV, off-peak	0.06		7.07		0.53	0.68
HGV-Rigid, peak	3.82		26.00		1.40	1.84
HGV-Rigid, off-peak	3.77		12.75		1.39	1.57
HGV-Artic, peak	7.57		33.45		0.99	1.42
HGV-Artic, off-peak	7.55		19.81		0.99	1.41
PSV, peak	5.74	78.73	20.31	−14.43	3.82	3.17
PSV, off-peak	4.93	80.10	12.31	−14.86	3.69	3.15

Note: PSV = Public Service Vehicle.

Source: Sansom *et al.* (2001).

cities and on congested sections of motorways and trunk roads is justified (CFIT, 2002b), while the government's proposals for a kilometre tax on heavy goods vehicles offer the means to go a long way towards correcting the distortions in the freight market (DfT, 2002). But opposition to these developments remains intense and there is no sign of such pricing being implemented beyond London and perhaps one or two other cities, whilst the freight proposals currently are 'revenue neutral' and will not remove current undercharging.

A survey by Vicario (1999) has shown that, if they did not use the train, some 60 per cent of interurban travellers and 40 per cent of urban travellers would otherwise use a car (the remainder mainly using a bus or ceasing to travel). On the basis of these figures it may readily be seen that, relative to their marginal cost, rail services are on average well worth providing.

For instance, for regional services the figures in Table 5.5 suggest that on average there is a shortfall of £2.22 per train kilometre in comparing revenue with marginal social cost for rail services. A typical regional service carries around 40 passengers and may therefore be diverting some 24 passengers from the car, or with an occupancy rate of 1.5 relieving the roads of 16 cars. If we suppose that the roads concerned are 50 per cent outer suburban motorway and 50 per cent rural motorway, Sansom *et al.* (2001) suggests a benefit of 15.4p per car km, or £2.464 per train km. This leads to a net benefit of £0.244 per train km. If some of the roads were urban, the benefits would be greater. On the other hand, if using rail actually attracted car trips into the urban area to gain access to the station, the benefit would be less or even negative. Clearly the whole door-to-door journey must be considered and the provision of appropriate public

Noise	Climate change	VAT not paid (PSV)	Total	Fares (PSV)	Vehicle excise duty (part)	Fuel duty	Value added tax on fuel duty	Total	Difference Costs – revenues
			Revenues						**Difference**
0.01	0.12		14.4			3.86	0.68	4.5	9.8
0.01	0.12		8.2			3.86	0.68	4.5	3.6
0.02	0.19		15.5			3.86	0.68	4.5	11.0
0.02	0.18		8.5			3.86	0.68	4.5	4.0
0.06	0.44		33.6		2.25	13.11	2.29	17.6	15.9
0.06	0.43		20.0		2.25	13.11	2.29	17.6	2.3
0.07	0.72		44.2		2.50	14.47	2.53	19.5	24.7
0.08	0.71		30.5		2.50	14.47	2.53	19.5	11.0
0.09	0.58	13.33	111.3	76.19	0.61	5.26	0.92	83.0	28.4
0.09	0.55	13.49	103.5	77.10	0.61	5.26	0.92	83.9	19.6

Table 5.4 Marginal cost and revenue analysis, by area type and road type (car, pence/km, low cost estimates)

Categories	Costs							Revenues			Difference
	Infrastructure operating cost & depreciation	Congestion	External accident costs	Air pollution	Noise	Climate change	Total	Fuel duty	Value added tax on fuel duty	Total	Costs – revenues
Central London											
Motorway	0.01	53.75	0.01	0.57	0.04	0.11	54.5	3.86	0.68	4.5	49.9
Trunk & principal	0.04	71.09	1.68	0.77	0.03	0.16	73.8	3.86	0.68	4.5	69.2
Other	0.08	187.79	1.68	0.87	0.04	0.19	190.6	3.86	0.68	4.5	186.1
Inner London											
Motorway	0.01	20.10	0.01	0.42	0.03	0.11	20.7	3.86	0.68	4.5	16.1
Trunk & principal	0.04	54.13	1.68	0.61	0.04	0.16	56.6	3.86	0.68	4.5	52.1
Other	0.08	94.48	1.68	0.66	0.03	0.17	97.1	3.86	0.68	4.5	92.6
Outer London											
Motorway	0.01	31.09	0.01	0.31	0.02	0.10	31.5	3.86	0.68	4.5	27.0
Trunk & principal	0.04	28.03	1.68	0.40	0.02	0.14	30.3	3.86	0.68	4.5	25.8
Other	0.08	39.66	1.68	0.45	0.02	0.16	42.0	3.86	0.68	4.5	37.5
Inner conurbation											
Motorway	0.01	53.90	0.01	0.47	0.02	0.11	54.5	3.86	0.68	4.5	50.0
Trunk & principal	0.04	33.97	1.68	0.55	0.02	0.14	36.4	3.86	0.68	4.5	31.9
Other	0.08	60.25	1.68	0.66	0.02	0.17	62.9	3.86	0.68	4.5	58.3
Outer conurbation											
Motorway	0.01	35.23	0.01	0.25	0.02	0.10	35.6	3.86	0.68	4.5	31.1
Trunk & principal	0.04	12.28	1.68	0.30	0.02	0.12	14.4	3.86	0.68	4.5	9.9
Other	0.08	0.00	1.68	0.32	0.02	0.13	2.2	3.86	0.68	4.5	-2.3

Categories	Costs							Revenues			Difference
	Infrastructure operating cost & depreciation	Congestion	External accident costs	Air pollution	Noise	Climate change	Total	Fuel duty	Value added tax on fuel duty	Total	Costs – revenues
Urban >25km²											
Trunk & principal	0.04	10.13	1.68	0.25	0.02	0.12	12.2	3.86	0.68	4.5	7.7
Other	0.08	0.72	1.68	0.26	0.02	0.13	2.9	3.86	0.68	4.5	-1.6
Urban 15–25 km²											
Trunk & principal	0.04	7.01	1.68	0.25	0.02	0.12	9.1	3.86	0.68	4.5	4.6
Other	0.08	0.00	1.68	0.24	0.02	0.12	2.1	3.86	0.68	4.5	-2.4
Urban 10–15 km²											
Trunk & principal	0.04	0.00	1.68	0.17	0.02	0.11	2.0	3.86	0.68	4.5	-2.5
Other	0.08	0.00	1.68	0.19	0.02	0.12	2.1	3.86	0.68	4.5	-2.4
Urban 5–10 km²											
Trunk & principal	0.04	2.94	1.68	0.15	0.02	0.11	4.9	3.86	0.68	4.5	0.4
Other	0.08	0.00	1.68	0.16	0.02	0.12	2.1	3.86	0.68	4.5	-2.5
Urban 0.01–5 km²											
Trunk & principal	0.04	1.37	1.68	0.13	0.01	0.11	3.3	3.86	0.68	4.5	-1.2
Other	0.08	0.00	1.68	0.14	0.01	0.12	2.0	3.86	0.68	4.5	-2.5
Rural											
Motorway	0.01	4.01	0.01	0.11	0.00	0.13	4.3	3.86	0.68	4.5	-0.3
Trunk & principal	0.04	8.48	0.30	0.10	0.00	0.11	9.0	3.86	0.68	4.5	4.5
Other	0.08	1.28	0.30	0.10	0.01	0.10	1.9	3.86	0.68	4.5	-2.7

Source: Sansom *et al.* (2001).

Table 5.5 Marginal cost and revenue analysis for passenger rail (£/train km, low cost estimates)

| Category | Costs | | | | | | | | | Revenue | Difference |
	Marginal infrastructure usage	Vehicle operating	Electricity	Congestion	Mohring effect	Air pollution	Noise	Climate change	VAT not paid	Total	Costs – revenue
Inter city	1.116	11.79	0.483	0.15	-1.55	0.279	0.122	0.067	2.46	14.92	14.07	0.85
Regional	0.149	5.04	0.068	0.09	-0.67	0.041	0.042	0.031	0.54	5.33	3.11	2.22
London	0.406	6.68	0.371	0.28	-1.19	0.067	0.088	0.037	1.48	8.22	8.47	-0.25
Passenger sector	0.424	7.07	0.228	0.18	-1.05	0.098	0.076	0.040	1.32	8.38	7.52	0.86

Note: Low cost estimates apply to environmental categories only.

Table 5.6   Marginal cost and revenue analysis for rail freight (£/train km, low-cost estimates)

Category	Costs						Revenue	Difference
	Marginal infrastructure usage	Vehicle operating cost	Air pollution	Noise	Climate change	Total		Cost – revenue
Bulk	1.79	8.60	0.166	0.170	0.131	10.86	13.01	−2.15
Other	0.88	9.70	0.166	0.170	0.131	11.05	13.61	−2.56
Freight sector	1.19	9.28	0.166	0.170	0.131	10.94	13.41	−2.47

Note: Low cost estimates apply to environmental categories only.

transport access and park and ride facilities will be important to realization of the potential benefits of rail services.

It would appear from the evidence cited above that a suburban service might attract a somewhat smaller proportion of its users from the car but that car occupancy rates would be lower and the extent that urban roads were relieved of traffic much greater. On the assumptions listed in Table 5.7 the net benefit of the rail service is now much higher, at £2.78 per train km. In the South East,

Table 5.7   Net benefits of different types of train

	Regional (interurban)	Regional (suburban)	Inter city passenger	Freight
Mean train load (passengers or freight tonnes)	40	40	160	300
Road vehicle load (passengers or freight tonnes)	1.5	1	1.5	20
Type of road relieved	50% outer suburban motorway, 50% rural motorway	45% rural motorway 45% suburban motorway 10% urban road	10% outer conurbation motorway 90% rural motorway	10% outer conurbation motorway 90% rural motorway
Net benefit per train km (£)	0.244	2.780	1.810	5.830
Trip length (km)	50	20	200	100
Net benefit per train (£)	12	56	363	583

Source: Derived from Sansom *et al.* (2001).

where revenue is already on average covering marginal cost and roads are more congested, the benefits will be much higher. Table 5.7 shows similar calculations for inter city passenger and freight on stated assumptions.

These figures will exaggerate the benefits in that, in the continued absence of appropriate pricing for roads, any relief of road congestion is likely to generate more road traffic and thus reduce the benefits. A model of this process such as that contained in CFIT (2002b) would be needed to get a more accurate measure of the benefits of rail subsidies. It is also the case that Table 5.7 averages over peak and off peak; both rail marginal costs and marginal benefits will be higher in the peak. Moreover, if we are concerned with whether to maintain or increase train frequencies as opposed to whether to provide longer trains as a way of increasing capacity, it is strictly only the increase in traffic from higher frequencies that should be considered rather than the average train loading. But the figures in Table 5.7 do serve to show that existing subsidies are not necessarily out of line with the benefits train services produce.

Nevertheless there remains a doubt about whether the Passenger Service Requirements (PSR) specifications for all TOCs reflect value for money, for two reasons. Tables 5.8 and 5.9 show the payment per passenger kilometre under the franchise agreements. These include fully allocated rather than marginal track costs. Thus part of these payments reflects the allocated track costs that would not be avoided if the service in question ceased to run unless there were simultaneous changes to other services and/or route capacity. But the high level of this figure for regional services certainly suggests that the argument for maintaining infrastructure used predominantly by these services needs re-examining. Clearly some of the TOCs have average load factors and average levels of subsidy far worse than for the sectors as a whole and within these overall averages they will still have a wide range. Looking for cheaper ways of providing the most poorly patronized services (bus, light rail), whether these are for entire routes or for late night or Sunday services, should certainly remain on the agenda.

The second reason takes us back to the issue of the allocation of capacity. These track costs do not include any charge for the opportunity cost of capacity that might be used to operate more valuable services. We return to that issue in the next section.

5   INCENTIVES TO TRAIN OPERATING COMPANIES

One of the problems with the current regime is that, despite a lot of thought having been given to the design of performance regimes, the incentives on train-operating companies are inadequate and in some cases even perverse. They are provided with a subsidy to enable them to provide at least the minimum level of service required by the franchise agreement. This reflects the attitude of previous governments over a long period to rail services; governments did not dare to cut them, but sought simply to keep them running at minimum cost to the taxpayer.

The ten-year plan of the current government (DETR, 2000) actually sees rail in a different light, as contributing to the solution of transport problems by carrying an increasing share of the market. But the existing franchise agreements are poorly structured to achieve this. There are penalties for failing to provide the agreed services (initially these were largely confined to the heavily subsidized TOCs, but they are gradually being extended to all franchises). But there are no bonuses for attracting extra traffic to rail. Such bonuses need to be aligned to the social benefits of attracting the traffic, so that there will be a much greater bonus in general for attracting peak commuter traffic than for off-peak leisure. OPRAF examined the best ways of quantifying those benefits and produced its planning criteria (OPRAF, 1999). But it is clear that the original passenger service requirements were drawn up largely before such criteria had been implemented, and owed more to a political desire that rail privatization should not be seen as a way of withdrawing rail services than to any economic analysis of their benefits.

Table 5.8   Subsidies, by market sector

	2000–2001 net[*] subsidy, from SRA and PTEs combined (£m)	Passenger kilometres (bn)	Net subsidy per passenger kilometre
Strategic routes	190	13.0	1.5p
London and south east	245	19.3	1.3p
Regional networks	855	6.7	12.8p
Total	1 290	39.0	3.3p

Note: [*] Includes premium payments from TOCs.

Source: SRA (2002b).

This is not to say that under present conditions those benefits are not substantial. The latest evidence, reviewed in the last section, points to the fact that they are. But this evidence has so far had little influence on the passenger service requirements, and is not translated into appropriate incentives to the train operating companies in terms of the ways in which they develop their services. Indeed in some circumstances the incentives are perverse. For instance, take a typical commuter rail operator. The raison d'être of its subsidies, and indeed its services, may well be to keep peak hour commuters off the road. However, if it has an increase in numbers of peak commuters, it is most unlikely that the extra revenue will cover the cost of provision of extra rolling stock. So it has incentives to avoid growth in numbers of commuters. The most obvious ways of doing this – increases in fares, failure to provide adequate capacity and so on – are closed off by fares regulation, and by penalties for overcrowding. But, to the extent that the operator can find other ways of discouraging growth in commuter numbers, it has an incentive to do so, and it certainly has no incentive to find ways of attracting additional commuters from the roads (in some cases, the franchise agreement does compensate TOCs for the costs of growth in commuting beyond some threshold, but again it does not provide any incentive).

In a sense the problem of perverse incentives is made worse by the way in which fares regulation has driven down the level of real fares for commuters, and has done so faster where performance has been poor, including where services are most overcrowded (SRA, 2002a). On the other hand, the degree of underpricing already noted for road means that substantial pricing below marginal cost for rail commuter services may also be justified.

What is needed, therefore, is a regime that links the level of subsidy to the social benefits provided. This might work by identifying a small number of categories of passenger kilometre (peak suburban, off-peak inter-city and so on), measuring the net social benefit attached to additional passenger kilometres of these categories and paying a subsidy per passenger kilometre in accordance with these. Provided that the rate was known at the time of franchising, the main effect should be not to change the train operating companies profits but to change the way in which subsidies are paid to improve incentives (although by increasing the revenue risk borne by the TOCs this could make long franchises more problematic, as explained above). Freight subsidies are already more closely aligned to this principle, being directly related to the benefits provided by particular flows of traffic.

At the same time the structure of track access charges similarly failed to provide appropriate incentives. Initially the proposed structure of charges for franchised passenger operators as described in section 2 meant that, on average, only 8 per cent of the charge was variable and most of this was the charge for electricity; 37 per cent of the charge represented the long-term incremental cost of meeting the operators' need for capacity, while 43 per cent was an essentially arbitrary allocation of common costs (of which about half, arising at below the zone level, were allocated on the basis of planned vehicle miles and half arising at national or zonal levels,were allocated on the basis of budgeted revenue). The remaining 12 per cent were station and depot access charges, which again were an essentially arbitrary allocation.

Table 5.9 Subsidies to train operating companies, 2000/2001

Company	Subsidy (£m)	Train miles (m)	Subsidy/train mile	Pass. miles	Pass. miles/train mile	Subsidy/pass. mile
Anglia	18.85	5.60	3.37	414.00	73.93	0.05
Arriva Mersey	5.91	3.60	1.64	158.00	43.89	0.04
Arriva Northern	109.78	21.80	5.04	885.00	40.60	0.12
c2c	23.99	3.80	6.31	487.00	128.16	0.05
Cardiff	16.98	2.20	7.72	70.00	31.82	0.24
Central	103.05	21.30	4.84	820.00	38.50	0.13
Chiltern	9.31	4.80	1.94	339.00	70.63	0.03
Connex SC	40.96	17.30	2.37	1610.00	93.06	0.03
Connex se	44.62	17.60	2.54	1998.00	113.52	0.02
Cross Country	79.95	11.00	7.27	1378.00	125.27	0.06
Gatwick	−11.75	1.60	−7.34	125.00	78.13	−0.09
GE	−4.91	7.80	−0.63	1120.00	143.59	0.00
GNER	6.68	11.80	0.57	2444.00	207.12	0.00
GWR	42.77	10.40	4.11	1492.00	143.46	0.03
Island	1.94	0.19	10.19	3.70	19.47	0.52
Midland	−217.00	7.10	−30.56	682.00	96.06	−0.32
NW	78.65	16.50	4.77	522.00	31.64	0.15
Scotrail	110.29	23.10	4.77	1205.00	52.16	0.09
Silverlink	25.69	6.30	4.08	643.00	102.06	0.04
SW	48.06	23.50	2.05	2589.00	110.17	0.02
Thames	11.15	8.60	1.30	629.00	73.14	0.02
Thameslink	−27.21	7.10	−3.83	802.00	112.96	−0.03
WAGN	8.18	11.60	0.71	1245.00	107.33	0.01
Wales & W	51.87	12.20	4.25	498.00	40.82	0.10
West C	57.84	11.30	5.12	2076.00	183.72	0.03

Source: SRA Annual Report, 2000–2001.

Where new access rights were required, the price for these would be negotiated at a level in between avoidable cost and the value of the path to the operator on the basis that Railtrack would be entitled to a greater share of the revenue the more it was bearing risk.

The regulator's conclusions on the original structure of track access charges were published in Office of the Rail Regulator (1994b). While the regulator argued that it would be desirable for a greater proportion of access charges to be variable with use, he did not consider it appropriate to change the structure of charges in the short term. Instead, he introduced procedures for the renegotiation of access rights and charges, in the hope that this would give Railtrack an incentive to 'buy back' scarce capacity where it could put it to better use. He also commented that different operators would vary in the quality of the paths they required and in their peakedness, and suggested the possibility of the variable element of the charge varying according to these factors (ORR, 1995).

In order to incentivize all parties a series of performance regimes were put in place. The track access agreements provided for Railtrack to compensate train operators for performance below a certain benchmark; where performance was above this benchmark the operator paid Railtrack a bonus. Operators also paid Railtrack if they were the cause of delays. There were also performance regimes between OPRAF and the TOCs which relied heavily on subsidy for their income, based on penalty payments for failures in reliability, punctuality and overcrowding (and incentive payments for performance above benchmarks). For the more commercial TOCs it was argued that commercial pressures alone were adequate.

The first periodic review of track access charges started with the publication of a consultation document in December 1997 (ORR, 1997). The regulator considered that charges should:

- incentivize Railtrack, train operators and funders to maximize the efficient use and development of the network;
- avoid undue discrimination between operators;
- appropriately reward Railtrack for changes in the level of output;
- meet the government's overall transport objectives.

Problems with the existing structure of charges were the following:

- negotiations for freight and open access operators were complex and time consuming, while negotiations on variation of access rights for franchisees were simply not working;
- the charging structure for franchisees gave no incentive for economy in the use of scarce capacity and no adequate mechanism for the replacement of existing low-value services by higher-value ones. Operators were not

adequately charged even for wear and tear, and not charged at all for congestion and opportunity cost of slots;

- circumstances had changed significantly since the charges were originally set. There had been a rapid growth in both rail traffic and train kilometres, leading to much greater congestion and requirements for investment in new capacity than had been anticipated, and it was the policy of the new government that this growth should continue. However incentives to expand the network were poor;
- the ability of Railtrack to negotiate charges according to the ability of a TOC to pay led to extreme secrecy about demand on the part of TOCs, to the detriment of service and investment planning.

During the review, Railtrack provided evidence of substantially higher wear and tear costs than allowed for in the existing charges, and also quantified congestion costs in fine detail by track section and time period (Gibson, 2000). Consideration was given to improving the incentive for Railtrack to expand the network by also incorporating the capital costs of expansion into the variable element of the access charge on the basis of a calculation of long-run marginal cost; however it was found that this varied enormously with the location, size and nature of the additional capacity required.

The recommendations of the regulator at the end of the process (Office of the Rail Regulator, 2000; 2001) were as follows:

- an increase in the variable part of the track charges to reflect the full wear and tear cost and 50 per cent of the quantified congestion cost;
- a move to a published tariff for all operators, with franchised operators continuing to pay on a two-part tariff, but freight and open-access operators paying only the variable element of the tariff; however open access continued to be heavily restricted, and the regulator subsequently suggested that, where open access was permitted on routes where franchises currently had exclusive rights, the entrant might be required to compensate the franchisee for loss of profits;
- an incentive payment to Railtrack based on increases in traffic in order to encourage expansion of the network. Because this was not funded through the variable part of the track access charge, there was no corresponding disincentive to train operators to expand, as there would have been had train operators paid this directly.

In the event not all of the costs falling on Railtrack as a result of these decisions were added to the fixed element of franchisees' charges; the Strategic Rail Authority agreed to pay for the removal of the contribution to joint and common costs from freight operators, and a substantial part of the general increase in Railtrack's costs following reassessment of the state of the infrastructure, through direct payment to Railtrack. This avoided a situation whereby franchisees' fixed payments would have increased, but under the terms of the franchise agreements SRA would have had to compensate them for these increases anyway. By entering into a direct financial relationship with Railtrack, arguably SRA would have more control over the way the money was spent.

As noted above, in the case of freight services, the previous system of negotiated tariffs was replaced by a tariff based solely on variable costs, which would form the basis of all future access agreements. Fixed costs attributable to freight services, and the cost of a new volume incentive paid to Railtrack in respect of freight traffic, will be borne by SRA (ORR, 2001). The result of this is roughly to halve the amount paid by freight operators for access to the rail network, thus offsetting some of the competitive advantage gained by road as a result of increased vehicle weight, freezing of fuel duty and reductions in vehicle excise duty. The cost to Railtrack of these changes will be compensated for by direct payment by the SRA. It remains the case, however, that for the main operator the variable element of the freight access charge has substantially increased. Hence the need the SRA has identified for other measures to achieve the target 80 per cent increase in freight tonne kilometres.

We commented in the introduction that infrastructure charges should also meet the external accident and environmental costs of additional services. Given the low accident risks, and the fact that railway companies are responsible for their own insurance, it seems unlikely that the external accident cost is very large. Environmental costs have been quantified in a recent study (Sansom *et al.*, 2001) and are shown in Tables 5.5 and 5.6. Although these are much smaller for rail than for road, it is clear that they are typically significant relative to the marginal infrastructure usage costs and should therefore be included.

As was seen above, one of the most difficult issues to deal with in rail infrastructure charging is that of scarce capacity. Ideally charges would give train operators appropriate incentives to expand services only where the value of the service is at least as high as the costs it causes, and, where capacity is scarce, to ensure that it is used to provide the services of greatest value. This issue has become one of great importance given the growth of traffic and the high costs of expansion and the consequent need to make the most effective use possible of what capacity is available (Bowker, 2002)

Charges need to reflect two different costs of capacity utilization: the cost of expected additional delays to other services as a result of running an additional train, and the costs of not being able to obtain a path at the desired time. The costs of additional delays may be estimated by means of modelling (Gibson, 2000). For instance, the approach taken by Railtrack was to use historical data on delays and capacity utilization to specify a function which could replicate the observed delays. This involved identifying appropriate measures of delay and of capacity utilization, identifying appropriate functional forms and then testing the strength of the relationship between incremental delay and capacity utilization. The result was a proposed tariff broken down into several thousand track sections and by time of day. However the regulator both simplified the structure and halved the level of charges before incorporating this element of costs in the tariff. It seems that he was concerned at the degree to which levying the full congestion charge might reduce demand (and it must be said that the proposed charge was based on existing, rather than equilibrium, levels of congestion. On the other hand, given the expected underlying growth in demand, it may reasonably be expected that congestion will get worse rather than better).

In addition to the expected delays there is the issue of scarcity: use of a particular slot by one train operator leads to inability of others to obtain their desired slots. This is a particularly difficult issue to deal with. The most attractive solution to this problem in theory is to 'auction' scarce slots (Nilsson, 2002). There are many practical difficulties, however, including the complicated ways in which slots can be put together to produce a variety of types of service, and the need to acquire an appropriate set of slots to provide a sensible timetable with good utilization of resources. It is also the case that the willingness to pay for the slot by the train operating company will only reflect its social value to them if appropriate subsidy regimes are in place to reflect the user and non-user benefits of the service as discussed above. In practice it is therefore usually accepted that any degree of price rationing of scarce slots will have to be on the basis of administered prices rather than bid prices, although some countries, including Britain, allow for a degree of 'secondary trading' in which slots change hands between operators at enhanced prices (strictly this must take place through Railtrack, so it is not secondary trading in the sense forbidden by EC directive).

A second possibility is to simply impose a price and see what happens to demand, and then iterate until demand equals capacity. The risk is, however, that serious distortions may occur while the price is adjusting, and that strategic game playing may occur to force the price down by withholding demand, where competition is not strong.

A third approach, recommended by NERA (1998), is to identify sections of infrastructure where capacity is constrained and to charge the long-run average incremental cost of expanding capacity. However, as explained above, this is a very difficult concept to measure (the cost of expanding capacity varies enormously according to the exact proposal considered, and it is not easy to relate this to the number of paths created, since they depend on the precise number and order of trains run). It may be argued, however, that more appropriate incentives are given to infrastructure managers if they are allowed to charge the costs of investment they actually undertake, rather than for the scarcity resulting from a lack of investment. Directive 2001/14 seeks to get round this by requiring infrastructure managers to undertake studies to determine the cost of expanding capacity, and to test whether this is justified on cost–benefit grounds, where scarcity charges are levied.

Given the difficulties with all these approaches, it may be thought that the best way of handling the issue is to permit direct negotiation between operators and the infrastructure manager over the price and allocation of slots, including investment in new or upgraded capacity. However British experience of this approach is that it is complex and time-consuming, given the number of parties involved and the scope for free-riding. It is also difficult to ensure that this does not lead to the abuse of monopoly power. An alternative is for the track-charging authority to attempt to calculate directly the costs involved. For instance, if a train has to be run at a different time from that desired, it is possible to use studies of the value people place on departure time shifts to estimate the value to its customers of the cost involved. Similarly the costs of slower speeds may be estimated from passengers' values of time.

Given the current degree of excess demand for slots, it is likely that the failure to charge for scarce capacity, together with the undercharging for congestion and the exclusion of certain other elements of marginal social cost, is leading to a situation where slots are substantially underpriced, compounding the problem of capacity shortage by leading to incentives to train operating companies to run too many trains, to have too strong a preference for frequent short trains rather than less frequent long, and to seek particular timings that are wasteful of capacity.

One counterargument should be considered first, however. That is the argument that the infrastructure of other modes, including road and air, is also not charged for in a way that adequately reflects marginal social cost, and in particular congestion and scarcity costs. Indeed the study referred to above (Sansom *et al.*, 2001) found substantial undercharging for the road mode on average, and too little differentiation in the current charges (primarily fuel tax) between locations and times where congestion is a problem and those where it is not. It might therefore be argued that to charge rail operators for these costs when road operators do not have to pay them is counterproductive.

This is, however, a very simplistic view of the appropriate approach to such 'second-best' conditions. The extent to which particular services divert passenger or freight traffic from congested or environmentally damaging roads or airports will differ with the type of service and how heavily it is loaded. The appropriate way of dealing with such second-best considerations is therefore to pay train operating companies incentives to reflect the benefits elsewhere of diverting traffic from other modes, as discussed above.

We have already discussed (in section 4) the average benefits of different types of train service. This may give some indication of the typical values to be attached to different types of train, although the point is made there that what we really want to know is the value of the marginal train. For passenger services, this will typically be below average, as the result of failing to run a particular train is simply a less frequent service, for freight, it is more likely that the consequence would be that the freight ceased to move by rail.

Table 5.7 brings together the estimates made in that section. They are crude, and based on a particular set of assumptions which may not even reflect average circumstances, let alone the circumstances of any particular case. They also leave out any benefits to users from being able to travel when they wish rather than at less convenient times. But for what they are worth they have some interesting implications. Firstly, it is certainly not apparent that the best way of dealing with shortages of capacity is to abandon freight traffic, as has been suggested in a recent report (RAC Foundation, 2002). Even if freight trains do typically take up more than one passenger path because of their slower speed, and are less certain actually to run, they appear to provide quite high social benefits. Secondly, amongst passenger services it is not immediately apparent that the most profitable, inter city, should take precedence over less profitable regional suburban trains.

There is an important further point to make here, however. This is that the failure to provide a path at a particular bottleneck may make it impossible to run the train in question over its entire length. For instance, if there is a bottleneck where a particular path could be used for an interurban regional train running 50km, a suburban train running 20km, an inter-city passenger train running 200km or a freight running 100km, then we would need to multiply the benefit per train kilometre by the distance each train is running to find the most desirable use of the path. As the table illustrates, on these assumptions the freight train retains the highest value, but the inter-city passenger train is more valuable than the shorter distance and more lightly loaded regional trains. If, however, the freight train displaces two inter-city passenger trains, inter-city passenger remains the most valuable use of the capacity in question.

What this example illustrates is that it is possible to provide at least a crude estimate of the value of using capacity in alternative ways. This calculation should be at the centre of any decisions on capacity utilization allocation, and could form the basis of a capacity charge based on the opportunity cost of the capacity which would give at least a simple incentive to economize in the use of capacity at critical times and places. Getting an accurate figure is very complex again because of the host of ways in which capacity may be used and the fact that some trains will require larger amounts of capacity than others (Nash *et al.*, 2002). Nevertheless the absence of a charge for the opportunity cost of capacity in the figures in Tables 5.5 and 5.6 represents a serious understatement of marginal costs, and wherever the operation of a short-distance passenger service currently displaces freight or long-distance passenger services that are running at capacity, it is likely that there is a serious misallocation of resources. When that in turn leads to major investment proposals to increase capacity on routes that would have adequate capacity if it was used more efficiently, the waste may be grossly multiplied.

6   LONG-TERM PLANNING AND INVESTMENT

A key problem identified by the Mercer report (2002) was the lack of leadership in the industry, leading to a lack of strategic planning and a failure to identify an appropriate investment strategy. Indeed the same point was made soon after taking up his position by the current chairman of the SRA (Bowker, 2002). Commenting that the existing investment planning framework was not fit for the purpose, he said: 'We need one plan, where all costs, benefits and risks associated with investing in rail can be clearly identified and analysed.'

As originally set up, the structure of the privatized rail industry appeared to rely on two organizations as the driving forces for investment. The first was Railtrack, for investment in infrastructure, and the second was the ROSCOs (Rolling Stock Leasing Company), regarding rolling stock. Railtrack was to have adequate incentives for replacement investment as a result of the performance regime and the penalties that would ultimately come its way if it failed to maintain the system; for enhancement, either it would invest at its own risk where it saw opportunities for selling capacity at commercially attractive prices, or it would rely on voluntary agreements with train-operating companies to pay for enhanced infrastructure. If OPRAF saw a case for enhancement, it would build that into the franchise agreement, and the regulator would allow Railtrack to recoup the cost and make an appropriate rate of return through the track access charges. ROSCOs would presumably invest in rolling stock on the basis of expected future lease income, again even if the current user only had a short franchise and therefore would only enter into a short-term lease. TOCs typically had a seven-year franchise and were not likely to invest in projects which would not provide a payoff in that time scale. OPRAF did have powers to underwrite both rolling stock leases and track access charges but was reluctant to use them, as it sought to maximize risk transfer to the private sector.

There were a number of problems with this structure. First and foremost, there was no organization really in a position to produce a strategic plan for the future of the railway around which other players could build their investment strategies. What made this crucial is the fact that the railway is a set of strongly interdependent components. It is no use one operator investing in rolling stock to increase or expand services if it does not know whether the appropriate infrastructure will be available to exploit it. As soon as capacity constraints begin to bite, hard decisions are needed on priorities and on investment in new capacity. But both would inevitably depend on the attitude of the government to the future requirements and funding for rail services, as expressed in particular in future passenger service requirements at franchise replacement and in future grant aid for freight.

At the same time, other questions should have been asked about whether the entire network had a long-term future. For many years the railway had been operated on the basis that the government did not dare to close it down, but wished to keep it going at minimum cost to the taxpayer. The new structure improved on this to the extent that OPRAF was in a position to study appropriate levels of support and investment for the passenger sector as a whole (although the fact that Railtrack was funded on the basis of the need to renew all its assets in modern equivalent form presupposed that the size of the network would remain unchanged, and some of the investment in refurbishing little-used stations that did take place appeared a very questionable use of resources).

OPRAF may have been able to play this role for the passenger business, despite its lack of a direct formal relationship with Railtrack, but it had no direct responsibility concerning freight. Railtrack may have been the strategic leader of the industry, in that its assets are the most long-term and fundamental to the ability of the industry to reconcile the competing demands placed on it, but as a privatized company sensitive to short-term share price fluctuations it was inevitably short-term and risk-averse in its outlook. Moreover the fact that it was negotiating prices for access with TOCs, who saw it as a profit maximizing monopolist, made the relationship between the parties antagonistic and the TOCs were certainly not willing to share data and information with Railtrack. It was certainly not the role of the regulator to tell the industry what its strategy should be. No other body had a wide enough viewpoint to play this role.

This situation is of course the one that led directly to the creation of the Strategic Rail Authority, and it might be thought that the problem is therefore now solved. But the SRA initially appeared a little reluctant to take on the above role. Indeed, in the *Strategic Agenda*, the then chairman of the SRA commented that the SRA should 'guide and lead, but not command and control' (SRA, 2001). Even the *Strategic Plan* (SRA, 2002b), when it did finally appear reads more as a collection of projects rather than a strategy. Moreover, it appears that the objectives given to the SRA emphasize meeting quantitative targets for traffic growth (50 per cent in passenger kilometres and 80 per cent in freight tonne kilometres) in a way that drives the investment strategy unduly. The *Strategic Plan* refers repeatedly to projects having been added to the list to ensure meeting the targets for traffic growth without their value for money having yet been tested. It is clearly stated in the plan that the pursuit of these projects does require that they be found to offer value for money under the SRA's criteria, but what happens if the SRA's obligation to obtain value for money from its spending conflicts with the targets for traffic growth set by the secretary of state is not said.

Whilst targets that are derived from an examination of strategic alternatives may be a useful monitoring device, targets of this sort that are maintained even when circumstances (and particularly the cost of reaching them) change dramatically are a recipe for waste. At the same time the SRA has come under intense pressure to invest in schemes thrown up by the Multi Modal Corridor studies, and from the PTEs to allocate funding and capacity to their areas, despite concerns about the costing of some of the former, and whether or not they make sense as a use of scarce capacity from a national strategic point of view for rail.

The result is to leave the SRA in a very difficult position, under political pressure from a number of sides, and yet charged with an overall duty to get value for money from the funding it provides. Clearly the new chairman of the SRA has made a determined start, has strengthened the organization in terms of its strategic planning role, and has declared that 'there are no sacred cows' (Bowker, 2002). Whether he will be able to produce and drive through a plan embodying the sort of changes that are needed remains to be seen.

CONCLUSIONS

We have in this chapter identified five key problems with the current position of the rail industry in Britain: (a) timetabling and the allocation of capacity, (b), cost escalation, (c) determining what services to provide, (d) providing appropriate incentives to operators, and (e) developing an appropriate strategic plan. Of these it is clear that strategic planning and determining what services to provide are the responsibility of the Strategic Rail Authority. It has strengthened its ability to tackle these, but is subject to many competing pressures. The efficient use of resources within the rail sector depends heavily on the SRA being able to overcome the pressure for actions which achieve short-term political gain, and to use its resources in the way which yields greatest benefits. That will undoubtedly mean looking carefully at the potential for reducing frequencies of lightly used rail services or replacing them with buses and concentrating investment and capacity where flows of traffic are dense.

Allocation of capacity is a shared responsibility; the SRA has made capacity utilization a priority, but ultimately it is the role of the regulator to adjudicate on disagreements about the allocation of capacity. The way in which capacity should be used will clearly emerge from decisions on what services should be provided and on long-term strategy and investment. But the processes by which these decisions are translated into day-to-day decisions on the allocation of capacity remain complex. I have already commented on the lack of clarity in the current decision criteria on the allocation of capacity. For the regulator to adopt decision criteria which clearly made the social value of the service the overarching criterion in capacity allocation decisions would help in this process.

Cost escalation and provision of appropriate incentives also concern both SRA and ORR. It is not clear how best they can tackle cost escalation, which in part arises as a result of the actions of another government body, the Health and Safety Executive. There are particular issues regarding the appropriate approach to incentives for Network Rail, given that financial penalties will not hurt shareholders, but the rail industry itself. Improved incentives for the train-operating companies require alterations both to franchise and track access agreements and therefore again involve both SRA and ORR.

Given that so many issues affect both SRA and ORR, one question that is often raised is whether both bodies are still needed. Indeed, in a previous lecture in this series, Dieter Helm (Helm, 2000) argued for their merger. The future need for an independent regulator may be further questioned now that Railtrack is being replaced by a not-for-profit organization with the SRA and the industry as its members. As long as the private sector is expected to invest in railways, I do see the need for an independent regulator, to provide a buffer between the decisions of government and the profitability of the private sector. The particular role of the regulator is to ensure fair and equitable treatment of the different bodies involved in the industry, and it is very difficult for a body under direct government control to do that, and to convince the private sector that it will do that. Talking to people in the industry I get the impression that they see even more need for protection against decisions of Network Rail than they did Railtrack, since they see it as more under the control of the SRA and, ultimately, government. However strange it may be to see two bodies, both appointed by the government, needing to draw up a Concordat explaining that they will work together, and however much there will inevitably be difficulties in the relationship between them, it does seem to me that the two bodies are both needed, and that the current obligations on the regulator, which oblige him both to aid the SRA in furthering its policies and to ensure that the private sector participants in the industry are treated fairly and can finance their activities, are right.

In short, then, in response to the question, 'what to do about the railways?' I have no easy answers. I think economic analysis can shed a lot of light on what should happen to services and fares, but the political difficulties in implementing the necessary changes are large. In terms of structural change it is not clear what needs to happen to address the many problems that have been identified. But I do believe that recent developments are a step in the right direction. There is hope that Network Rail will prove able to take a more long-term approach to issues than Railtrack did, although ensuring that it operates efficiently will be a challenge. Relationships between the various parties in the industry have already improved. The Strategic Rail Authority is clearly the appropriate body to tackle many of the issues raised above, and is doing so, but will need support from the regulator, while recognizing the separate duties the regulator has to fulfil. There remain a number of challenges. It is clear that some services are currently operating that cannot possibly justify their costs, especially where there is an important opportunity cost of the track capacity they occupy. As part of refranchising, the SRA will need to tackle this issue and ensure that all rail services give value for money. The regulator will need also to keep value for money in the foreground in his decisions regarding conflicts over track capacity. Alongside this, SRA will need to take a sufficiently prescriptive role to ensure that a sensible timetable is produced, while not excessively displacing the commercial judgment of the operator. That is a difficult balance to strike. And, finally, further improvements will be needed to the incentives to train operating companies to develop their services in the most socially desirable way, and to make the most efficient use of limited track capacity. This is perhaps the most important area where further progress is needed.

REFERENCES

Bowker, R. (2002), 'Britain's Railway – time for a new radicalism', Sir Robert Reid lecture, Institute of Logistics and Transport, London.

Caves, D.W. *et al.* (1987), 'Network Effects and the Measurement of Returns to Scale and Density for US Railroads', in A.F. Daugherty (ed.), *Analytical Studies in Transport Economics*, Cambridge: Cambridge University Press.

Commission for Integrated Transport (2002a), 'Fact Sheet 10. The implementation of railway safety measures', CFIT, London.

Commission for Integrated Transport (2002b), 'Paying for Road Use', CFIT, London.

Department of the Environment, Transport and the Regions (2000), 'Transport 2010 – the 10 year plan'.

Department for Transport (1993), 'Gaining access to the Railway network. The Government's proposals', DfT, London.

Department for Transport (2002), 'Modernising the Taxation of the Haulage Industry. Progress Report 1', DfT, London.

Fowkes, A.S. and C.A. Nash (2002), *Rail Privatisation in Great Britain – lessons for the rail freight industry*, Paris: ECMT.

Gibson, S. (2000), 'Charging for the Use of Railway Capacity', in Chris Nash and Esko Niskanen (eds), *Helsinki Workshop on Infrastructure Charging on Railways*, VATT discussion paper 945, Helsinki.

Helm, D. (2000), *A critique of rail regulation*, Beesley lectures in regulation, London: IEA.

Jones-Lee, M.W. *et al.* (2000), *Valuation of benefits of health and safety control: final report*, Sudbury, Suffolk: HSE Books.

Joy, S. (1971), 'Pricing and Investment in Railway Freight Services', *Journal of Transport Economics and Policy*, **5**.

Mercer Management Consulting (2002), *The GB Rail Industry: in its own words. Problems and Solutions*, London: Mercer.

Nash, C.A., S. Coulthard and B. Matthews (2002), 'Rail track charges in Great Britain – the issue of charging for capacity', paper presented at the 8th International Conference on Competition and Ownership in Passenger Transport, Rio de Janeiro, September 2003.

NERA (1998), *An examination of rail infrastructure charges*, London: NERA.

Nilsson, J.E. (2002), 'The institutions of Sweden's railway sector; the past, the present and the future of pricing for track use', paper presented at the second Imprint-Europe seminar, Brussels.

Office of Passenger Rail Franchising (1996), *Passenger Rail Industry Overview*, London: OPRAF.

Office of Passenger Rail Franchising (1999), *Planning Criteria*, London: OPRAF.

Office of the Rail Regulator (1994a), 'Framework for the Approval of Railtrack's Track Access Charges for Franchised Passenger Services, A Consultation Document', ORR, London.

Office of the Rail Regulator (1994b), 'Railtrack's track access charges for franchised passenger services. Developing the structure of charges. A Policy Statement', ORR, London.

Office of the Rail Regulator (1995), 'Railtrack's charges for passenger rail services: the future level of charges. A Policy Statement', ORR, London.

Office of the Rail Regulator (1997), 'The periodic review of Railtrack's access charges: a proposed framework and key issues', ORR, London.

Office of the Rail Regulator (2000), 'Periodic review of Railtrack's access charges: final conclusions', ORR, London.

Office of the Rail Regulator (2001), 'Review of freight charging policy: provisional conclusions', ORR, London.

RAC Foundation (2002), 'Motoring Towards 2050', London.

Railway Reform Group (2000), 'Perfect Timing. A national strategic timetable to make transport integration work', York.

Railway Safety (2002), 'The ERTMS Programme Team Final Report', London.

Sansom, T. *et al.* (2001), 'Surface Transport Costs and Charges. Great Britain 1998', Institute for Transport Studies, University of Leeds.

Strategic Rail Authority (2001), *A Strategic Agenda*, SRA, London.

Strategic Rail Authority (2002a), *Future fares policy – seeking your views*, SRA, London

Strategic Rail Authority (2002b), *The Strategic Plan*, SRA, London.

Vicario, A.J.B. (1999), 'Diversion factors and cross elasticities', unpublished MA dissertation, Institute for Transport Studies, University of Leeds.

CHAIRMAN'S COMMENTS

Tom Winsor

Chris Nash discusses five issues: timetabling and allocation of capacity, cost escalation, the services which should be provided, the long-term strategic vision for the railway and providing incentives to operators. My reactions to those points, and a few questions, are as follows.

As regards timetabling and use of capacity, Chris Nash says the relationship whereby the government buys services from the infrastructures users, who then buy services from the infrastructure provider, probably could never work; the government should be deciding what capacity to buy. I think that is going to change now with the Strategic Rail Authority's Capacity Utilisation Policy. He also says the ORR decision criteria, D4, would be very complicated to apply, there would be uncertainties about the outcome of any particular application of the criteria and a simpler approach might be better. Let me tell you some of the history.

In 1993 I attended a conference of railway professionals in Peterborough, and I, and one or two other lawyers (because that is what I was at the time) sat at the back of the hall and watched the railway professionals (one or two of whom are in the room now) jumping up and down at whiteboards, coming up with very complex mathematical formulae showing how capacity would be allocated and how an individual timetabling decision would be taken in any particular set of circumstances. One of my fellow lawyers said, 'This looks like it is going to turn into the pool rules for the electricity industry but I don't think we will be able to design them in the ten days we have to do it, because the pool rules took longer.' The railway professionals were becoming more and more excited, they were wanting weighted averages for social cost–benefit analysis and many other things, and then they had to get the same formula that would apply to every decision on the network. So it was going to apply to the highly subsidized services, the profitable inter-city services, freight and so on.

These ideas were going nowhere. During all this frenetic activity, I and one of my fellow lawyers at the back scribbled down in timetabling terms what we thought the regulator's section 4 duties (section 4 of the Railways Act 1993) would look like if you put them into timetabling criteria, because the section 4 duties are very general as well. I drafted these duties in five or six minutes, and apart from the odd tweak they are still the same today. When the whiteboard had been covered and the formulae had run into the sand, we produced this draft. The assembled guys said, 'Well, it is not as sophisticated as ours would have been but we will have it for now.' And it lasted for the best part of nine years. It is general, but one of the remarkable things is that there only has been one appeal to the Rail Regulator (in 1996) on the application of those criteria even though there have been 120–130 cases before the industry's timetabling dispute resolution tribunal. There is, therefore, no superior case law on those decisions, and maybe it would be better if there were.

On the issue of cost increases, Chris Nash mentioned transaction costs, compensation for possessions, legislative requirements, attitudes to risk and other matters. Again, I am surprised in terms of projects, in terms of network changes, that there has never been an appeal to the regulator under Part G of the network code, which is the appropriate mechanism, even though it has been there for nine years. Railtrack always appears to settle these cases. It negotiates TOC compensation for any particular project. The TOCs often propose very large figures. Railtrack appears to believe that it has to reach agreement on these matters and the TOCs just fold their arms and say, 'Pay me or I just will not agree.' Railtrack in my understanding just pays up. And the costs of projects rocket. There are some projects where the cost of TOC compensation can be as much as 40 per cent and yet Railtrack has never once appealed any of those questions to the regulator to get some case law established. Take the West Coast project, which is the most troubled railway project probably in the world. On two occasions in two successive years I said to those in charge of the project: 'Given that such a high proportion of the costs of this project is TOC compensation, why do you never appeal these questions?' The project manager, the most senior Railtrack project manager, said, 'I didn't know I could.' And the second thing I said was, 'Well why, if you think the rules are too generous for the train operators, don't you propose a change to the rules themselves under the change procedure under the network code?' And he said, 'I didn't know I could, I will have a word with Headquarters and make sure they do.' And the next year I asked the same questions and he said, 'I forgot.' Now 40 per cent of these enormous costs should not be falling down the cracks like this.

In terms of transaction costs and so on, under section 21 of the Railways Act, the regulator is empowered to publish and require the use of model clauses, standard clauses for access contracts, and we have been engaged in this (we lost a year, because of the administration of Railtrack, otherwise we would have finished by now). Our programme is to establish these model clauses to reform the relationship between the infrastructure user and the infrastructure provider so it has a simpler, clearer, stronger relationship, a true relationship of a joint venture recognizing the intensity of the interdependence of the infrastructure user and the infrastructure provider in so many things. As Chris Nash says, trains do not carry electrons or molecules of gas but people and goods, and they care where they get on, where they get off and what it was like on the journey, and they write letters when they don't like it. It is immensely complicated. And therefore the relationship between the infrastructure user and provider needs to be as much a joint venture in the truest sense as possible, so we must create a culture of compliance, where there is a simple strong clear specification of what each of you brings to the party, what you have to do in this relationship, and secondly what happens if things go wrong. And if you have no culture of conflict, you are not arming either side for the inevitable battle, it is not a lawyers' bonanza, it is actually a recipe for compliance, and for knowing your obligations and therefore honouring them.

We are also planning, through the model clauses programme, to reform the network code so as to improve these things. Again this was one of the shortcuts taken at the time of privatization and it has been immensely expensive in terms of transaction costs and attitudes to risk. The network code is the central commercial code for the railways. It is like the Pooling and Settlement Agreement and the Grid Code all rolled into one in the electricity industry. And yet this document was put together in a tearing hurry. For a long time it was in the hands of Railtrack, and those of us who were then working on all this saw 1 April 1994 rapidly approaching. This document was nowhere near ready and fit for purpose for the 1 April deadline. So the drafting of the document, and the policy decisions in relation to the document, were taken away from Railtrack by two government departments, OPRAF and ORR. And I remember sitting in a room, at a leading firm of solicitors one Saturday and Sunday, writing the whole document so that it would be ready and fit for purpose for 1 April 1994. But we knew then that this was nothing more than a framework on which the industry should build for the future. It deals with matters of timetabling, capacity allocation, operational disruption, vehicle change, network change and environmental protection. Apart from a few forays to tinker with the timetabling regime and one or two very minor other things, the industry has left this code alone. My intention is to rewrite the whole thing and make it fit for purpose, in consultation with the SRA, the Department and the people that have to work with it, that is Network Rail and the train operators.

Chris Nash argues that the services which should be provided are not purely a commercial decision for the railways. I entirely agree, but they never were. Those who are interested should read the leading judgment of the Lord Chief Justice in the case that we had in the Court of Appeal in June 2002, when he made it clear that the role of the regulator is superior to those of the administrators in capacity allocation and other matters, and emphasized that the Railways Act allows the regulator in matters of capacity allocation to depart from the wishes of both the infrastructure user and provider. The way the Lord Chief Justice said it orally in court (although his written judgment was different) was: the regulator not only is entitled in these matters to go off on a frolic of his own, he is *required* to do so. He is required to look outside the individual commercial interests of the two parties before him, and take a wider view of the proper and efficient allocation of capacity. What we have lacked for too long is an engaged and competent Strategic Rail Authority, which can give us their view on what the shape of capacity should be, so that when we are making these decisions we can make them in the light of that. We almost have to make them in a vacuum. Now, with Richard Bowker at the SRA, with the SRA's development of their capacity utilization policy (and there is a difference between utilization and allocation: utilization is what he does, allocation is what I do, but it comes together and it is coherent and rational), things are much better. With that we are going to be able to make much better and much faster decisions.

Then there is the issue of long-term planning and investment. Chris Nash says no organization was placed in the position to produce a strategy. Well it was, but it just did not know it, and the name of the company was Railtrack. They were the company established forever (they lasted five years). They did not have a short franchise, they had a 35-year licence that could only be terminated after year ten, on 25 years' notice. They were there for good. They had something the railway never had before, which was a secure revenue stream with an independent regulator operating according to statutory public interest criteria, subject to challenge on public law grounds but not the interference by politicians in determining what their revenues were for the efficient and competent management of the network. What a birthright! How was it thrown away? Only Railtrack could have done it. And indeed, if Railtrack had risen to the task, there would have been no need for the invention of the Strategic Rail Authority. Because Railtrack did neglect its birthright and shrank from the task for which it was established, it was necessary for the SRA to be invented.

Chris Nash also says it is not the role of the regulator to tell the industry what its strategy should be. I totally agree. It is the function of the regulator to act as a referee, not as a player, and that is why the SRA was needed and indeed has come. Dieter Helm mentioned a couple of years ago the possibility of a merger of the ORR and the SRA. This would, at a stroke, cast independence to the wind. But let us not go into that argument because it has been won in favour of independent economic regulation. The last Secretary of State for Transport appeared to regard independence as a disposable commodity. The present Secretary of State for Transport regards it as an essential continuing requirement and said so in his published statement on 12 June 2002: 'Independent economic regulation for the protection of the interest of users and the protection of interests of lenders, so as to secure private investment in the railway.' And if you want private investment, you must have independent economic regulation. But let us be clear. If you do not want private investment in the railway then my job is pointless and we should just pack it up and put it all under state control with the Strategic Rail Authority taking directions from the secretary of state and from the Treasury. It is a perfectly legitimate model. It is called nationalization. Many countries have it. But I think we have moved a bit further from there. And if you look at the government's proposals and platform in the last general election it was very much one of getting private investment in the provision of public services. That seems to me to be pointing in favour of private investment in the railways and therefore you need independent economic regulation.

Finally, I entirely agree with Chris Nash's comments that the accountability between the infrastructure user and the infrastructure provider needs to be strong. And indeed in my statement when I was consulting on the interim review, and saying what my approach would be to the acquisition of Railtrack by Network Rail, I made it very clear that I regarded the relationship between infrastructure provider and infrastructure user to be unchanged by the advent of Network Rail (a company without shareholders) and said that I believed that it was necessary to ensure that the accountability was as strong with Network Rail as it would have been with Railtrack. That is why we have continued and indeed strengthened even further Railtrack's network licence and, subject to the consultation period that is at present going on, we will be introducing a number of new and strengthened licence conditions, we will finish the model clauses programme and we are doing the interim review. That is the review that we were thinking would not be taking place just a year ago.

6. Liberalizing utility markets in the European Union

Frits Bolkestein

THE INTERNAL MARKET

At the moment the European Union is a global trading power ensuring a respectable degree of wealth and prosperity for its citizens. By the end of 2002, it will have been a decade since Europe's Internal Market without borders was launched. The Internal Market is one of the Union's proudest achievements. Its success is based on a liberal market economy. European integration is the most liberal project for which liberals were never credited.

Some people seem to believe that the Internal Market has long been finished and consider it yesterday's issue. Some may take the fruits of the Internal Market for granted, but I am sure that UK citizens whose cars have been seized by British Customs because they had purchased too many goods on the Continent realize that the Internal Market is not finished. Improving its performance is a process, not an event. Ten years after the magical '1992 deadline' there are still holes to be plugged and barriers to be removed, for example in the area of services and taxation. A single and open market (backed up by a strong single currency) provides the essential basis for future economic growth in the Community. Therefore we must be adamant that agreements which underpin the strength of the euro are adhered to. A dilution of commitments will inevitably undermine confidence in the single currency, generate inflation and thus erode the pension claims of the elderly, an ever growing segment of the electorate.

At the European Council in Lisbon, in March 2000, the heads of state and governments formulated the ambitious political and economic aim of becoming the most competitive, dynamic and knowledge-based economy in the world. The Lisbon summit urged the European Union to accelerate the liberalization of major parts of the utility markets such as the transport sector, electricity and gas, and postal services. Although the Lisbon agenda makes slow progress, this ambition ought to be set in stone because, if realized, it will ensure much economic growth.

ENERGY

In particular the security of energy supply is of strategic importance. The European economy is a notorious energy consumer but its own supply of energy is limited. As a result, external dependence on energy is constantly increasing. Currently 50 per cent of European energy requirements are imported, 45 per cent of oil imports come from the Middle East and 40 per cent of natural gas from Russia. If no measures are taken, dependence will increase from 50 to 70 per cent by 2030.

Energy dependence may be seen in all sectors of the economy. Transport, the domestic sector and the electricity industry largely rely on oil and gas and are at the mercy of international prices. Enlargement will exacerbate these trends. A rise in oil prices as a result of political events in the Middle East would cast gloom over the European economy which is already in difficulties with volatile financial markets. Energy dependence is the weakest point of the European economy now and will remain so for decades to come.

At the moment, Europe can rely on a strong, competitive energy sector which has been stimulated by liberalization. Member states have started opening up their gas and electricity sectors on the basis of European legislation. Some have gone faster than prescribed. The progressive opening of the gas and electricity markets has shown interesting results because it has gained its own dynamic. Around 70 per cent the European electricity market is currently open to competition. This will rise to 82 per cent by 2005. For gas, 80 per cent on average of European demand is open to competition. All member states except France and Luxembourg envisage a full market opening by 2005. At the moment, all member states except Germany have a system of access for electricity involving an independent regulator. All but Germany and France have that for gas. Liberalization of the energy markets has thus gained momentum, but it is still incomplete because two big players, Germany and France, lag behind.

LIBERALIZATION

Liberalization of the energy markets has generated benefits for industry as well as citizens. Prices of electricity have fallen and the service has become more affordable for consumers with low and average incomes, even though households have not gained as much as large consumers. Gas prices have shown a similar pattern, but there still remains a lot to be done in order to improve the performance of the internal energy market. There are still significant price differences across the European Union, highlighting the need for more integration. Markets are segmented by physical bottlenecks and inadequate domestic deregulation.

In spite of these benefits a polar wind now blows through the concept of this liberalization. It is often depicted as a recipe for disaster, a failure to supply essential services to citizens. The fear of liberalization and privatization is fuelled by the energy failure in California, a high-profile state. In size, California is the sixth largest economy in the world. If in Siberia a state-owned electricity company breaks down it will go largely unnoticed. But in California a similar event is noticed by the whole world.

CALIFORNIA

In 1996, California decided to privatize electricity, but something went wrong. The true reason for the electricity breakdown was not the transfer of legal property from the state to shareholders. No, the real causes were threefold: the environmental movement, smooth-talking politicians and ill-organized deregulation.

During the 1990s electricity demand in California increased by 30 per cent, mainly as a result of robust economic growth, but supply only rose by 6 per cent. So California was confronted by a huge gap between demand and supply. Electricity companies wanted to construct new power stations but failed to obtain licences from the authorities. Environmental groups protested at all possible construction sites. Even in Silicon Valley, the most notorious energy consumer, no additional capacity could be generated. The environmentally led resistance was labelled 'Banana'. It stands for 'build absolutely nothing anywhere near anybody'. The conclusion was evident: California went bananas! Banana resulted in an increasing electricity shortage in a booming market.

The second cause of disaster consisted of wobbly politicians who were more interested in votes than in good policies. California wanted to please citizens by keeping energy prices low. The instrument for this was a price cap which only remained feasible as long as feedstock prices stayed low. But in 2000, oil and gas prices increased steadily. Electricity companies, not being allowed to build additional capacity, were forced to buy electricity on the spot market at a high cost, but to sell it at a low price. As a result, electricity companies were loaded with debt while industry and citizens lavishly consumed energy because prices stayed low. Politicians and citizens only realized what had happened when electricity companies went bankrupt.

Thirdly, the Californian energy market did not let competition take place. Newcomers on the market were forced to contribute to the costs incumbent companies had already incurred in order to build power stations. Having to share the cost of the existing infrastructure resulted in a high entry ticket. The threshold to enter the market was made even higher by the price caps. The Californian market simply became unattractive for newcomers.

The experiment was bound to fail: there was no supply, there was no system of prices geared to costs and there was no competition. Despite some claims to the contrary, a 'Californian situation' cannot easily emerge on the European market because conditions there are different. In the European Union there is an adequate supply of electricity, prices reflect real costs and competition increases. There is no evidence to support the thesis that liberalization has a negative impact on the energy market. On the contrary, the gradual process of increasing competition has made markets stronger, companies fitter and prices more affordable. Universal service is guaranteed at a high quality level.

Those who point at liberalization and privatization as dangers to a reliable energy supply are barking up the wrong tree. The real danger is rising energy dependence and the European Union's exposure to the volatility of international oil and gas prices. This issue was acknowledged by the Founding Fathers of the European Community. The aim of the Euratom Treaty, signed in 1957, was to provide the European Community with an alternative source of indigenous energy in order to bring a halt to its growing dependence on oil from the Middle East. The treaty was meant to enable Europe to develop its know-how and obtain the means of exploiting nuclear energy for civil purposes. Euratom is still at the heart of European energy policy.

The Commission has now decided to increase the Euratom lending instrument which supports the financing of investments in nuclear installations from four to six billion euros. At the same time the Commission has adopted a package of initiatives to enhance nuclear safety.

NUCLEAR ENERGY

In some larger member states energy consumption relies heavily on nuclear power stations. At present 77 per cent of French electricity demand is met by nuclear energy. In Germany it is 31 per cent, in Britain 23 per cent and in Spain 29 per cent. Some smaller member states also rely on nuclear power. In Sweden, 50 per cent of electricity demand is met by nuclear power stations, in Belgium 58 per cent and in Finland 31 per cent. Recently Finland decided to build another nuclear power station because it has come to rely on a single fuel, gas, from a single source, Russia. Finnish prime minister Paavo Lipponen warned that all of Europe runs the risk of becoming a 'fossil monster' if it renounces nuclear energy.

I am aware that the issue of nuclear energy is contentious, but nuclear energy is not an aim in itself. It serves two important objectives of Community policy. Firstly, nuclear energy provides the technical capacity to increase energy diversification, which is needed to reduce external dependence. Currently 41 per cent of overall energy demand is covered by oil, 22 per cent by gas, 16 per cent by hard coal, 15 per cent by nuclear and 6 per cent by renewable energy sources. If nothing is done the pattern of energy consumption will change by 2030 to 38 per cent oil, 29 per cent gas, 19 per cent solid fuels, 8 per cent renewable energy (wind, solar, biofuels) and only 6 per cent nuclear.

The second aim is to meet the environmental challenge, in particular the issue of climate change and the commitments made in the Kyoto protocol. With the current pattern of energy consumption (which emphasizes the role of oil, gas and coal), the Kyoto requirements remain out of reach. The current use of nuclear energy avoids creating 312 million tons of CO_2 per year, which is 7 per cent of all greenhouse gases emitted in the Union or the equivalent of the CO_2 emissions of some 75 million cars.

Nuclear energy is a crucial contributor to a long-term European energy policy. An increased use of nuclear energy would reduce the external dependence of the European Union. It would also increase diversification, which would enable the European Union to cope with volatile oil and gas prices. And finally nuclear energy makes an excellent contribution to the Kyoto requirements. The paradox of current policies is that nuclear energy does not attract the political priority it deserves. Instead it is debated on the moral high ground and on the basis of often unjustified emotions.

As a result an increasing number of member states are either freezing the current use of nuclear energy or leaving the field altogether. Five (Sweden, Spain, Netherlands, Germany and Belgium) out of eight member states with nuclear power have adopted or announced a moratorium. Italy renounced nuclear energy following a referendum in 1987. Only France and the United Kingdom remain active in this field. Germany, traditionally a strong supporter of nuclear energy, announced the shutdown of its last reactors in 2021. Belgium will do the same in 2025. Both countries will have to import a great volume of energy. Germany will rely strongly on gas from Russia. The Russian government has announced the construction of an additional 30 nuclear plants to satisfy its own needs because oil and gas are mainly exported in order to acquire foreign currency.

Furthermore the European Union will remain vulnerable to external events, such as political crises in the Middle East. The European Union is eager to outline a common foreign policy which demonstrates a self-confident, independent position and global ambitions. But any foreign policy goal would be subject to pressure from oil-producing countries in the Middle East because the European economy, and in particular the employment of millions of Europeans, depends on an uninterrupted oil supply. Europe experienced two oil shocks in the 1970s which were highly disruptive. Representatives of member states went to the Middle East to beg for oil. The same may occur if oil prices rocket following a war in Iraq which is opposed by most Arab nations.

Europe should not only reduce dependence on oil, it should also prepare itself for higher energy prices in the future. The price of oil and gas can only rise because of limited availability in the long run and higher costs of exploitation in less accessible areas.

There are still problems in the field of nuclear energy which remain to be solved, but the difficulties are being reduced and they do not justify the total phasing out of nuclear energy now carried out by a number of member states. We have arrived at a crossroads in energy policy. Decisions taken today will affect future generations. The goals of Lisbon highlight transport, gas, electricity and postal services. Liberalization of the transport sector has produced tangible results for consumers, in particular in the area of civil aviation. Flying has become affordable for nearly everyone. Market opening in the telecommunications sector has produced benefits which were unthinkable ten years ago. Liberalization of the energy markets is well under way and in the postal sector it is gaining momentum.

WATER

But one segment of the utility market is always omitted: the water sector. We should also look at market forces here. In The Netherlands the water sector is not following the trend towards liberalization. Worse still, some people want to have nothing whatsoever to do with it.

We have to bear in mind that liberalization is not a dogma; it is a practical instrument for establishing the correct relationship between price, quality and the standard of the service provided. Water will be a scarce commodity in the future. The demand for water is rising as a result of an increase in population and economic growth, while the amounts of relatively clean and cheap groundwater are decreasing. And there is the problem of desiccation, resulting particularly from the large amounts of water used in agriculture. This is already serious in Spain. Drinking water is used for everything nowadays, including washing cars and flushing toilets. From an ecological point of view one may wonder whether the water sector does not need to be more subjected to market forces if supply and demand are to be better matched. The question is logical and legitimate.

Some may say that the British experience in the water sector has not been very positive. But here there is a lesson to be learned. In 1989, Britain started to privatize the water companies but not to liberalize the market. That was putting the cart before the horse. One should begin by opening up the market and giving consumers a choice, only then letting government and companies decide on the structure they wish to adopt for operating on this market. In a nutshell: first liberalize and then, if you want, privatize. The privatization of the British water sector did not come out of the blue; the sector was in a state of severe neglect – and in government hands. The people of Britain had long assumed that water supplies and water purification were not a problem. It turned out that they were wrong.

During the privatization process, a major investment project was launched with a view to improving the quality of drinking water and the purification facilities. Many British water companies both produce drinking water and treat waste. The price of water in the United Kingdom went up because the country had to meet the EU's environmental standards. The high costs of treating waste were increasing the price of drinking water. Privatization was seen as a way of restoring the strength of the entire sector. The market had to make up for the government's negligence. But market forces had no influence at that time. When presenting the budget in 1999, the British government proposed greater competition in the water sector. It was thinking in particular of competition between regional networks. On the Continent, one often hears the argument that the water sector in Britain is in a bad state because of privatization, this being a danger for public health or the environment. This is tub-thumping. The sector was neglected when it was in government hands.

More generally, on the European level, steps towards opening the water sector market are feasible. First, diversification is an important factor, since consumers – and particularly businesses – increasingly want given amounts of a given quality. Major consumers in new sectors of industry are starting to install double pipelines in order to differentiate between water products. They simply want to be more economical with water because prices are rising. After all, there is a big difference between drinking water, rinsing water and cooling water. You can use rainwater for watering plants. Nowadays high-quality drinking water is used for too many purposes and the groundwater level is falling as a result.

Another possibility is competition between networks. Supplies of drinking water are at present regional, so companies depend on a regional supplier. It is possible, however, for a water company to connect a pipeline to a neighbouring distribution network in order to supply a given customer or group of customers. This means the consumer has a choice. It also means that an inefficient water supplier would run the risk of losing customers to another regional distributor. This would be an incentive for providing good service. The British government is particularly keen on stepping up regional cross-border competition with a view to improving the performance of privatized water companies. I am pleased to note that the UK government's paper on its future water policy, recently released, ('Directing the Flow') states that it intends 'to introduce greater competition in the supply of water for larger users, to encourage further innovation, greater efficiencies and keener prices'.

Thirdly, we must also consider technological developments. Time does not stand still. In telecommunications, technology did much to open up markets. In the water sector, membrane technology is making decentralized and small-scale water production possible. With the aid of a fairly simple installation, a company can purify and use water itself, thus reducing dependence on water companies. The water sector is not stagnant, therefore, and it will become better if it makes preparations for new developments rather than depending entirely on government support.

Another possibility would be a form of competition based on concessions along French lines. With this approach, the government issues a public invitation to tender for the production and distribution of water and the company offering the best terms gets the contract for a given period. All the essential agreements are made within a legal context and the private concession holder has access to the capital market and may form partnerships. The World Bank vigorously promotes the concession model.

The market presses on, also in the water sector. The water sector has been 77 per cent privatized in France and 87 per cent in Great Britain. In Spain, privatization is well under way and Portugal and Italy are moving in that direction. It is also interesting that, in Germany, which has a large number of water companies, the government is dismantling the drinking water monopoly. The water company serving the capital, *Berliner Wasserwerke*, has been privatized to a considerable extent. The City of Berlin holds 51 per cent of the shares and market operators 49 per cent. The Ministry of Economic Affairs considers that German water companies are inadequately prepared to act as international operators and that the water sector is too fragmented. Liberalization should provide German water companies with an incentive to modernize and increase the scale of their operations. We can therefore expect a wave of mergers and alliances between German and foreign water companies.

The current trend will also take on a European dimension one day. As far as water is concerned, the Commission has hitherto concentrated on quality. In September 2000, the European Parliament and the Council of Ministers adopted the Framework Directive on Water, which should be implemented in national legislation within three years. As soon as this has been done, we will be better placed to look at water as a cross-border product. The Framework Directive provides for cross-border trade in water if certain ecological standards are observed.

General De Gaulle is supposed once to have said that the economy is like the train of an army: it follows. The opposite is true. In utility markets, economic developments and free markets show the way. The legislator will follow, sooner rather than later.

CHAIRMAN'S COMMENTS

Philip Fletcher

The Commissioner's chapter addresses a wide range of issues. There is his robust analysis of the Californian problem and his stout assertion that there are few lessons from that for us in Europe. There is his very stark warning of the danger of energy dependence, and especially of the importing of oil and gas. There is his comment on the incompleteness of the liberalization of the energy market across the Union, with his finger firmly pointed at Germany and France as the laggards. A point of even greater interest is his defence of the nuclear option. All of us, whether we are involved directly in the energy sector or not, await with huge interest the British government's statement on energy policy which has been deferred again, and will now appear some time in 2003, rather than before Christmas 2002.[1] And there is his comment on the interesting development in the Commission's own policy, on moving further into the field of ensuring nuclear safety across the Union.

There is a convention, one simply of self-preservation, whereby utility regulators, sectoral regulators, like me in the case of water, do not start commenting on the business of other sectoral regulators. So you will not find me commenting on Graham Corbett's business in relation to the post, or Callum McCarthy's in relation to energy. Thankfully Mr Bolkestein went on to comment on water, which gives me at least an opening. Let me try and respond to one or two of his points.

The Commissioner drew attention to General de Gaulle's remark that the economy follows the legislator and stoutly rebutted it. I entirely accept that true price competition reaches parts that no legislator, no regulator can hope to reach. But problems arise with something as essential to health and life as drinking water if the product is left unregulated. We sit here in the centre of a city which experienced the free market in its rudest and rawest form in relation to water, 150 years ago. Different companies supplied households on the basis of different sources of water, and different networks. This caused a few problems. It was first of all a very unregulated market in which all sorts of malpractice went on: both the European Commission and domestic national regulators would frown on such things as breaking up your competitors' networks and then going on, on the back of that, to sell your services to the deprived householders. More seriously it provided the foundation for the first great epidemiological study based on the different sources of water. This demonstrated that cholera was water-borne and, what is more, that it was related to sewage. A lot of the pipes were drawing water from just below the sewer outfalls. It is not a surprise that London suffered greatly from cholera in the first half of the nineteenth century.

Now that is not to dispute the point Mr Bolkestein was making, it is really to take to an extreme the fact that a market requires regulation within the context of its freedom.

I would like to make one other point. As the Commissioner rightly said, there are those in Europe who say 'we should never privatize' and couple that with 'we should never liberalize water markets – look what has happened in the UK'. I would hope that all of us would now feel confident in rebutting such an argument. Given the fact that we have not liberalized water fully in the United Kingdom, and there are reasons for that which I will touch on, we have certainly seen, following privatization, huge advances in meeting the requirements of the Community and the Union and in delivering the requirements of water customers here. To give just a few examples: drinking water, which only ten years ago failed the quality tests at the tap one in 100 times, now fails the test in one in 700 times. Ten years ago, 84 per cent of our rivers were 'fair to good' in terms of their chemical and biological quality. Now 94 per cent meet these criteria, a lot of them moving to 'good'. Even the Thames is starting to move in that direction, and we can look at a whole host of other indicators. There is a reason behind the improvement and it is the reason Mr Bolkestein identified: prior to 1989, within the public sector, the water industry was deprived of the necessary investment. Freed into the private sector, and completely freed from dependence on the taxpayer, the level of investment has more that doubled. We are seeing levels of investment consistently since 1989 of roughly five to six billion euros every year in England and Wales. That is what underlies the improvement. The customers have paid, bills have gone up 20 per cent in real terms, but they have not paid anything like as much as they would have done without the huge efficiency gains which monopoly companies had made under the twin pressures of regulation and shareholder demand for profit.

As the Commissioner indicated, the government has now moved to say what it wants to happen on competition. There are all sorts of reasons, and I fully understand them, why the government has said we are very unwilling to move competition fully into the domestic sector for water. But they are saying they want to see competition stretching beyond the regulator's reach into large business users and they are setting out a framework. We await the Queen's Speech which will formally tell us whether or not the starting gun has been fired for a Water Bill[2] this coming session in the British Parliament. That bill would put this new system in place to allow true competition – and incidentally to encourage a regulator in the water sector to seek to ensure that we do not have oligopoly substituting for monopoly. You will forgive me if I express a little scepticism on the French model, which is very heavily dependent on just two or three companies for the operation of the concession system.

NOTE

1. The White Paper on energy policy was published in February 2003. See chapter 9.
2. The Water Act 2003 received Royal Assent in November 2003.

7. Measuring the success of postal regulators: best practice in postal regulation

Ian Senior

INTRODUCTION[1]

In 1970, I wrote a paper,[2] published by the Institute of Economic Affairs, arguing that the letter monopoly in the UK should be abolished. My conclusions received support from *The Economist*, but elsewhere encountered a resounding silence. When I developed the arguments in a further paper in 1983,[3] also published by the IEA, and suggested privatizing the Post Office, I was taken out to lunch by the Post Office's public relations department, which represented progress of some sort.

Since 1970, I have developed my ideas in various publications and talks, but my starting point remains that competition is desirable in supplying postal services in general and letter services in particular. This is the first time I have specifically addressed the question of whether and how postal regulation should be used to bring a fully competitive postal market into being in the UK and beyond.

1 BACKGROUND

In the 1980s and 1990s, Mrs Thatcher's administration embarked on a major programme of privatization, a word that had not been coined in 1970. Not only were organizations such as British Airways that clearly operated in a competitive market privatized, others such as water, gas and electricity were included even though the possibilities for the creation of competing physical structures were, and are, far less promising.

Postal services, embodied in what then was called the Post Office, remained curiously absent from Mrs Thatcher's shopping list. Only when John Major became prime minister did the privatization of the Post Office enter the debate, but the proposal was abandoned because the then government's wafer-thin majority would have prevented Michael Heseltine's bill getting through Parliament. Today the European Community has accepted the case for significant liberalization of the letters market with reductions of the reserved areas coming into force on 1 January 2003 and 2006. In 2003, the reserved area became letters below 100g or priced at three times the standard letter. In 2006, the upper limits of the reserved area will be reduced to 50g or 2.5 times the standard letter, and a review will take place to decide whether a third reduction should take place on 1 January 2009. This could be anything between total liberalization and no further change.

In this chapter I shall look at the issues that regulators must address and I shall suggest some criteria for judging their operations. But first I begin with some general observations about postal markets generally and hence whether regulation of them is needed at all.

2 IS POSTAL REGULATION NEEDED AT ALL?

The primary justification for regulation in any sector is to correct market failure, actual or potential. A secondary justification may be to enable a smooth transition in a market from monopoly to competition. Sharp discontinuities caused by opening up a market may create short-term inefficiencies of production and hence additional costs to end-users. These inefficiencies are likely to be self-correcting within, say, three years of the market being opened to full competition.

The first justification for having a regulator specific to the postal industry is the experience of full postal liberalization in Sweden and New Zealand, where, after five to ten years, the original incumbent has still retained up to 95 per cent of the market. Massive market dominance might provide a similarly massive scope for the abuse of market power and for inefficiency in providing service. In fact in both Sweden and New Zealand the incumbents reduced staff numbers significantly to handle about the same volumes of mail, showing that the mere presence of competition is a spur to efficiency in the incumbent even when its market share remains dominant.

A postal service differs from other utilities because its output is highly heterogeneous. The output of the electricity industry is a kilowatt-hour, whatever the inputs. The output of the gas industry is a cubic metre of gas of a measurable and largely uniform thermal value. The outputs of the postal industry are delivered items ranging from postcards, letters with contents specific to the addressee, light letters, flat letters, heavy letters, bulky letters, direct mail letters, urgent letters, non-urgent letters, magazines, newspapers and small packets such as photographic film. The processing of all these items from acceptance to final delivery is sufficiently complex to justify the creation of a specialist regulator, at least while the market is in transition from monopoly to a free market.

During and after the transition, and possibly for many years, the incumbents are likely to wish to squeeze out new competitors, for example by predatory pricing. A regulator's role is to ensure that this does not happen. Further, if new entrants raise complaints against the actions of incumbents, the right forum for arbitration of disputes may well be a knowledgable, independent and specialist postal regulator rather than the general competition authorities or the law courts.

Other arguments for having specialist postal regulators could be put forward which, I suggest, are much less important. The role of watchdog, split in the UK for no clear reason between Postcomm and Postwatch, is seen as protecting small firms and individual senders of mail, yet their mail costs are tiny in relation to all their other outgoings. The big senders such as the direct mail houses, the mail order firms, the banks and the utilities have plenty of muscle and need no protection. As for individual users, who are among the most vocal when their mail arrives late, they have not paid to have it sent. Not having paid the piper, they have no right to call the tune.

In sum, the justification for specialist postal regulators boils down to this: they are required to manage transition and to ensure that new entrants to the market do not suffer from incumbents' abuse of a dominant position. From this analysis it follows that both Postcomm and Postwatch should be seen as transitional institutions. When the UK letters market has been fully liberalized in 2007 and is seen to be working well over, say, the next three years, both organizations should be phased out and their residual responsibilities handed over to the general competition authorities of the day.

3 A FINAL MILE MONOPOLY, UNIVERSAL DELIVERY OBLIGATION AND CREAM SKIMMING

It is well known that there are significant economies of scale in mechanized letter sorting,[4] bulk transport between production centres and delivery over the final mile. This being so, when full access to the market is open in legal terms, only parts of the market may be contestable in practice.

An incumbent monopolist with the sole final mile delivery network could unilaterally decide to cut out deliveries to uneconomic addresses and therefore, it is argued, must be prevented from doing so by a universal service obligation (USO). Incumbents have supported this argument, saying that permitting competitors to enter just part of the market without a commitment to universal service would result in cream skimming. However they have never acknowledged that providing universal delivery has a positive value. Mailers large and small require it, and the cost of setting up a duplicate competing final mile network from scratch seems prohibitive at present. If the positive value of universal service could be quantified, which is difficult, it might outweigh the negative value of delivery to sparse areas.

However the profitability of cream skimming so far has proved much less attractive than previously thought. Attempts in Sweden and New Zealand by new entrants to provide even localized services of collection and delivery have frequently failed, and many new entrants have left the market. Furthermore, the proportion of significantly uneconomic deliveries in the UK was shown by NERA's study for the European Commission in 1998 to be tiny. Of about 17.3 billion inland mail items carried by Royal Mail in 1996–7, about 0.3 billion, or 1.8 per cent, were significantly uneconomic to deliver.[5] If it was felt that this burden on the Royal Mail Group was intolerable, it could be eased by allowing deliveries to such areas to be made every second day: that is, three times a week. This would enable the number of staff to be halved and the number of items to each address to be doubled on each delivery.

In essence, the loud complaints over the years by the Post Office about the cost of the universal service obligation and the threat of cream skimming have little merit. Experience in Sweden and New Zealand suggests that the Royal Mail Group in the UK and incumbents elsewhere can expect to retain at least 90 per cent of their national letters markets for at least five years following full liberalization. This should be ample for them to make profits. Posten in Sweden and NZ Post have both continued to make profits since market liberalization, but at lower levels than under monopoly. Thus the 'natural monopoly' argument is no longer an issue, nor is cream skimming, and the 'cost' of the USO burden may even be positive.

4   THE GOVERNMENT'S REASONS FOR POSTAL LIBERALIZATION IN THE UK

More Commercial Freedom

In 2000 the UK government passed the Postal Services Act. Its declared intention was to give the Royal Mail Group[6] more commercial freedom and to open the market to competition. Additionally the government decreed that the USO must be maintained: not less than one delivery to every address and one collection throughout the land each working day. The Act requires a universal service at a uniform tariff.

The argument about giving the Royal Mail Group greater commercial freedom was only partly valid. During the 1990s, the Post Office raised its prices when it wanted and made good profits. True, it was compelled to pass some of those profits as cash loans to the Treasury but the Post Office did not grumble that it was short of cash to do the things it wanted. Its current claim that it was not allowed to 'invest' is untrue. It made a number of investments in overseas letter and parcel operations, and there was no suggestion that it was being thwarted from mechanizing or modernizing its domestic services. In essence, it had enough freedom and cash, but its management was poor. It chose to protect a monopoly rather than get ready for competition.

Social Engineering

Most would agree that postal services are a utility and should not be an instrument for social engineering. Unfortunately the Postal Services Act embodies two clear instances of social engineering and the obligation to implement such social engineering has been imposed on Postcomm.

The first is the requirement of a uniform tariff. Section 4 of the Act lays down that there should be 'a public tariff which is uniform throughout the United Kingdom'. Presumably this is a well-meaning attempt at social inclusiveness on the grounds that poor country mice should not be charged more for their mail than fat-cat urban dwellers. In fact, the cost of letter delivery is often the opposite. Big houses with long drives in stockbroker Surrey take more delivery time than closely grouped dwellings, whether in a village or in a city centre. The uniform tariff probably benefits the country's top 5 per cent income bracket more than anyone else.

The EC Directive 97/67/EC[7] does not contain any requirement for a uniform tariff, and it is evident that the present government's imposition of a uniform tariff was a political and not an economic decision. It is enlightening to consider the origin of the uniform tariff. In his seminal monograph of 1837, Rowland Hill wrote:

> I therefore propose that the charge for primary distribution, that is to say, the postage on all letters received in a post-town, and delivered to the same or any other post-town in the British Isles, *shall be at the uniform rate of one penny per half ounce.*[8] ... In the present state of things, the secondary distribution of letters to places of inferior importance is in some places a source of loss. This appears to me to be undesirable: every branch of the Post Office ought, in my opinion, to defray its own expenses.[9]

Today we accept that the tariff for utilities such as water, gas and electricity should vary according to the supplier. A uniform tariff that is willingly offered as such by a supplier is acceptable, but there is no economic justification for forcing a uniform tariff on Royal Mail's letters. In practice, the uniform tariff for letters exists only for individuals and small business users. Large mailers rightly get substantial discounts for work sharing, notably for presorting mail.

The 'Uniform Tariff' is a Fiction

Royal Mail Group recently gave a body blow to the concept of a uniform tariff. It announced a pilot scheme under which businesses that receive fewer than 20 letters a day and wish to receive them before 9.00 a.m. should pay a fee of £14 per week or £728 per year. On this basis a firm receiving 19 letters a day, five days a week, would pay a delivery surcharge of 14.7p per letter. Allan Leighton, Royal Mail Group's chairman, announced that he had first heard these figures on the radio and immediately countermanded them, but the concept has not been withdrawn.

The scheme is notable in being a reversion to times when posters did not pay for the mail and addressees were charged for receiving it. Some of them refused and the mechanics of the present scheme appear similarly flawed. Who will count and record the letters for relevant addresses each day? What happens if an addressee's average fluctuates during the year around the figure of 20 items per day and ends up at, say, 19? What happens when Firm A receives an average of 15 letters per day and Firm B next door receives 25? If Firm A declines to pay a surcharge and Firm B gets its letters at 8.45 a.m. anyway without a surcharge, Royal Mail then must make a point of bypassing Firm A at 8.45 a.m. It must then deliver to Firm A later at extra cost, or deliver the mail to Firm A at 8.45 a.m. without the surcharge, making a mockery of the entire scheme.

However this new proposal has one merit: it opens up the possibility of specialized operators collecting the mail free from Royal Mail's offices to deliver to Firm A and others who want to receive it before 9.00 a.m. This would be welcome as the start of an embryonic 'final mile' delivery network.

Other Forms of Social Engineering

Within the Postal Services Act, Postcomm has also to conduct further overt social engineering:

> The Commission shall have regard to the interests of –
> (a) individuals who are disabled or chronically sick,
> (b) individuals of pensionable age,
> (c) individuals with low incomes, and
> (d) individuals residing in rural areas,
> but that is not to be taken as implying that regard may not be had to the interests of other descriptions of users.[10]

To date Postcomm has rightly given priority to other issues, but the time may come when, under the Act, it is obliged to favour those of pensionable age, including Bernie Ecclestone, with cut-price postage stamps. Despite the difficulties facing Formula 1, Mr Ecclestone cannot yet be said to be of low income.

With the exception of Christmas, old people probably send no more than one or two letters a week. Ten per cent off 54p is 5.4p or £2.70 per year. It is likely that the cost of administering the scheme would far outweigh that. Taking the Act as a whole, its thrust is in the right direction of freeing the market, but it is flawed by aspects of social engineering.

5   CRITERIA BY WHICH TO JUDGE GOOD POSTAL REGULATION

Against this background, I now come to the main theme of the chapter. It might be thought difficult to devise measures to show whether a given postal regulator is doing its job well or badly. A cynic might say that, the louder those who are regulated squeal, the better the regulator is performing, but I do not accept this. Instead I now suggest ten criteria against which to judge postal regulators in the UK and elsewhere.

Compliance with EC Law

The EC postal services directive was signed on 15 December 1997 and should have come into force 12 months later. Key clauses of the directive have still not been implemented in some member states. Notable examples are the creation of an independent regulator, and requiring incumbents to produce separate accounts for their reserved and unreserved services. While national legislatures rather than postal regulators are to blame for failure to set up independent regulators (see below), the regulators should take responsibility for requiring incumbents to produce separate accounts.

Full Independence from Government

As noted, the postal directive 97/67 requires the creation of independent national regulatory authorities. Austria, Belgium, Denmark, France, Italy and Spain have chosen to ignore the directive on this point, and their postal regulators are a ministry. A ministry, by definition, is an arm of government whose job is to look after the interests of its nationals in general. A ministry is influenced by national considerations rather than by the creation of a correctly working market within its jurisdiction.

Belgium can be identified as a case where the absence of an independent national regulator allowed a serious breach of market competition to occur. La Poste introduced a new service whose clear aim was to undercut the Belgian business of Hays DX, the British document exchange company. In the absence of an independent regulator, appeal to the Belgian ministry by a British company against the actions of the Belgian postal incumbent would have been fruitless. Hays DX therefore took its case direct to the European Commission and won. La Poste's service was declared illegal and, presumably, La Poste will pay damages to Hays DX.

Although this case achieved a satisfactory outcome, it is clearly undesirable that postal competition matters relating to a national market should have to be heard in the first instance by the European Commission. The Commission has massive executive and legislative functions already. It should not have unnecessary judicial functions in addition.

Milestones and a Deadline for Full Liberalization

Full postal liberalization in Sweden and New Zealand took place as a 'big bang' for which both incumbents were given about five years' advance notice. Both administrations are on record as having welcomed their governments' decision to liberalize their markets. By contrast, the British Post Office and France's La Poste, for example, have consistently opposed liberalization tooth and nail.

The alternative to a big bang is for the regulator to set milestones, for example a reduction in the weight limit of the reserved area or the opening up of market segments such as direct mail. Postcomm has chosen the milestone route. It is hard to say whether the big bang or milestones are the best. In the past, a big bang would have seemed more risky. It is virtually impossible to undo a big bang, whereas milestones can be postponed if problems emerge. However the outcomes of big bangs in Sweden and New Zealand suggest that there is less risk of Railtrackian chaos than was thought.

What is definite is that a clear path to liberalization, whether by milestones or a big bang, is essential to bring competition to the market and to allow incumbents to prepare for it.

Current Size of the Reserved Areas

As noted, all EU member states are faced with the new directive's milestones. However experience is that many states are late in complying with EU legislation. If six states have still not implemented the directive of 1997, they may take just as long to implement the directive of 2002. Those incumbents that enjoy a larger reserved area at any time will have an unfair advantage over others. The larger the reserved area, particularly when coupled with high prices, the greater the potential for supernormal profit and hence for cross-subsidized foreign acquisitions. From Table 7.1, it can be seen that currently the Netherlands has the smallest reserved area and France the largest. Deutsche Post has the smallest reserved area for direct mail.

Even if all member states had implemented the new directive by 1 January 2003 the UK market, opened by Postcomm to mailings of 4000 or more identical items irrespective of the weight of each unit, is much more radical because each item can be charged at any tariff.

Table 7.1   Current reserved areas in four EU states

	October 2002	EC's new postal directive from 1.1.2003
France	Up to 350g or 5 times the basic letter	100g or 3 times price of standard letter
Germany	Up to 200g for ordinary mail and up to 50g for direct mail	Ditto
Netherlands	Up to 100g or 3 times the basic letter rate	Ditto
UK	Items up to £1, i.e. about 3.7 times the basic letter rate but from January 2003 the market will be liberalized for mailings of over 4000 items	Ditto

Liberal Licensing Policy

I suggest that postal regulators should award licences to provide any form of postal service without restriction. They are in no position to judge the commercial risk entailed either for applicants or for operators already in the market. The main purpose of licensing should be that of knowing who the players are and monitoring what is occurring in the marketplace.

Up to June 2000, the German postal regulator had received 850 licence applications, of which only two had been rejected. By contrast, up to 12 September 2002, Postcomm had received just 15 applications, including that of the Royal Mail Group. All to date have been granted in an average time of four months. Why the disparity in number of applications? One possible explanation is that Deutsche Post's basic tariff in June 2001, when adjusted for purchasing power, was 36.9p for standard letters up to 20g and 73.8p for standard letters weighing 20–50g. These were the highest in the EU and so offered a much larger margin to attract new entrants than was the case in the UK.

Other possible explanations are that the operations for which German licences have been granted are more clearly defined, whereas Postcomm has effectively said to applicants: do lots of homework, show us your business plans and then we will decide whether we will grant you a licence; and/or Postcomm's licences have been for one year only, meaning that licensees have no certainty that the licences will be renewed or that the conditions will remain the same. Whatever the reason, Postcomm needs to eliminate any impediments that currently discourage new entrants to the market.

If postal regulators issue licences freely, why have licences at all? The answer is that they provide the possibility of controlling anti-competitive behaviour by operators in the market, notably the former incumbents. Reverting to the Belgian case, if Belgium had had an independent postal regulator in the Hays DX case (which represented a clear abuse of a dominant position by La Poste) the regulator could have instructed La Poste within days or weeks to cease and desist.

To ensure compliance, a regulator's ultimate sanction is the withdrawal of any operator's licence. This should give a measure of confidence to users considering using the services of new entrants because cowboy firms could quickly have their licences revoked and be removed from the market.

Commercial Separation of Incumbents' Main Businesses

As noted, the EC postal directive of 1997 requires incumbent administrations to produce separate accounts for their businesses that are in the monopoly areas, notably letters, and those that are not, notably parcels and express services. For years the Post Office published separate accounts for its three main businesses which showed among other things the regular subsidy to the parcel service paid by the letters operation. The then Post Office or Consignia began to bundle its accounts for the three main services so that they provided less information and concealed the subsidy to Parcelforce. Similarly, in Germany Deutsche Post was found by the European Commission to have subsidized its loss-making parcel division from profits on letters and was fined for providing illegal rebates to customers as part of this.

The ability to split incumbents into their main operational components may fall to national governments rather than regulators, but the latter need to ensure that incumbents publish accounts that separate their main businesses. Separate accounts are a second best option to separate companies.

In passing, it should be noted that the appalling fiasco of segmenting Railtrack from the operating companies is *not* an argument against segmenting letters, parcels, counters, banking and express services. Train operating companies require rails to run on. By contrast, the overlaps in the UK between the functions of letters, parcels, counters, express delivery and banking services are small.

Intervention on Service Quality

The level of service provided in a correctly working market should be determined by what suppliers offer and customers demand. Postcomm has made much of requiring Royal Mail to meet a target of delivering 92 per cent of first class mail on the next working day (D+1). Given the declining importance of mail as a medium of time-sensitive communication, it is likely that making Royal Mail perform to targets set by Postcomm is counterproductive. There is a tradeoff between quality of service and the cost of supplying it. Major mailing houses may prefer slower deliveries and lower tariffs, they may prefer a higher standard of service at higher prices, or they may want day-definite deliveries. In a liberalized market it should not be part of a postal regulator's job to assume the function of interpreting what customers want.

The price difference between first and second-class mail should be sufficient to allow customers to express their choice between D+1 or D+3 deliveries. If big mailing houses want something different they should talk directly to Royal Mail and to new entrants, not to Postcomm or Postwatch.

It could be argued that, if Postcomm did not impose any quality standards on Royal Mail, D+1 delivery might fall, say, to 50 per cent and no penalty would be imposed. This seems unlikely. Royal Mail has belatedly scrapped the second delivery. The duration of the single delivery, I have regularly argued, should be spread over eight hours, from 8.00a.m. to 4.00p.m. which are in daylight throughout the year. Business areas would receive early deliveries and residential areas later ones. I have further argued that every posting box in the land should be marked with a latest posting time for next day delivery of first-class mail. In rural areas, this might be noon or earlier. Combining earlier collection with extended delivery times should enable Royal Mail to aim for 100 per cent D+1 delivery of first-class mail.

Direct Intervention on Individual Operators' Prices

As noted, letter mail is *not* a commodity akin to water, gas, electricity or telecommunications. Delivering an inner-city letter that is presorted and typed with a bar code is far easier to handle than one that is handwritten, lacks a postal code and is addressed to the Isle of Mull. A stamped letter requires different treatment from one that is franked or whose payment is printed on it. A letter weighing 50 grams that is flat is different from one of the same weight containing a 35mm film. A letter with a first-class stamp requires more urgent treatment and hence different handling compared with a second-class letter.

When the Royal Mail Group developed its model to cost the USO, it took these and other differences to the extreme, and came up with 30000 different types of mail (misleadingly called 'routes'). Regulators should not attempt to model a postal system with its heterogeneous traffic, its varying cost elasticities in relation to traffic volumes and its varying demand elasticities in relation to price. Such a model requires huge effort, is dependent on the incumbent's data and goes out of date rapidly. Therefore price regulation based on 'second-guessing' an individual operator's cost structure should be avoided as far as possible. The one exception – setting charges for access to Royal Mail's final mile delivery network – is discussed below.

Access to the Incumbent's Final Mile Network

As noted earlier, the ability of competing operators to gain access to the incumbent's final mile network will be important in opening the upstream market. If, for example, consolidators can collect, process and transport mail more efficiently than the Royal Mail Group, they should be allowed to do so and to inject the mail into the final mile network at prices that still permit the incumbent to make a profit on final delivery.

Protection of New Entrants from Unfair Competition, Notably Predatory Pricing

New entrants to the market can expect hostility from incumbents. Given the complexity of cost accounting within postal networks, it would be easy for incumbents to apply predatory prices while still arguing that their new, lower prices made a valid contribution to costs.

Of the ten criteria suggested above, the final two are of highest importance, and I now propose practical ways for Postcomm and other postal regulators to approach them.

6   ACCESS TO ROYAL MAIL'S NETWORK FOR DELIVERY OVER THE FINAL MILE

If it is accepted that access to Royal Mail's final delivery network should be obligatory in order to stimulate upstream competition, then on what terms? If the price of access is set too low, Royal Mail will lose money; if set too high, the tariff will keep upstream competition out of the market.

Big mailers, of whom the top 500 in the UK account for about 75 per cent of letter traffic, can bar code their mail for mechanical sorting or print mail in an order that corresponds to postmen's walks. In doing this work before transferring their mail to Royal Mail, they obtain substantial discounts. I suggest that assured access to Royal Mail's delivery network is desirable. I also suggest that finding a tariff that is attractive to upstream consolidators and still profitable to Royal Mail may be simpler than many have thought.

We can assume that Royal Mail's current Walksort tariff provides a margin that makes Royal Mail a profit. We do not know the extent of this margin or the profit but we do know that discounts increase with volume up to a maximum of 42 per cent. In other words, at the limit, Royal Mail receives 58 per cent of the full tariff of the letter concerned. We also know that in 1996–7 Royal Mail's delivery costs were 38.4 per cent of its total costs.[11] These two figures give a bracket within which the tariffs for access to Walksort could be set.

In Table 7.2, we see that the margin on Walksort letters may be about 19.6 per cent of the full tariff for the letter, namely 5.3p for the delivery of a first class Walksort letter and 3.7p for a second class letter. This suggests the Royal Mail could cut the tariff for the final mile delivery of Walksort mail to, say, 50 per cent of the full price tariff and still make a margin on the final mile. If Postcomm were so minded, they could divide Royal Mail's current margin equally between Royal Mail and third-party consolidators.

Clearly the figures in Table 7.2 are a first approximation and might be refined. However the best is the enemy of the good, and I suggest that if Postcomm required the Royal Mail Group to provide access to bulk, walksorted mail at a discount of 2p per item *below the current maximum discount* Royal Mail should still have a sufficient margin from which to make a profit.

I emphasize that third-party mail gaining the full discount would have to be fully walksorted and would need to be input to those Royal Mail offices with machinery that would meld walksorted mail with Royal Mail's own mail stream. Unwalksorted mail deposited at a delivery office would require hand-sorting that would warrant a higher tariff. Even fully walksorted mail, if deposited at unmechanized delivery offices, would require a melding process that would be far less economical than having it melded mechanically further upstream.

Table 7.2   Walksort mail: Royal Mail's revenue and costs per unit of final mile delivery

	%	1st class p	2nd class p
Total	100.0	27.0	19.0
Revenue per final mile delivery	58.0	15.7	11.0
Cost per final mile delivery	38.4	10.4	7.3
Margin	19.6	5.3	3.7

7   HOW TO PREVENT PREDATORY PRICING

The potential for predatory pricing by Royal Mail or other national incumbents could distort a liberalized postal market. In this context I suggest a new price-change mechanism that would be transparent and simple to operate. Its purpose would be to prevent dominant operators in defined market segments from making sudden price changes to drive competitors from the market. The merit of my concept is that it would be mechanical, and it would control the way incumbents change their prices without requiring complex and intrusive intervention by Postcomm on a case-by-case basis.

The letter market could be segmented as shown in Table 7.3. I am aware that the Royal Mail Group is considering a tariff based on the shape of the mail akin to the concept of 'Post Office Preferred sizes' which the Post Office tried half-heartedly to introduce about 40 years ago.

Table 7.3   Possible market segmentation

Type of mail	Weight
Flat items	Up to 20g
Flat items	20–50g
Flat items	50–250g
Flat items	Above 250g
Non-flat items	Up to 100g
Non-flat items	Over 100g

The concept of the price-change mechanism that I propose is based on four principles. First, the larger a supplier's share of any market segment, the longer it would have to wait to change its prices in that segment and the more limited would be the percentage by which it could change its prices. A supplier with over 55 per cent of a given market segment would have to wait 24 months before changing its tariff for that segment and then would be restricted to the change in the retail price index (RPI), plus or minus 1 per cent. Second, above a share of 35 per cent in a given segment, suppliers would be obliged to publish their tariffs. Third, above a segment share of 75 per cent, no special deal discounts to individuals would be permitted. Between a segment share of 35 and 75 per cent, special deals would be permitted but the individual deals would have to be published. Finally, below a market share of 15 per cent in a given segment, suppliers would have no constraints on pricing at all.

The system looks complex but is easy to understand when set out as in Table 7.4, which shows how the system might work in practice. In essence, it would enable new entrants to the market to change their prices at will and without publishing their tariffs. Equally, the incumbent could respond only more slowly and publicly. As new entrants became bigger and incumbents lost market share the restrictions on new entrants would increase (to allow the next wave of new entrants to come to the market) while incumbents (having lost market share) would have their restrictions reduced.

Table 7.4   Price change limitation table

Segment share (per cent)	Maximum frequency of price changes (months)	Maximum change (per cent)	Obligation to publish tariff	Discounts for individual customers permitted?	Deals with individual customers published?
>95	24	+ or – (RPI * 1.0)	Yes	No	
>85	24	+ or – (RPI * 1.1)	Yes	No	
>75	24	+ or – (RPI * 1.2)	Yes	No	
>65	24	+ or – (RPI * 1.3)	Yes	Yes	Yes
>55	24	+ or – (RPI * 1.4)	Yes	Yes	Yes
>45	18	+ or – (RPI * 1.5)	Yes	Yes	Yes
>35	18	+ or – (RPI * 1.6)	Yes	Yes	Yes
>25	18	+ or – (RPI * 1.7)	No	Yes	No
>15	12	+ or – (RPI * 2.0)	No	Yes	No
< 15	No restriction	No restriction	No	Yes	No

Note: Asterisks mean 'times'.

Source: Ian Senior, Triangle Management Services.

Clearly an accurate knowledge of market shares would be necessary to operate the system. Postcomm would require all licensed operators to provide a simple return once a month or once a quarter, stating the volume of their traffic within each segment. As part of this data-gathering exercise, Postcomm would feed back to operators their market shares in each segment – information that would be necessary to make the scheme work and which would also be of immense value to managers.

The attraction of such a system is that it would be transparent to all participants and would be applied mechanically. Postcomm would intervene only if an operator broke the rules, and the penalty for doing so would be the temporary or permanent suspension of its licence. Such a system would also serve to rectify a significant flaw in both the postal directive and the Postal Services Act. The EC's Directive 97/67 says: 'the application of a uniform tariff does not exclude the right of the universal service provider(s) to conclude individual agreements on prices with customers'.[12] This clearly permits former incumbents or dominant suppliers to do special deals behind closed doors with individual customers and, as in the Belgian Post Office case, invites predatory pricing.

Similarly the UK Postal Services Act 2000, clause 4 states: '(b) the conclusion with customers of individual agreements as to prices, shall not be taken to preclude the provision of a universal postal service'. Given the huge dominance of the former incumbents in the liberalized Swedish and New Zealand postal markets, the Royal Mail Group should not be given the right to do special deals behind closed doors with individual customers. My proposal would prevent this.

8   TESTING THE CRITERIA IN RELATION TO POSTCOMM

I shall now apply the criteria from section 5 in the form of a 'first term report' on Postcomm.

Compliance with EC Law

The fact that Postcomm has set milestones and a date for full market liberalization suggests that Postcomm abides by EC law and passes this test.

Full Independence from Government

The Postal Services Act gives final decisions concerning the closure of individual post offices to the secretary of state. However, in postal matters, Postcomm appears to have full independence. Presumably the government of the day has the power to appoint and remove Postcomm's chairman and other members of the Commission, but I imagine that this would be used only in extreme circumstances. Postcomm passes the test of independence.

Milestones and a Deadline for Full Liberalization

As noted, in January 2003, Postcomm opened up the market for bulk mailings of 4000 items or more, representing 30 per cent by value of the postal market. Upstream consolidation will be permitted. From 1 April 2005, further liberalization will open another 30 per cent of the market. From 1 April 2007, all restrictions on market entry will be lifted.

Postcomm therefore has set clear milestones and a deadline for full market liberalization. It passes this test with flying colours.

Current Size of the Reserved Areas

As noted earlier, the UK reserved area is roughly in line with those in France, Germany and the Netherlands, but the progressive reduction of the reserved areas under Postcomm's milestones may be quicker. Indeed, from January 2003, the liberalization of the market for mailings of 4000 identical items means that the reserved area in the UK will be more radically reduced than is required by the EC.

Postcomm's milestones are well in advance of those in the new Postal Services Directive and Postcomm passes the test with distinction.

Liberal Licensing Policy

As noted, by 12 September 2002, Postcomm had issued a licence to the Royal Mail Group and 14 others in an average of four months. No applications had been refused, but the information that Postcomm requires may be unduly onerous and interim licences are unattractive. It is uncertain whether Postcomm passes this test. Certainly it could do much better.

Commercial Separation of the (Former) Incumbents' Main Businesses

The Royal Mail Group's 2002 annual accounts give details of the profit and loss on the main business operations: mails, logistic solutions, parcels and counters. This is an improvement over preceding annual accounts. If this results from Postcomm's actions, Postcomm passes this test.

Intervention on Service Quality

Postcomm has considered the concept of fining Royal Mail for failing to meet a given standard of quality but has held back from implementing fines, given the parlous nature of the Royal Mail Group's finances. How a fine should be calculated is problematic. What is the damage that a firm or individual suffers if a letter is delivered one day late? In most cases the answer must be none or very little. A birthday card that is a day late does not represent financial damage. Truly time-sensitive items such as contractual bids ceased to be sent by first-class mail years ago.

Postcomm has threatened Royal Mail with fines if a standard of 92 per cent D+1 delivery for first-class mail is not reached. By intervening on standards of service that should reflect users' requirements rather than Postcomm's preconceptions, Postcomm fails the test.

Direct Intervention on Individual Operators' Prices

In May 2003, Postcomm permitted the Royal Mail to increase its prices by 1p on both the first and second-class letter. A 1p price increase was not enough to enable the Royal Mail Group to break even. Even after the increase its prices, when adjusted for purchasing power, were among the lowest in Europe. An increase of at least 3p on basic stamp prices was needed. Postcomm should have confidence that its steps to open up the market are the right way forward. Direct price control at this or any stage is a retrograde step.

Postcomm's reported proposal to couple an increase of 1p on basic postage with a weighted average price cap of 29.1p per unit seems objectionable in every way. It may make Royal Mail lose yet more money, it will take no account of changes in patterns of traffic, it will direct management effort into seeing how to tweak prices rather than tackle the basic inefficiencies of the service, and it has the unwelcome characteristics of a command economy.

Postcomm should draw back from this completely wrong-headed approach. Even if it does so but still persists in granting Royal Mail only a one-penny increase, Postcomm fails this test badly.

Access to the Incumbent's Final Mile Network

Postcomm has carried out extensive consultation into this question and at the time of writing no decision has been announced.

Protection of New Entrants from Unfair Competition, Notably Predatory Pricing

New competition has yet to emerge in the UK.

Table 7. 5 summarizes the report on Postcomm.

Table 7.5   First term report assessing Postcomm by ten criteria

Criterion	Assessment
Compliance with EC law	Pass
Full independence from government	Pass
Milestones and deadline for full liberalization	Pass
Current size of reserved area	Pass with credit
Liberal licensing policy	Could do much better
Commercial separation of incumbents' main accounts and businesses	Pass
Intervention on service quality	Serious failure
Direct intervention on individual operators' prices	Serious failure
Access to the incumbent's final mile network	Postcomm still considering
Protection of new entrants from unfair competition (predatory pricing)	Too early to judge

9   CONCLUSIONS

I suggest that the following main criteria by which postal regulators in any country should be judged are the following:

- regulators must be fully independent and not a government ministry;
- they should issue licences freely and without requiring onerous detail;
- they should not intervene on quality of service, which should be determined by users' needs and competition when it arrives;
- they must set charges for access to the former incumbents' final mile networks as a high priority and then leave the market to determine whether new, possibly localized, entrants can offer keener prices than the incumbents;
- apart from enabling access to the final mile networks they should not intervene on the prices of individual operators, but to prevent predatory pricing they could consider a form of transparent price change mechanism on the lines I have suggested;
- they should set a clear date for full market liberalization, with milestones on the way; and
- they should envisage that, once a fully liberalized postal market has been established, their roles as specialist regulator and watchdog should be phased out.

In conclusion, overregulation of postal services will hasten the decline of an industry whose future is far from certain. In postal regulation less is more. It is far better that some postal service providers make too much money before competition and the Internet slim them down than that they be starved to death by overzealous regulation.

Fat cats are more useful than dead ones.

NOTES

1. This chapter concerns the liberalization of letter mail only. I thank colleagues at Triangle Management Services, particularly Paul Jackson, for comments on a draft.
2. Ian Senior, 'The postal service – competition or monopoly?', IEA, background memorandum 3, 1970.
3. Ian Senior, 'Liberating the letter – a proposal to privatise the Post Office', IEA research monograph 38, 1983.
4. Above certain volumes, sorting machinery becomes economic, saving costs compared with manual sorting. The latter does not provide economies of scale if the number of sorter-hours is aligned to the volume of mail.
5. NERA. 'Costing and financing of universal services in the postal sector in the European Union', Appendix C, p. 221, October 1998.
6. I use 'Royal Mail Group' since the name 'Consignia' is to be scrapped.

7. 'Common rules for the development of the internal market of Community postal services and the improvement of quality of service', December 1997.
8. Rowland Hill, 'Post Office reform: its importance and practicability', 1837, p. 27.
9. Ibid., p. 38.
10. Postal Services Act 2000, s. 5.
11. NERA, 'Costing and financing of universal services in the postal sector in the European Union', October 1998, p. 220
12. 'Directive 97/67/EC of the European Parliament and of the Council of 15 December 1997 on common rules for the development of the internal market of Community postal services and the improvement of quality of service', *Official Journal*, L 015 , 21/01/1998, pp. 0014–0025, Article 12.

CHAIRMAN'S COMMENTS

Graham Corbett

Ian Senior gives a comprehensive and challenging view of what postal regulation might have been, or perhaps should be, and provides his own first-term report on Postcomm's performance so far. I hope he will forgive me for concentrating (and indeed perhaps he would even expect me to concentrate) my own remarks on his assessment of Postcomm's performance: five passes, one could-do-better, two serious failures and two 'the jury's still out'. Not, I think, a very glorious result. I have an uncomfortable feeling that, if I were to find myself in front of that Great Regulator in the sky, trying desperately to tuck this report away behind my back, he would suggest that I had come to the wrong place altogether. However, as Ian has predicted, I do have to say that I find myself in very close sympathy with the A-level students who found that the goal posts had been moved when they were not looking. Ian approaches our role from the standpoint of a very market-oriented economic regulator, and away with all the stuff of social engineering, flight paths: just go for the jugular. Parliament could, of course, have asked us to do just that, but it did not. It made our number one priority the preservation of the universal service, which included uniform pricing – for good or for ill – and only if we are satisfied that it is safe are we then enjoined to further the interests of users wherever appropriate by promoting competition, and even then having regard, of course, to the interests of the disadvantaged groups that Ian Senior listed.

I do not think it matters very much that I happen to think that these are worthy and proper regulatory objectives, whereas Ian is equally convinced that they are not. What does matter is that, in a parliamentary democracy, in this case that is what the law requires of us and if Postcomm's commissioners did not like the remit that parliament had given us, they should never, frankly, have applied for the job. But, having done so, I do think they are entitled to be judged by their performance against the job spec, rather than against any other job spec that might have been more palatable to Ian Senior. So Ian, while being duly appreciative of the pass marks you have given us and frankly very much in support of your desire to see postal regulation have the shortest life practicable, I would like to revisit each of the three areas in which you have given us less than a pass. In doing so I will try to respond in a way which will, I hope, stimulate debate.

Let us start with the question of the liberal licensing policy. Ian Senior downgraded us for having instigated an interim liberalizing policy, which he says many applicants have found unattractive. But remember that we had to ensure that there would be no material damage to the universal service, at least until we have done the analysis to underpin the long-term market-opening scheme, effective from 1 January 2003. That interim scheme was designed quite specifically to permit a low-level activity enabling all players, ourselves, Royal Mail and the operators, to familiarize themselves with what would be involved and in particular to bring forward the start date for the critical discussions on terms of access. And all of this was able to happen while the extensive examination of the characteristics of the universal service was being completed: its costs, benefits and its vulnerability. Only when we had established to our own satisfaction that our market opening proposals would not put the universal service in jeopardy, and exposed our thinking through a series of consultation documents to a wide range of commentators, did we feel justified in moving on to the next step. By a happy coincidence I am able to tell you that our long-term licence decision document was released earlier today, providing for licences with a minimum of seven-year terms and alongside that decision document are the first consultation documents for the first applications for long-term licences from Hays, TNT and TPG. So this is a good day, when the interim licensing regime comes to an end, and in my view it has fulfilled its important but time-limited function with considerable distinction.

We move on to intervention on service quality. Here I think Ian Senior's serious failure rating stems even more directly from the same monocular view of what we should be trying to do. If there is one message that comes back through every survey that we or Postwatch have carried out it is of dissatisfaction with the quality of the postal service, with its reliability and with its lack of responsiveness, and that is coming from bulk-mailers, from individual householders, all the way across the spectrum. And that is nearly always allied with the frustrations of not being able to turn to an alternative supplier.

So let us return to our remit which was to 'further the interests of users wherever appropriate by promoting effective competition'. Just note that 'wherever appropriate'. What it means is that, if competition were not to be the right answer, or if it were to take too long to become effective, that does not let us of the hook of furthering the interests of users which is an obligation that is placed on us here and now, today. I find it frankly inconceivable that we could have contemplated opting out of service standards, opting out of penalty provisions, opting out of compensation arrangements on the grounds that competition would solve all these problems by itself. Indeed it might – someday. And I do believe that in the meantime we can justifiably point with some satisfaction at the new emphasis on quality standards coming within the Royal Mail, stimulated even by the threat of market opening. But please do not expect miracles any time soon. And for myself I have no doubt at all that I would much rather stand in front of the Great Regulator guilty of having interfered in such matters than of having sat placidly with my arms folded waiting for the market to do it for me.

I move on, then, to direct intervention on individual operators prices. I hope you forgive me for being a bit more cagey on this front as we are, as you know, still in the middle of a formal consultation process. But we can certainly discuss the points of principle at stake here. First of all let me clarify that it is not our intention to control the prices charged by any operator other than Royal Mail. But, for as long as Royal Mail remains the dominant player, its prices will be subject to Postcomm's oversight, since by definition its pricing behaviour will not be sufficiently constrained by competitive threats, nor will it be immune from the temptation of reducing prices selectively to ward off new entrants. And none of that, let me emphasize, is a criticism of Royal Mail. Indeed, if we want Royal Mail to become more competitive in its' behaviour, we should expect it to take any opportunities that are available to it, to maximize its market share and its net revenues. But it is then our job to make certain that this does not foreclose the market or result in excessive price increases. Secondly, we agree with Ian Senior that it is undesirable for the regulator to control each of the hundreds of different prices in Royal Mail's range of services. Interestingly, that is precisely what we were being pressed to do from a number of quarters, not a million miles away from Royal Mail itself. We have explained in our consultation document that, by contrast, we were keen to find a price control mechanism that would give Royal Mail the freedom within quite broad limits to modify its pattern of tariffs, whether to respond to competitive pressures or to support its own marketing strategies. The average pricing structure that we favour did just this. But we did recognize in our document, and indeed in the press release that accompanied it, that that carried the possible disadvantage of being insensitive to changes in product mix, a problem that we acknowledged called for further study, which I can assure you it is now actively receiving. But to suggest, as Ian does, that we could rely on a competitive market to leap into effective existence from day one and to control improper pricing activity would in my view be to fly in the face of experience, of logic and of common sense and be an abandonment of our responsibility to users of postal services. So my response to this serous failure rating is a resounding 'not guilty'.

But let me, in closing my remarks, try to step back a bit, try to draw out some of the big issues that I think flow from the rather different views that Ian Senior and I have put in front of you. First and foremost, should a society like ours, through its elected representatives, be asking its regulators to involve themselves in soft issues of social policy or should they stick exclusively to a more narrowly defined economic regulator role? Second, even if the narrower role were to be preferred, how practical is it to seek to divorce economic decisions from their social and environmental consequences?

Third, to what extent, if at all, do we want regulators to impose service quality standards through the licences process? And if we do want them to do so, how muscular should they be in monitoring them and penalizing non-performance? Fourth: is all price control misguided?

Fifth, perhaps: should the Great Regulator let me and my colleagues in after all?

8. Can regulation address the investment problem? Examples from aviation

Doug Andrew

INTRODUCTION[1]

Simon Cowan in his excellent review paper[2] on the principles of economic regulation concluded with the observation that it is not clear that price cap regulation provides the optimal incentives for investment in utilities. He goes on to note that developing robust mechanisms for investment without encouraging gold-plating (excessive costs) will be important. This will be the central focus of this chapter, but first some context.

Aviation is often regarded as the first of the major regulatory reforms in Western economies, starting with the USA in the 1970s. Europe and others followed in the 1980s. The benefits are seen to be substantial. Steven Morrison and Cliff Winston's recent work estimates a 27 per cent reduction in airfares due to deregulation.[3] It also emphasizes the benefits of competition or the threat thereof. The benefits to European travellers from deregulation has become more recently apparent with the rapid growth of the 'low frills' carriers, commencing in the UK perhaps as a result of its more commercial airline market.

It is important to emphasize that the USA started from a private commercial airline industry. The infrastructure was and substantially is state-owned, either local or federal government. In the UK and on the European continent, there were high levels of state ownership of airlines. Regulatory reform and privatization were linked. In the UK, airline deregulation and the privatization of British Airways (BA) were closely linked, although BA continued (and continues) to have substantial advantages from highly restrictive bilateral international agreements. The UK extended the reform model to infrastructure with the privatization of the British Airports Authority (BAA) in 1987, following the British Telecom (BT) privatization in 1984. More recently, it partially privatized the air traffic control provider, National Air Traffic Services (NATS), as the first public–private partnership (PPP) in the UK. The latter was noteworthy also for the fact that it is a statutory monopoly.

BAA, NATS and local government owned Manchester Airport (MA) were subject, not only to general competition law including the Competition Act

1998, but also price control via specific economic regulation under the Airports and Transport Acts.

The title of this chapter promises a discussion of investment and regulation, but, as the introduction suggests, its theme is the broader issue of clarity of property rights, governance (state or private ownership), how that is influenced by market structure, ownership and regulation and the resulting congruence with social aims. The conclusion is that the more commercial approach has worked well and needs to be built on, rather than eroded. This reflects a judgment on the balance of risks: market versus government failure, reflecting experience locally and internationally over the last 20 years.

The chapter proceeds by defining the public policy problems that need to be addressed, what the policy objectives might be, the framework for analysing the problems and options for achieving the objectives. It ends with a case study of the Civil Aviation Authority (CAA) approach to incentivizing investment at regulated airports used in its advice to the Competition Commission in February 2002.

THE PROBLEM

As is indicated in the introduction, the downstream aviation market in the European Union (EU) is not subject to any government-imposed economic entry barriers except on international routes outside the EU. Subject to safety and limited consumer protection regulation, any EU-owned and controlled airline can operate within the EU. The gains were modest initially,[4] but more recently the rapid growth of 'low frills' carriers has brought forward obvious benefits to customers as well as placing pressure on incumbent airlines to improve their performance.

The policy issues are now related to preventing the creeping reregulation of airlines and completing the liberalization agenda internationally. In the latter case the ends are broadly agreed but the means are more contentious, depending as they do on assessments of intergovernmental negotiating strategies and domestic political constraints. The USA has its 'Open Skies' model, while the EU has its Trans-Atlantic Common Aviation Area (TCAA). The former is generally implementable bilaterally, removing government-imposed economic entry barriers to airlines owned by nationals of the two nations. It does not permit the development of airlines owned internationally, thus restricting the gains from establishing the most effective governance structures and gaining access to the most efficient capital markets. This problem is presumably bigger the smaller the domestic capital market, as the recent Australian debate concerning QANTAS indicated.[5]

The TCAA is probably harder to implement but does (eventually) allow for airlines to be owned anywhere, with access to the most efficient ownership arrangement given the particular business model in question. It has to be the kernel of the desired long-term solution in that the output and capital market are both liberalized, provided it is an open regional arrangement that other countries can join.

Both in the USA and in Europe, the problems faced by airlines are increasingly infrastructural in nature: limited airport and air traffic management capacity in key areas. Ownership and regulation play a much bigger role here. Specifically there is excess demand for aviation infrastructure in the UK south east. Elsewhere in the UK there is capacity available. The recent government studies broadly confirm this point looking out over a 30-year period. Slot values at Heathrow are high.[6] Newspaper reports suggest capital values of a single slot pair in the £2 million range.

It is conventional wisdom that aviation infrastructure investments are 'lumpy', although, with a more commercial approach, incremental development has become the rule, suggesting 'lumpiness' is perhaps less of a problem. However investments such as Terminal Five at Heathrow, with its £3.7 billion total price tag remain substantial. With this, and when real option costs are allowed for,[7] commercial developers will probably undertake the investments a little 'late' compared to the timing that a benevolent social planner would prefer. So some excess demand is probably optimal with efficient prices. However the excess demand that currently exists in the UK south east, and its likely persistence, probably go well beyond that, with substantial welfare costs.

A second fundamental problem is the importance of externalities associated with the development of the aviation market and consequential infrastructure pressures. Local impacts such as noise are well known and perceived. Global impacts are increasingly seen as important, as aviation continues to be one of the industries, increasing its share of contributions to greenhouse gases, despite improvements in technical efficiency. High-level estimates prepared by the Department for Transport[8] using available studies suggested that in aggregate, current special taxes on air travel (the Airline Passenger Dub) are roughly in line with external costs. The design of the fiscal instruments is obviously far from optimal in addressing the environmental problem. The current planning system struggles to cope with major airport developments, as the recent Heathrow Terminal Five inquiry demonstrated.

THE PUBLIC POLICY OBJECTIVES

Fundamentally, economic efficiency would seem to be the benchmark for public policy objectives: maximizing the size of the 'national pie' in standards of living terms. Practically this would suggest that policies should allow the downstream aviation market to expand or contract so that marginal **social** benefits and costs are in line over time. By 'social' we mean that costs and benefits should include externalities such as pollution. As this is a major subject in its own right, this is not covered further in this chapter beyond the stating of this principle, consistent with current government policy.[9]

The signals from the downstream market should be transmitted by a range of vertical linkages (markets, contracts, vertical integration and so on) to the upstream infrastructure markets to achieve the same outcomes in those markets, lumpiness permitting. More practically this would suggest that the policy problem is how to ensure (a) least-cost production: productive efficiency, (b) best use of scarce outputs: allocative efficiency (including environmental costs), and (c) optimal investment: projects only proceeding when the expected net present value exceeds zero and costs include option values: dynamic efficiency.

FRAMEWORK

The conventional approach to the analysis of this problem is a market one, the interaction between consumer preferences and firms reflecting fundamental cost structures, focusing on market failures and interventions to address them. A richer, more realistic, approach is the comparative institutional approach articulated by Ronald Coase, where market failures and government failures are taken into account in designing optimal policy responses in a world where perfect competition (for example, no fixed, let alone sunk, costs) is merely a pedagogical tool and information asymmetries are inherent.

The focus in this chapter is on problems in the upstream aviation markets, where 'lumpy' investments and fixed, sunk costs are prevalent. In assessing answers to problems we need always to focus on the public policy mantra of evaluating an option in relative terms: 'compared to what'? If we are thinking about new airports, expanded airports or better performing air traffic management, it may be illustrative to consider the traditional decentralized market approach alongside public sector management models. There are a range of governance variants in-between: Buchanan's user clubs, franchise bidding and not-for-profit models, for example.

'Public interested' governments acting on behalf of their societies arguably want to achieve economic efficiency, which means addressing each of the subobjectives above. Public choice theory suggests that interest group capture of public policy diverts governments from this goal. Niskanen's model of bureaucratic behaviour suggests that empire building by bureaucrats is an important motive explaining government behaviour.

The traditional critique of the market approach to infrastructure (an approach which by that stage had built 'roads', railways and canals) is highlighted by the case of a proposed new project such as a bridge. These projects are regarded as having high fixed and sunk costs and broadly zero marginal costs until it becomes congested. Private provision funded by user charges would lead to underutilization as prices would exceed marginal costs and cause a loss of economic efficiency. Private provision may come later than is ideal as the private developer may not be able to price discriminate sufficiently to obtain all the consumer surplus that would feature in the social cost benefit assessment. A tax-funded subsidy could address this problem. Under public provision the publicly interested government would undertake a cost–benefit analysis, trying to judge the expected demand schedule for the bridge and assess the costs through to implementation, all against the best alternative. If the bridge were built using tax revenues, no charge would be levied, achieving best use.

This example illustrates the classic public policy problems:

- the government's ability to obtain the best information on demand and costs;
- the government's ability to remain 'public interested', avoiding 'capture' by local or construction interests and effectively addressing the principal–agent problem including stopping bureaucrats who merely want to expand their empires;
- the deadweight costs of taxation to finance the bridge; versus
- private provision being 'later' and using a toll resulting in a lower traffic volume.

The example also leads to the issue of regulation. Under private provision, if the project is unsuccessful the developer bears the loss. If it is successful the developer may/will be exposed to the risk of subsequent regulation to reduce perceived excess profits. The sunk investment could be exposed to partial expropriation through price control or nationalization.

The more standard textbook analysis of market failure in this area was the decreasing cost problem due to lumpy investments. Charging efficient marginal costs, while leading to optimal utilization, resulted in the project running at a loss. The leap from this situation to regulated statutory monopolies protected by government-imposed economic entry barriers (US model) or state provision (UK model) is a big one. In a single bound insights from Ramsay and non-linear pricing are overlooked, without mentioning regulatory or governance issues.

After the Second World War the state sector, including the infrastructure area, grew, perhaps reflecting views of widespread market and coordination failures. Concerns with performance in the sector grew, but with a lag.[10] Governments found it difficult to implement efficient pricing. Generally underpricing predominated, with occasional overcharging, such as for long-distance telephone calls. Governance issues, in the sense of ensuring that the enterprise managers acted in accordance with the government's objective, were and are always problematic. The government objectives for the enterprises were often multiple and changing as the result of new developments: for example, concern about job losses or local unemployment.

Resulting financial losses became increasing burdens on governments and the entities were subject to increasing government control and cash rationing. The economic cost to countries became an issue. Investment was affected. Governments (re)learnt the hard way about principal–agent problems. Public sector cost–benefit analysis became only loosely linked to the investment decision.

Poor performance (Vickers and Yarrow) and fiscal pressures led to policy change and privatization. By and large, market restructuring and liberalization were not initially integral to privatization in the UK, in contrast to the approach in, say, New Zealand where government-imposed economic entry barriers were removed immediately. BT was only exposed to limited competition via the statutory duopoly with Mercury. BAA from the start had a dominant market position in two regions. It was also sold with a golden share making hostile takeovers more difficult.

Sector-specific economic regulation was introduced to protect consumers 'until competition arrived'. Starting with Oftel, an alternative approach was followed in contrast to the then prevailing US regulatory commission model. Critically the regulators, generally as single persons, were statutorily independent of the government, although appointed by the government. This was seen as important to reduce the risk of dominant market positions being abused and later of the government intervening post-privatization to keep prices too low and so at least partially expropriate the investment by private investors. The recommended regulatory paradigm was price cap regulation as against cost of service regulation because of its expected superior performance. The UK regulatory institutions are relatively new compared to those in the USA and the constitutional settings are different.

STRENGTHS AND WEAKNESSES

The commercial model with private ownership, in contrast to the public sector alternative model such as a department or state-owned enterprise, would normally look to achieve more cost-effective operation: productive efficiency. In aviation it is impressive to see the degree of contracting out undertaken by BAA at its UK airports, reflecting its perspective as a commercial owner on where the 'make' versus 'buy' boundary is. More broadly the evidence[11] on the relative superior efficiency of commercial versus state provision is now strong and generally in accordance with common sense. The only qualification would be that the existence of economic regulation that takes account of the firm's own costs to some degree somewhat weakens this incentive.

There are arguments that capital market failures may limit pressure on incumbent management.[12] As was emphasized above, the 'compared to what' question is the relevant one with information asymmetries and principal–agent realities. One is struck by the amount of monitoring effort of firm performance in the private sector: banks, controlling interest shareholders, equity analysts, re-inforced by information from the bond and equities markets when securities are listed. The private sector CEO tenure span can be short. The premiums to share prices generated when takeovers are announced suggest that the threat of takeovers is an important part of the governance process.[13]

Public sector monitoring of public sector enterprises and their cost-effectiveness seems limited in comparison. Objective functions of the 'principal' in the public sector are usually more complex than those of private owners, reflecting the inevitable pressures in an open democratic society. It is harder to write and enforce optimal contracts between the government and the heads of government departments and agencies. Large bonuses are harder to defend in the public sector. Sanctions are harder to implement because objectives may be less clear and ministers are probably less willing to end up in employment tribunals and courts.

Where there is market power and economic regulation imposed, the regulatory regime can adversely affect cost-effectiveness. Regulatory schemes can be characterized by the following stylized equation:

$$p = A + \beta.C$$

where p is the allowed revenue/price, A is a fixed fee, C is the firm's costs and β is the fraction of the costs passed through to customers. Pure cost of service regulation sets A at zero and β at one. Pure incentive regulation sets β at zero. The latter applied to a commercial firm obviously gives the maximum incentive to operate cost-effectively and expand output until incremental revenue and marginal cost are equal, that is, performing as in a competitive market. The time period for the scheme is critical depending on the nature and payback periods of the efficiency-enhancing projects available to the firm. It is possible for the allowed revenue to be out of line with true costs, leading to business failure that might or might not be desirable. Setting the revenue or price is problematic but benchmarking, optimized depreciated replacement cost or incremental costs are usually considered.

Concerns about rents, regulatory reneging and downside risks usually mean that regulatory plans have β set closer to one (with incentives being increased by the plans having the characteristics of multi-year price caps). The incentive power decreases accordingly. The tradeoff is stark. In competitive markets prices adjust rapidly to supply and demand shocks. Where there are monopolies and incentive-compatible regulatory schemes are applied, economic efficiency suggests moving to high-power incentives and fixing maximum prices for a longish period. However, when concerns over profits and dealing with risk are taken into account, perhaps we should not be surprised that actual plans have β closer to one and the right to pass through unbudgeted costs or revenue shortfalls exist.

Allocative Efficiency

Allocative efficiency would also be assisted by the commercial approach. Commercial firms, compared with state-owned businesses, would presumably have stronger incentives to define and price outputs. They generally would be reluctant to continue to provide outputs from existing capacity at prices below short-run incremental costs. They would be unwilling to invest unless prices would be expected to cover long-run incremental costs. The significant innovations in pricing in aviation (dynamic yield management systems) and telecommunications over the last decade or so are indicative of the gains. For example, BAA has been steadily introducing new charges for specific services it provides. Work by Crandall[14] and Winston[15] hase emphasized the importance and benefits of better pricing, usually implicitly linked to better governance of the suppliers. Transport remains one area where pricing policies are clearly suboptimal: the lack of road pricing and airport pricing/slot mechanism problems in the UK south east are two well-known examples. We will return to airport pricing below.

The commercial approach, compared to the public interested public sector alternative, does raise concerns about allocative efficiency where dominant market positions are involved as a result of significant sunk costs. With market power, and even in the absence of government-imposed economic entry barriers, commercial firms have stronger incentives to price excessively, with resultant losses in economic welfare. It is useful to think further about the likely behaviour of firms with dominant market positions in the absence of explicit price control. Such firms would wish to avoid the output loss if they could do so profitably. Price discrimination allows a reduction in the output loss and hence aggregate welfare loss.

As the aviation example shows, such price discrimination is possible and beneficial. The Competition Act guidelines from the Office of Fair Trading are also supportive of price discrimination within limits consistent with protecting the competitive process. In the case of airports, Peter Forsyth[16] has argued that relevant elasticities will be low and, with profitable price discrimination, output losses as a result of pricing above efficient levels may also be low. This is partly because airport and air traffic control charges generally make up a small portion of airline costs: the importance of being 'unimportant'. Starkie and Yarrow[17] point out that the existence of competitive retail outputs, complementary to airport outputs, also reduces the incentive for an unregulated airport to price airport outputs excessively where there may be output losses.

There will be distributional consequences of price reform when prices are well out of line with incremental costs and values, however, and in the real world and, without perfect lump sum taxes and transfers, these matter. Many sound pricing reforms have foundered on opposition from the losers and the weakness of support from the future winners. The constituency for the dynamic gains is often confined to think-tanks, some treasuries and potential new competitors around the world.

The traditional response where entry barriers are significant is the imposition of economic regulation. Ironically, while the argument for economic regulation in efficiency terms is to avoid the losses of allocative efficiency, economic regulation may not help much and may make it worse. Traditional cost-of-service regulation keeps maximum prices in line with average historic accounting costs, preventing excessive returns on the historic capital invested. While this should give protection to invest in respect of their investment these prices may or may not coincide with relevant economic incremental or opportunity costs. The cost base and hence allowable prices are gradually adjusted for the costs of new investments. Presumably then prices adjust to incremental costs over time.

Fundamentally the objective is to have a regulatory incentive plan, if competition is likely to be inadequate, that encourages the regulated firm to expand output to the point where prices and marginal costs are equal. The literature has some interesting models that illustrate the issue and the problems. Information asymmetries are at the heart of the problem. The insight from the Loeb–Magat model[18] is that, if the regulator is able make a payment equivalent to the social or consumer surplus, the firm will expand output to optimal levels. However the regulator needs to 'know' the demand curve and have a source of revenue.

Over time models have developed that reduce the information requirements and eliminate the need for the regulator to have access to sources of funding. The idea is to have regulatory plans that give the monopoly an incentive to expand output. One interesting example was Sibley's[19] paper, which had low information requirements, relying on the requirement for the firm to offer a default two-part tariff linked to the previous period price and rents in addition to any other pricing plan it wishes to offer. Sibley shows that the firm has an incentive to expand production incrementally until prices fall to marginal costs. The CAA, picking up on advice from Sibley,[20] proposed the idea of a default price cap in the airport regulatory regime to encourage 'win, win' contracting within the allocation of property rights given by the cap and competition law.

Price cap regulation can offer slightly or dramatically improved performance over this benchmark. The simplest model is merely translating accounting costs and volume projections into a multi-year cap which is reset periodically on the basis of newer information. There are some incentives in this approach for improved pricing along with operating cost efficiencies if permitted by cap operation. For example, the airports price caps have single till-based average revenue caps. BAA and MA are constantly introducing or increasing charges for particular services, often to the consternation of airlines and other airport users. By and large, we are supportive of this as the process incrementally better defines what services the airports actually produce and their costs. They certainly have a financial incentive to define and price outputs but there remain concerns about excessive pricing. The Competition Act 1998 potentially constraining such behaviour is a relevant factor. The till approach used in airport regulation means that other regulated prices are reduced next time around as a result of this pricing innovation.

Dynamic Efficiency and Optimal Investment

Against the public sector approach of political decision making aided by cost–benefit analysis and within budget constraints the commercial model as illustrated by the bridge example has strengths and weaknesses. Profitable projects should be able to be financed in the capital markets with the appropriate mix of debt and equity, depending on risk and appropriate accountability/incentive structures to address agency problems.[21] In the public sector infrastructure projects are competing with bids from health, education, crime prevention and so on within constraints set by overall fiscal policy and broad political imperatives. The principal–agent problems may be more fundamental and also harder to address.

Over the life of the project, revenues must be expected to cover total costs discounted at the project's risk-adjusted cost of capital. There are strong incentives for cost-effective provision of new projects. Only with perfect price discrimination will the developer be able to obtain the available consumer surplus: a potential weakness compared to the 'public interest' version of the public sector approach. This will not happen but the developer will have incentives to maximize the recovery, such as contracts with potential users, which may have fixed-cost elements allowing lower marginal usage costs.[22] Arguably agency problems will be better addressed under the commercial model. The developer can appoint her own people to manage the implementation and operation of the project. Such people may see their long-term interests aligned with those of the developer. There will be more market tests available of demand and cost projections, such as actual project net earnings. These can be linked into incentive schemes to encourage 'truth-telling' and continued commitment. Where there is market power the commercial model will, as an integral part of its commercial strategy, underprovide capacity as the corollary of its ability to overprice. This might be manifested as 'late' investment from a social perspective.

As discussed above, economic regulation to address market power concerns can have unusual effects on investment. The standard cost base model (a high β scheme) can allow all and any investment to be remunerated at the regulatory cost of capital, regardless of the investment's inherent social profitability. This is discussed further below. US regulators have spent considerable resources examining investment programmes to address the resulting adverse selection problem *ex ante*. At the extreme is the state regulation of investment decisions by hospitals in the USA. Certificate of Need programmes require a hospital to obtain approval before undertaking certain investment programmes.[23] Regulatory risk such as the exclusion by regulation of some investment from the allowed regulatory cost base *ex post* also qualifies this assessment and may force regulated firms to behave more prudently or excessively risk-adversely. The price cap approach probably increases incentives for regulatory 'gaming', with regulated firms having incentives to seek price caps to fund investment programmes and then under spend on the projected programmes to gain the cash-flow and hence business value benefit within the control period, managing the regulator's response at the next review.[24] The regulator's problem is to distinguish between desirable efficiency gains in investment programmes and undesirable delays of adding valuable capacity. The CAA has had to wrestle with this, given the delay over Terminal Five at Heathrow. (In February 2002 the CAA recommended a 50 per cent clawback in an attempt to strike a balance.)

The more fundamental answer has to be better output specification and pricing thereof. In terms of the fundamental regulatory equation outlined above, if β is set at zero the firm's own costs do not affect prices: price is exogenous to the firm. This replicates the marketplace. A commercial operator then has an incentive to deliver the output, cost-effectively. If they do not deliver, they do not get paid. The regulated price has to be output-related, consistent with long-run incremental costs. The regulated firm carries the volume risk but regulation should not constrain (and should encourage) the firm from contracting with other parties to share risk and return if it is efficient to do so. Airlines would be an obvious contract counterparty for a major airport terminal development. It is well known that in US airports airlines often own terminals. Retailers would be other potential contractors to lay off the project and volume risk. Service quality is integral to the output specification problem. This is moderately straightforward where there are constant returns to scale but more difficult where there are increasing or decreasing returns where the issues of rent distribution or covering of losses arise.

Unfortunately this is a serious second-best problem and tradeoffs have to be made concerning the risks of regulatory reneging as higher than expected profits are disclosed versus incentive compatible regulatory plans aimed at expanding output to the optimal levels. As assets become more specific, sunk costs higher and investments long-lived the problem becomes starker and regulatory credibility becomes of more importance. Even price caps are unlikely to be set for more than five or so years. In competitive markets prices are constantly adjusting to new supply and demand factors even if the resulting prices are still exogenous to the individual firm. However, as market power increases, the competitiveness of markets obviously decreases. The problem of dealing with new information in regulatory regimes remains problematic given the tradeoff between high power incentives, rents, new information and time inconsistency problems. From an economic efficiency perspective, the bottom line is to push to increase the power of incentive schemes consistent with market fundamentals, provided the institutions are robust enough to resist opportunistic intervention when excess profits are earned. The CAA proposal to set the price cap for BAA at Heathrow and Gatwick as a long-term 'price path commitment' is an example of this. This is discussed further below.

THE SCORECARD

Integrating the foregoing assessments of strengths and weaknesses of the commercial versus (best practice) state sector management in terms of economic efficiency would indicate that the former on average dominates in terms of cost-effectiveness, still dominating but perhaps slightly less strongly in terms of allocative and dynamic efficiency. Where the firms have dominant market positions and economic regulation is imposed the assessment is less clear-cut, mainly as a result of the adverse effects of economic regulation. This may be summarized as follows:

Commercial versus state enterprise models

	General law	Plus economic regulation
Cost-effectiveness	✓✓✓	✓
Allocative efficiency	✓✓	✓?
Dynamic efficiency	✓✓	✓??

It might be argued that, if this analysis is robust, it is surprising that state production continues to be prevalent. Without getting into this wider discussion, the general trend internationally to commercialize state enterprises is consistent with the above analysis.

HYBRID GOVERNANCE OPTIONS

The foregoing has concentrated on discussing the commercial for-profit model in contrast to public sector models. As indicated above, there are a range of intermediate options that continue to be advocated and/or implemented. User clubs owning monopolies in theory internalize the risk of monopoly abuse. The free-rider problem may weaken clubs' ability at achieving cost-effectiveness and improving pricing. The investment story seems more ambiguous. So-called 'public interest corporations', albeit not explicitly owned by governments, seem to be taking the debate back to the concept articulated by Herbert Morrison, the Labour Minister in the Attlee government.

'The public corporation must be no mere capitalist business, the be-all and end-all of which is profits and dividends, even though it will, quite properly, be expected to pay its way. It must have a different atmosphere at its board table from that of a shareholders' meeting: its board and its officers must regard themselves as the high custodians of the public interest. In selecting the Board, these considerations must be in the minds of the Minister.'[25] It is hard to better the critique in Vickers and Yarrow of these models. The main points would seem to be similar to the weaknesses in the state enterprise model:

- unclear objective function: what does 'public interest' mean and what would constitute good or bad performance in terms of delivering this objective?
- do the managers have appropriate autonomy?
- can the managers be held effectively accountable with such an objective?
- how does the incentive structure for management match best-practice commercial models? (This is a point that Ofwat has raised in the context of the recent initiatives in the water market for mutuals and thin capitalisation models to replace the more conventional commercial models.[26] ORR has raised similar questions in respect of Network Rail.)[27]

In these situations regulators seem to be feeling the need to intervene within the firm to require the management of these firms to be incentivized as if the firms had conventional 'for profit' financial structures.

Work by Edward Glaeser[28] suggests that not-for-profits often evolve into organizations that resemble workers' cooperatives. The primary check on this tendency is the need for the organizations to compete in outside markets. It is thus of concern that the focus on such hybrid governance arrangements is in the regulated utilities where the competition is seen to be limited.

AN AVIATION CASE STUDY: THE CIVIL AVIATION AUTHORITY'S APPROACH TO DETERMINING AIRPORT PRICE CAPS

The CAA sets the maximum airport charges for BAA's Heathrow, Gatwick and Stansted airports and the local government-owned Manchester Airport under the Airports Act 1986. It does so following a recommendation from the Competition Commission. The Act requires the CAA to set the price cap most likely to further reasonable user interests, promote efficient and profitable airport operation, encourage timely investment and impose minimum restrictions.

Airports have traditionally been regulated under the standard UK approach. The adverse effects of conventional regulatory asset base economic regulation on pricing and investment are marked and are more fully illustrated with some simple business case arithmetic in the attached annex. The key message, however, is that, while caps give good (that is, normal) commercial incentives within the price control period, decision makers will be aware that at the next review costs turn into benefits. The cost base is adjusted, for both capital and operating costs. These translate into the allowed prices in the next period. The business case for investments for the regulated firm in discounted cash-flow terms in this is highly distorted compared to the conventional firm's. The only counter would seem to be that the unregulated dominant firm's business case analysis is even more distorted. The adverse effects of regulation discussed above do reinforce a subtle point made in our proposals, namely that, if a price cap is expected to be only marginally binding, it will still bring the distorting effects discussed above with the attendant costs. In this case there are likely to be net benefits if the cap can be made non-binding in the sense of not affecting the airport's behaviour. This is relevant particularly to Stansted in the CAA's February 2002 proposals.

The above analysis of the problems with economic regulation in addressing investment provides the context of some of the thinking behind the CAA's approach to setting airport price caps. This, the developments in market conditions, together with the Competition Act 1998, are all significant changes since the last review and we consider that regulatory policy needs to reflect this.

CAA Recommendations to the Competition Commission

In February 2002 the CAA recommended to the Competition Commission a set of regulatory policies for Heathrow, Gatwick, Stansted and local government owned Manchester for the five years commencing 1 April 2003.[29]

The problems being faced at each of the regulated airports are different. Heathrow and Gatwick runways are subject to excess demand and, while these airports are planning major investment during 2003–8, this situation is likely to continue. Manchester has capacity available due to the recent opening of a second runway. Stansted is experiencing high growth but has plans to expand to meet projected growth. The fifth terminal at Heathrow is the major project for the next five years.

Given the projected growth in the demand for air travel and that airport infrastructure developments are long-term undertakings, the CAA's proposals made in its recommendations to the Competition Commission aimed to deliver the best incentives for achieving the investment and service quality valued by users and also achieving, cost-effectively, the best utilization of existing capacity. The CAA has considered and evaluated a range of regulatory policy options in the knowledge that it has only one policy instrument: a price cap. These options ranged from the continuation of the traditional single till cost-based model, modifications of it to reduce regulatory coverage, incremental cost-based prices through to market prices.

While the CAA recommendation to the Competition Commission to move from the traditional 'single till' basis of price setting to a narrower revised regulatory cost base (RRCB) attracted the most attention, the innovation this chapter focuses on is the proposal of a long-term 'price path commitment'.

The Price Path Commitment

The long-term price path commitment is an example of the use of a high-powered incentive scheme aimed at addressing a performance issue. The idea behind this approach is that it would offer higher-powered incentives compared to the standard regulatory asset base (RAB) approach to addressing the problems in the market. The recommended long-term real price path allows higher prices only when additional services are delivered and output handled. Such a price path commitment improves the incentives to operate efficiently and invest effectively. It would provide a simple and transparent foundation for the major investment programme planned, minimize regulatory risk and bridge the gap between investment projects with long lead times and payback periods and price caps that are fixed for only five years.

Application to Heathrow

As prices at Heathrow are low, in relation to value and long-run incremental costs, the price path could be set slightly high, with little risk of efficiency losses, reducing the risk of the price path being set too low and investment being compromised. Apart from addressing remuneration of the proposed fifth terminal at Heathrow on an incremental output/incremental cost basis, the price path commitment also provides a long-term framework for addressing other major investments particularly runway developments.

Figure 8.1 illustrates the price path options and the recommended price path for Heathrow. As the CAA recommended policy would translate into lower real prices than those from existing (single till) policies, the CAA, for reasons of not reneging regulatory commitment, set the price path at no lower than single till levels for the 2003–8 period. This will also reduce the price 'spike' when the fifth terminal opens, consistent with the policy of gradualism.

A further benefit of the proposed framework is the flexibility it would have provided for addressing future capacity enhancements beyond Terminal Five. The government published a White Paper on future airport capacity in 2003. If this were to lead to BAA and/or MA adding new capacity additions to their plans, under this framework the CAA would identify the outputs the enhancement was expected to produce, and link a new revenue allowance to those outputs. The airport would have to judge, on the basis of the commercial business

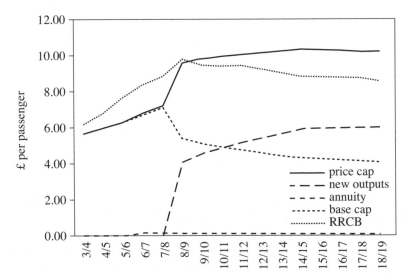

Source: 'Heathrow, Gatwick and Stansted Airports' Price Caps 2003–2008, CAA, February 2002.

Figure 8.1   Breakdown of contributions to the overall price cap

case, whether, when and where to proceed with an application for planning permission. There would not be a need to change the elements of the price path specified now.

This represents a different approach to incentive setting under economic regulation with a consequential shift in risk sharing. For this to be effective it has to be seen as credible over a long time period: certainly well beyond the traditional price control period. Regulatory structure and institutions are a major factor in delivering this. Relatedly, recognizing the strategic interdependencies between airlines and airports, the CAA has also proposed the development of a compact between the parties built around enhanced information disclosure by regulated airports relating to long-term business plans for the airports.

CONCLUSION

The commercial model has worked well in aviation, with substantial benefits to consumers. Additional benefits are available from further liberalization, completing the desired process of government disengagement.

The public policy problems are increasingly in the upstream infrastructure markets where service performance falls short of demand and excess demand is a significant issue in parts of the UK. The lessons from the downstream market of the benefits of a more commercial approach have transferred more slowly. Maximizing competitive pressures within which commercial firms operate is likely to deliver the maximum long-term gains. Where *ex ante* economic regulation is judged necessary it is desirable that the institutional structure encourage a credible regime that maximizes the incentive properties given the characteristics of the regulated firms.

ANNEX: INVESTMENT INCENTIVES UNDER A REGULATORY COST BASE APPROACH

The following is an illustration built around a likely standard business case investment analysis that a firm would undertake in deciding on an investment. The usual assumptions apply: for example, only benefits and costs that can be attributed to the project compared with the best alternative are relevant, real option values are incorporated in the project's costs and the project will only proceed if the net present value is positive at the firm's cost of capital for the project reflecting the equity beta for the project. The key parameters are as follows:

I = project investment cost in cash terms,

C = project annual operating cost,

Q = output volume,

P = price per unit output,

D = five year effective discount factor reflecting project's cost of capital,

π = economic profits per unit output from commercial activities,

r = regulated rate of return (%),

d = allowed depreciation for price cap purposes (%),

D_i = discount factor for periodic review time period reflecting project cost of capital and any regulatory risk.

Subscripts: s = single till; 1,2… = periodic review time periods.

1. Standard Unregulated Commercial Model

Investment in an aeronautical project with possible commercial spinoffs proceeds if

(1) $$0 \le \Sigma D_i [\Delta Q_i ((P) + \Pi_i^e) - C_i] - I.$$

2. Single Till Regulatory Asset Base Approach

The regulated airport in its investment analysis will allow for the single till RAB-based regulated price plus the *expected* net profits from the unregulated activities over the first five years multiplied by projected volumes. The investment and operating costs are a cost to the firm as in the commercial model in the first period.

In second and subsequent periods the single till regulatory asset base (RAB) approach takes away any excess earnings including profits from non-regulated activities and sets regulated prices relevant to the project to allow current operating expenditure and sunk capital expenditure to be recovered.

(2) $$0 \le \Sigma D_1 [\Delta Q((P_{si}) + \Pi_1^e) - C_1 - I_1] + D_2 [C_1 + (r + d)I_1] + \dots$$

One critical point is that the regulatory cost base approach distorts investment incentives, turning costs into benefits and taking away any superprofits.

3. Revised Regulatory Cost Base (Dual Till) Approach

Moving from the single till to the RRCB can be thought of as allowing the initial regulated price to be adjusted by best estimate of non-regulated net profits (probably the previous period's reported net profits would be the best unbiased forecast).

(3) $0 \leq \Sigma D_1[\Delta Q((P_{si}) + \Pi_0) - \Pi_1^e) - C_1] - I_1 + D_2[C_2 + (r + d)I_1] + ...$

4. Difference between Single Till and RRCB

A simple comparison between equations 2 and 3 suggests that all terms cancel out except

$$D_1 \Delta Q \Pi_0.$$

Unsurprisingly the abolition of the single till improves the profitability of aeronautical investments which increase throughput. In situations where there is excess demand for aeronautical outputs, increasing the supply of new capacity seems the logical response. A movement to the RRCB from the single till is one way of achieving this.

5. Social Optimization

It is instructive to contrast the investment decision rule under RAB regulation with a simple social optimization objective function whereby projects should proceed if the gains in consumer surplus[30] exceed the social costs of the project.

$$0 \leq \int Q^{-1}(P)dq - C - I.$$

Where there is market power (for example because of lumpy investments) the unregulated monopoly objective function takes account of falling marginal revenue as output expands with the first derivative of the inverse demand curve replacing the inverse demand curve in the objective function.

$$0 \leq \int Q^{-1'}(P)dq - C - I.$$

The policy aim is to close the gap between the demand curve and the marginal revenue curve. Again the effect of the move from the single till to the RRCB would be likely to shift the marginal revenue function to the right.

NOTES

1. I would like to acknowledge the assistance of Nienke Hendriks in the preparation of this chapter.
2. Simon Cowan, 'Developments in Regulatory Principles: the UK Experience', *Regulation of Network Utilities*, Oxford: Oxford Unviersity Press, 2001.

3. Steven Morrison and Clifford Winston, 'The remaining role for Government policy in the deregulated airline industry', *Deregulation of Network Industries*, Washington, DC: AEI-Brookings, 2000.
4. Civil Aviation Authority, 'The Single European Aviation Market', CAP 685, 1998.
5. *Financial Times*, 14 August 2002, p. 24.
6. Civil Aviation Authority, 'Airport Quinquennial Review, Heathrow, Gatwick and Stansted Airports Price Caps 2003–2008: CAA Recommendations to the Competition Commission', Chapter 1, February 2002 (www.caaerg.co.uk).
7. A cost of undertaking a mutually exclusive project at time *t* is not being able to undertake it at time *t*+1.
8. Department for Transport, 'Demand for Air Travel: impact of meeting the costs of external costs from climate change and other developments', mimeo.
9. 'A New Deal for Transport: Better for Everyone, the government's White Paper on the Future of Transport, 1998', (www.dft.gov.uk/itwp/index.htm).
10. John Vickers and George Yarrow, *Privatisation: an economic analysis*, Cambridge, MA: MIT Press, 1988, ch. 5.
11. William L. Megginson and Jeffry M. Nutter 'From State to Market: A Survey of Empirical Studies on Privatization', *Journal of Economic Literature*, June 2001.
12. Nicholas Crafts, 'Britain's Relative Economic Performance 1870–1999', IEA, 2002.
13. Gregor Andrade, Mark Mitchell and Erik Stafford, 'New Evidence and Perspectives on Mergers', *The Journal of Economic Perspectives*, Spring 2001.
14. Robert Crandall, 'A Time to End Regulation', in Colin Robinson (ed.), *Competition and Regulation in Utility Markets*, Cheltenham, UK and Northampton, MA, USA: Edward Elgar, 2003.
15. Clifford Winston, 'Government Failure in Urban Transportation', *The Institute for Fiscal Studies*, **21** (4), December 2000, 403–25 (www.ifs.org.uk).
16. Peter Forsyth, 'Regulation under Stress: Developments in Australian Airport Policy', mimeo, February 2002.
17. David Starkie and George Yarrow, 'The single till approach to the price regulation of airports' (www.caaerg.co.uk).
18. Martin Loeb and Wesley Magat, 'A Decentralised Method for Utility Regulation', *Journal of Law and Economics*, October 1979, 399–404.
19. David S. Sibley, 'Asymmetric Information, Incentives and Price-Cap Regulation', *Rand Journal*, **20** (3), Autumn 1989, 392–404.
20. David S. Sibley, 'Economic Analysis of the CAA's proposals for NATS', July 2000 (www. caaerg.co.uk).
21. Oliver Hart, 'Firms, Contracts and Financial Structures', *Clarendon Lectures in Economics*, Oxford: 1995.
22. Paul Joskow, 'Vertical integration and long term contracts: the case of coal-burning electric generating plants', *Journal of Law, Economics and Organisation* **1** (1), 1985.
23. W. Kip Viscusi, John M. Vernon and Joseph E. Harrington, Jr, *Economics of Regulation and Antitrust*, Cambridge, MA: MIT Press, p. 310.
24. Ofwat, 'Financial performance and expenditure of water companies in England and Wales, 2001–2002 report', Ofwat, 2002, p. 3.
25. John Vickers and George Yarrow, *Privatization: an economic analysis*, Cambridge, MA: MIT Press, 1988.
26. Ofwat, 'Proposals for the Modification of the Conditions of Appointment of Anglian Water Services Limited', April 2002, p. 6.
27. Office of Rail Regulator, 'The Proposed Acquisition of Railtrack by Network Rail', June 2002.
28. Edward L. Glaeser, 'The Governance of Not-For-Profit Firms', May 2002 # wp8921 (www. nber.org).
29. 'Heathrow, Gatwick and Stansted Airports' Price Caps, 2003–2008: CAA recommendations to the Competition Commission', February 2002; 'Manchester Airport's Price Cap 2003–2008: CAA recommendations to the Competition Commission', March 2002 (www.caaerg.co.uk).
30. Assuming that the project is relatively small in relation to the economy, so that relative price changes are negligible, allowing the use of consumer surplus.

CHAIRMAN'S COMMENTS

Andrew Sentance

From an airline industry perspective, we should thank Doug Andrew and his team at the CAA for one thing. As a result of the work they have done on the airport charges review, they have forced us all to think a lot more seriously about the system of airport regulation and how it operates. However it has not inclined us to agree with his solution. I want to talk about some problems that we have encountered with the ideas he has been through during the discussions we have had on the latest airports regulatory review. We are now at quite a crucial time because the Competition Commission has concluded its deliberations after hearings over the last eight months. It has delivered its report to the CAA, which will soon provide us with an assessment, which will then be the subject of further consultation. We have quite a prolonged process for reviewing airport regulation in the UK.

Let me emphasize one other point of agreement with Doug, his general approach. We should be looking for market-based or commercial models that deal with the problems that we face if we can. Doug has highlighted what he saw as good examples of the market working, but even in the areas he has covered, it is clear that the market does not solve all problems. In the airline industry, the volatility of demand interacts with a number of other industry characteristics, creating the opposite problem to the underinvestment that Doug is worried about. We have periodic periods of overcapacity as airlines invest quite heavily in the upswing and then find they have far too much capacity in the downswing. Entry is generally easier than exit; and it is difficult to take capacity out. That is partly because of the structure of regulation in the industry. But when you look at the combined valuation of airlines at present (particularly in the USA) I am not sure the shareholders of airlines would agree with Doug's observation that the market and commercial-based approach has worked well for them, though clearly consumers have benefited.

The standard analysis of regulated industries is that, if you move towards a more market-based deregulated solution, that has to be accompanied by moves to create a more competitive market structure. In other words, Doug's approach is part of a deregulatory agenda and the CAA have made that quite explicit. In fact, it is a bit of a misnomer to call Doug an economic regulator because it is quite clear from his chapter that his inclinations are deregulatory. But Doug is trying to promote a form of deregulation without a significant injection of competition. That approach creates quite a few problems for us.

I will identify four problem areas about his airport case study that he has highlighted. The first area of difficulty is that the attempt to incentivize investment using the mechanisms he has suggested is extremely costly for consumers. Doug has highlighted the emphasis on the long-run price cap and the attempt to take a longer-term view, but the CAA has also proposed a major shift in the regulatory base, in the way in which the regulatory system is operated, to create what is called a dual till as opposed to a single till. This dual till aspect certainly has caused us quite a few problems, as it creates consumer disbenefits as prices are pushed up. Now Doug is quite overt about this: he thinks airline 'rents' will absorb the higher prices and therefore it is a good thing in terms of investment incentives for prices to rise. But given that the basis of economic regulation is to contain market power, airlines are understandably very worried about proposals that end up pushing up prices – and allowing a monopoly to enjoy much bigger returns in the absence of competition.

The second issue is the complexity of the proposals. The dual till is a very complex system. Though the chart that Doug uses looks quite simple in concept, underpinning it is a set of very complex and arbitrary calculations. In effect, his regime involves carving up the airport, and in particular the terminals, into an aeronautical and a commercial stream. To give a rather vivid example of this, a baggage hall roof might look like an aeronautical facility to most people and should therefore perhaps fall in the aeronautical till. But if you look at the cost of the baggage hall roof, a large part of it arises from the need to reinforce it so it can support the retail facilities sitting above. This is just one very small example which is replicated across the airport. And when you get into a labyrinthine discussion about carving up the airport between these two streams, you blunt the simplicity of the investment incentives that Doug is looking for. If you want investment incentives, clarity and simplicity are essential. If that clarity is undermined by a very complex allocation of assets across what is essentially a common facility – an airport – we cannot be at all sure that investment will flow in an economically rational way.

The third issue is that we need stability in the system of regulation, not necessarily in the price cap itself. Doug made a lot of the need for long-term stability, and I would agree with that. But the five-year review process in the UK does strike a reasonable balance between the need for some degree of flexibility and the need to maintain stability because the structure of the system remains the same. The long-term price cap approach that he is suggesting is damaging. If it survives, it builds in quite a lot of inflexibility, as you set up a structure at a point now, and if the economic situation changes in a very volatile industry such as aviation, you do not have a chance to change it without undermining a whole regulatory approach.

The approach which the airline community prefers is to focus on the stability of the framework itself, rather than the price cap. We have a framework of five-yearly reviews in the UK that has worked, not perfectly but adequately, based on the concept of the single till. As far as investment is concerned, the single till remunerates the cost of capital. We have a debate every five years about what the cost of capital should be: that is not unknown in economic regulation circles. In most regulatory reviews, the cost of capital seems to be one of the most heavily debated matters. But if the cost of capital is right, there should be no disincentive to invest, and there are various ways of making sure you can set the price cap to deal with the problems of gold plating and so on that Doug referred to.

Finally the structure of the aviation industry means that consultation, if it can be made to work effectively, is a very powerful tool for incentivizing investment. Doug is obviously clearly keen to set powerful incentives. However the aviation industry is not like other regulated industries where you have a very fragmented and diverse user base of many millions of customers. In our industry, you have easily identified users who are operating competitive markets, as Doug has highlighted, and who are therefore well placed to signal to you what the appropriate investment streams might be. That does create a role for the regulator, as he or she has to police the process of consultation to some degree. But the way to get the right sorts of investment is to build on that process of consultation.

There are two powerful undercurrents to this whole debate. First, is the issue of market power, which we see as a very big problem in the airport industry in the UK, where you have an organization which controls the bulk of capacity in the south east of England and therefore has considerable market power. In this environment, you have to be careful about the way in which you use these incentives, not giving them too much leeway to exploit that market power. That is one of our major reservations about the approach that Doug was outlining.

The second undercurrent, again buried at the bottom of one of Doug's lines, is the key to the investment issue in the case of airports, which is environmental and planning constraints. As far as the airport system in the UK is concerned, that is the real problem. If the planning system in the UK worked as it did in France, for example, I think we would have Terminal Five at Heathrow up and running by now. It is the combination of cumbersome planning and an unclear airport strategy framework, alongside lack of clarity on how to deal with the environmental impact of the airport, that have been the biggest impediments to airport investment in the UK. We are going through a process of government consultation on these issues at the moment. We might imagine a world where we could disengage the government from the policy process, but that is not the world we inhabit. In reality, in the airport system, so many of the key parameters are in government hands. The best I think we can hope for is that we get a clear strategy from the government, a clear way of dealing with those environmental problems and a more streamlined planning system, so that, when investment proposals come forward, through dialogue between airports and airlines, they can go ahead and be financed expeditiously.

Doug makes some very valid points about the difficulty that regulatory systems have in dealing with investment, but in the airport case study he has highlighted we are really shooting at the wrong target. Investment incentives are probably adequate under the current regulatory system if it is applied properly with what we call very affectionately 'the single till'. What we need to develop is various mechanisms around that to make sure that the regulatory price formula is linked into the delivery of service quality, and the provision of adequate infrastructure through investment. If our objective is getting a better and more rational approach to investment in airport infrastructure, it is really a matter of getting a clearer airport strategy, dealing effectively with the environmental issues and establishing a more streamlined planning system.

9. Gas, electricity and the energy review
Colin Robinson

A TEXT

In 1993, Michael Beesley contributed a Foreword to a paper I had written about energy policy.[1] In it, he said,

> One of the abiding problems in establishing the credibility of economists in real government or business decisions is that their predominantly neo-classical training both encourages the idea of playing God in the machine and diverts them from studying how markets develop, not least in response to attempts to coerce them.

That is an appropriate text for this chapter because it discusses an apparent revival of attempts to 'play God in the machine' in energy markets.

THE YEAR OF ENERGY POLICY

2002 was the year in which energy policy returned. In earlier postwar times, from the late 1950s to the early 1980s, energy policy was a subject of some importance, meriting a specialist government department to administer it: the Ministry of Fuel and Power, the Ministry of Power and the Department of Energy. But, about 20 years ago, Nigel Lawson, then Secretary of State for Energy, killed the extant form of energy policy, as I shall explain.

The year 2002 has seen not so much a resurrection from the dead as a reincarnation: it has been more like the transference of the soul of energy policy into a new body which has a rather different appearance from the one that went six feet under in the early 1980s. It bears some resemblance to what went before but it has been spruced up to reflect present-day concerns. Its emphasis and its particulars are quite different from those of the old policy.

The flurry of activity started with publication in February 2002 of the *Energy Review* by the Cabinet Office Performance and Innovation Unit (PIU), following which, in May, the government produced its 'Key Issues for Consultation' paper. There have been some other less significant government documents on energy policy during the year.[2] By early 2003, a White Paper is promised[3] which, according to my calculations, will be the first White Paper on energy policy for 35 years (though there have been other, lesser pronouncements on the subject).[4] Moreover, during 2002, there were some momentous unplanned events which affected the energy industries, including the financial problems of British Energy, which not only gave the Department of Trade and Industry (DTI) an immediate problem of whether to bail out the company, but raised longer-term doubts about the role of nuclear energy, and the possibility of war with Iraq which raised crude oil prices and indirectly affected prices of other energy products. The influence of 'events', in the sense of Harold Macmillan's famous comment, is one of the issues to which I will return.

Not for many years has energy been so high on the political agenda. According to the DTI website, 'Maintaining a forward looking coherent energy policy is a major task for Government.' That statement could have been lifted from any one of the many attempts in the earlier postwar period to define and implement a policy for the energy sector. However a crucial difference this time is that the energy industries (apart from some aging Magnox stations) are in private ownership, whereas in previous times only the oil companies were private.

This chapter starts with a potted history of British energy policy since the Second World War to see what lessons we might learn. Then it discusses the theory of government intervention in the energy market. Finally it considers the main issues which the new form of policy emphasizes, whether they constitute a genuine basis for government action, and their impact on the privatized gas and electricity industries and their regulation.

A POTTED HISTORY

In the early postwar years, energy and coal were regarded as virtually synonymous, just as they had been 80 years previously in the days when Jevons was writing about coal in the mid-nineteenth century.[5] Both electricity and gas were produced from coal, oil was primarily a transport fuel, there was very little hydro power and no civil nuclear power stations had then been built. Returning coal production to its prewar level and then increasing it to permit the economy to grow seemed pressing concerns to contemporary writers and to the first postwar Labour government.[6] By 1952, coal production had returned to its 1938 level of some 230 million tonnes, but that proved to be its postwar peak: the downward trend of the inter-war years then resumed because of competition from relatively low-priced oil products and later from North Sea natural gas. Before the Second World War, production had fallen because of declining exports of coal: after the war, with exports very small, output fell as home consumption of coal declined.

For the next 30 years, what governments described as 'energy policy' was, in practice, a series of protectionist measures intended to aid British coalmining, with a subsidiary objective of promoting British-designed nuclear power stations.[7] The wall of protection which surrounded British-mined coal rose higher and higher as governments of both political parties tried to offset the forces which were turning consumers away from British-mined coal. Of course, support for coal was not in a form which explicitly violated world trade rules by imposing tariffs and quotas. Governments, both Labour and Conservative, implemented the policy principally by leaning on the nationalized electricity supply industry to make it burn more British coal than it would freely have chosen, by giving coal preference elsewhere in the public sector, by taxing fuel oil heavily from 1961 onwards and by keeping out imports of coal and Russian crude oil. Periodically financial assistance was given to the (then) National Coal Board by writing down or writing off the value of its assets. The policy had constantly to be adjusted, as circumstances changed, in a vain effort to stop new forces cutting away more of the coal market. For example, when natural gas was found in the North Sea, the government made plain to the oil companies which had made the discoveries and to the Central Electricity Generating Board (CEGB) that there was no question of gas being used in power stations. The *de facto* ban on gas use in British power stations is sometimes attributed to the EEC (as it then was), but that is incorrect. In the mid-1960s I was economic adviser on North Sea natural gas to one of the major oil companies and I know that the ban was imposed then, well before Britain joined the Common Market.

Despite increasing protection, British coalmining fell sharply, from 198 million tonnes in 1960 to 130 million tonnes in 1980, as relatively low-priced oil penetrated markets previously held by coal. Fuel oil sales in particular grew rapidly, displacing coal in industrial and commercial markets. Even the two oil 'shocks' of the 1970s failed to promote revival, though for a time the rate of decline slowed. Nevertheless governments, which were being pressed by the National Union of Mineworkers to establish a target annual output of 200 million tonnes, in their public statements remained determinedly optimistic about coal's future. Particularly unfortunate examples of this tendency came in two documents published in the mid-1970s which anticipated an expansion of Britain's coal output to 135 million tonnes in 1985 and 170 million tonnes in 2000.[8]

The nationalized electricity supply industry was also used as the instrument for favouring civil nuclear power, beginning in 1955 with the First Nuclear Power Programme (Magnox), followed in 1965 by the Second Nuclear Power Programme (Advanced Gas Cooled Reactors) and then by the lone Pressurised Water Reactor (PWR) at Sizewell. There were also plans to construct commercial fast reactors at some time in the future which were not dropped until the late 1980s. Some people in the CEGB had begun, around 1960, to doubt the wisdom of these ventures into nuclear power based on British-designed reactors. But the electricity supply industry did not resist too strenuously because it was, in effect, compensated by taxpayers and electricity consumers for its support both for British-mined coal and for British-designed nuclear stations. Britain's nuclear power industry was conjured into existence and then maintained by the state.[9]

A number of official documents have a bearing on government intervention in the energy industries in those years. Because three of the industries (coal, gas and electricity) were nationalized, the three White Papers on the nationalized industries of 1961, 1967 and 1978 are themselves relevant.[10] They were all attempts to ease the tensions that were building up between the boards of the nationalized corporations and governments. They set financial and other targets for the nationalized corporations and, in the case of the 1967 document – sometimes described as the 'welfare economists' charter' – advocated marginal cost pricing and improved investment appraisal methods. However there was not much sign that these documents had any influence on the behaviour of the corporations and, in any case, governments seemed to lose interest in them after publication.[11] More directly relevant were two White Papers on Energy Policy, issued only two years apart, in 1965 and 1967.[12]

I argued at the time[13] that these White Papers were no more than *ex post* rationalizations of numerous *ad hoc* interventionist measures taken as short-term responses to perceived problems by a succession of past governments. The White Papers described, and attempted to justify after the event, as 'policy' what had actually been a 'haphazard process of piling measure on measure'. Supporters of energy policies presumably expect policy formulation to come first, followed by action in conformity with the policy. In the case of 'energy policy' (and probably many other government policies too), the process was reversed, in a demonstration of the force of Macmillan's comment about the powerful influence of 'events'. Events came first, followed by responses to those events which were later dignified by the title of 'policy'.

Moreover there were the inevitable unintended consequences. Measures initially intended mainly to protect coal resulted in a protected fuel market, so that all energy suppliers in Britain were helped (and energy consumers were disadvantaged) by the high level of fuel prices. Governments of both parties increased coal protection and continued to favour nuclear power up to the early 1980s. The last act of this kind of policy came in February 1981 when, in a remarkable U-turn, the first Thatcher government, which had said it would reduce protection for coal, decided under the threat of pit closures to give the industry more aid.[14]

It was not until the arrival of Nigel Lawson at the then Department of Energy later in 1981 that a new attitude towards energy policy appeared. He realized right away that the planning mentality in the department was inconsistent with liberal market economics. 'Predict-and-provide' was the prevailing view in the department: project the demand for energy many years into the future, then project the supply of various forms of energy, then start to worry about the 'gap' between demand and supply which such exercises in 'gapology' invariably show. These gaps are spurious: they merely reflect human shortsightedness. People can see problems which might arise if present trends are extrapolated but, by definition, they cannot see the yet-to-appear solutions which human ingenuity will most likely provide. But the Department of Energy took these supposed gaps very seriously, using them as an excuse to justify protectionist measures which, it claimed, would fill the gap. As Nigel Lawson explains in his memoirs, he saw no value in these blueprints for the future and stopped the department working on them, giving it a major culture shock. Instead of an energy policy, he argued, the way forward was to price fuel realistically.[15]

The Conservative government did not immediately give up coal protection (the infamous 'Joint Understandings' which from 1979 committed the CEGB to take most of its coal from the (then) National Coal Board remained) and it continued to promote nuclear power until, in 1988, it cut the fast reactor programme sharply and the following year gave up the idea of a 'small family' of PWRs. But for the 15 years or so from the early 1980s to the end of the Major government in 1997, energy policy in the sense in which it had been understood in the earlier postwar period seemed at least moribund, if not dead, despite many momentous events in the British energy market. The year-long coal strike of 1984–5 was the most dramatic: after the 'defeat' of the main mining union the industry was never again the powerful pressure group it had been in earlier postwar years. Then there was energy privatization. I am not a great fan of the way the energy industries were privatized which, as I argued at the time,[16] left too much market power with incumbents. However, although in general the energy privatization schemes were not, in themselves, liberalizing measures, they were important enabling steps which over many years allowed energy regulators and the (then) Monopolies and Mergers Commission to open up energy markets. In 1986, gas was privatized, followed by electricity (except for nuclear power) in 1989 and coal in 1994, after many years of attrition during which it waited for the privatization scheme to be announced. Soon afterwards (1996) nuclear power, except for the Magnox stations, also went into the private sector.

The Lawson aim of moving towards realistic pricing seemed on the road to achievement through privatization. Moreover, with almost all the energy sector in private hands, the old form of energy policy – operated through the back door by ministers and civil servants making known to the bosses of the nationalized industries what government wanted them to do – had become impossible to maintain. Under nationalization, the electricity supply industry had been more an instrument of industrial and energy policy, supporting coal, nuclear power and the British heavy electrical industry, than a commercial operation. That kind of organization could not survive privatization.

However in the recent past it has been possible to spot some continuities with the earlier postwar period and an incipient departure from the liberalizing trend. The beginnings of the change can be traced back to 1997 when the government decided on an old-fashioned 'rescue' of the then recently privatized coal industry after threats of pit closures.[17] The package included an extremely ill-advised, albeit short-lived moratorium on the construction of gas-fired power stations which restricted entry to a generation industry already short of competition. Coal has continued to be supported, even if the scale of the support is now small compared with the past, given the extent to which the industry has shrunk. Perhaps even more significant was the aid the government offered that other, now privatized, favourite of the policy makers of old, nuclear power, when in the autumn of 2002 British Energy found itself in severe financial difficulties. Indeed the rescue of British Energy suggests that Macmillan's 'events' still dominate policy towards the energy industries, whatever plans governments may have. The events still come first and whatever short-term solutions are applied to them will no doubt later be dignified with the label of 'policy'. However that may be, another effort to write down a policy in advance of events is now taking place. I will describe the new policy more fully later, but first I want to discuss a topic which supporters of energy policy seldom bring into the open: the theory of energy policy.

THE THEORY OF ENERGY POLICY

I argued earlier that government energy 'policy' in the earlier postwar years was a long way from the considered, long-term strategy which supporters of energy policy would presumably like to see. It was just a collection of short-term interventionist measures which were subsequently written down and collectively described as 'policy' in government documents. Its consequences were both unintended and perverse. Presumably none of the supporters of an energy policy would have been happy with its outcomes: in particular, higher prices for consumers and an electricity supply industry which, as I shall explain, was primarily an arm of government industrial policy, had undiversified fuel supplies and therefore suffered from insecurity of supply and produced more pollution than if the market had been permitted to work. This tendency to 'adhockery' in policy making has re-emerged in the last few years. An important question is whether it is inherent in energy 'policy' or whether a wise and considered long-term government strategy for the energy sector is feasible and desirable.

The Neoclassical View and its Flaws

The idea that an energy policy is desirable rests essentially on the mainstream neoclassical economic notion that markets are 'imperfect' and 'fail'.[18] As Michael Beesley put it in the quotation at the beginning of this chapter, that view encourages 'the idea of playing God in the machine'. Government can be brought in, as *deus ex machina*, to improve on what would have been the market outcome, but there are many flaws in that view which are listed briefly below.

First, staying within the confines of neoclassical economics, attempting to move the outcome of one market closer to the outcome of a perfectly competitive market inevitably comes up against the second best problem pointed out by Lipsey and Lancaster nearly 50 years ago.[19] There is no reason to believe that such a move, while other markets remain imperfectly competitive (piecemeal welfare economics), will have beneficial effects. That is a very inconvenient result for mainstream microeconomists because it means there can be little faith in most of their policy prescriptions. The response of the majority of them is to carry on regardless, acknowledging but essentially ignoring the second-best issue.

Second, moving outside mainstream economics but nevertheless to well-established theoretical conclusions, there is the 'public choice problem'. After all the work of James Buchanan, Gordon Tullock and their followers it is hard to understand why economists interested in policy take so little account of the presence of government failure. If people in the government sector have similar motivations to those in the private sector, why should anyone believe that government servants are pursuing the 'public interest'? Such an interest is anyway difficult to define and identify and, unless ministers and civil servants are different beings from the rest of us, concerned only with the interests of others, why should they be assumed to be pursuing it? Of course, if there is government failure the case for bringing in government to set right the failures of the market is severely dented. Indeed it can be argued that, in general, government failure is the worse problem. The pursuit of self-interest in a competitive market is likely to lead to beneficial results in terms of welfare. But governments are not in competitive markets. They have monopolies of policy between elections and so government policy essentially represents the pursuit of self-interest in a monopolized market.

Third, and even more fundamentally, it is worth giving some thought to what is meant by 'imperfections' and 'failures' in markets. What mainstream economists mean is that conditions in the relevant market will not produce an outcome like the long-run equilibrium of perfect competition with price equal to long-run marginal and 'normal' profits. But that is a rather odd view of what constitutes an 'imperfection' or 'failure' since that equilibrium is not on offer as a possible state of the world, if for no other reason than that it assumes perfect knowledge – or, more precisely, it implies perfect knowledge of the future (as all decisions are about the future) which, all experience indicates, cannot exist. In effect, therefore, mainstream economics sets up as an ideal a state which cannot be realized, then treats as 'imperfections' and 'failures' departures from that state. All markets, when examined against such a criterion, are bound to be 'imperfect' and 'failing', so intervention by government will appear to be justified everywhere. Putting the matter another way, to justify government intervention by reference to supposed imperfections and failures is to indulge in what Harold Demsetz has aptly described as 'Nirvana economics'.[20] Instead, Demsetz argues, practical policy making should be about choosing among feasible states of the world.

Fourth, an allied question concerns what governments (including government-appointed regulators) can know. Most economists would probably now accept the impossibility of formulating a welfare function for society which reflects individual preferences. But perhaps a government could avoid such a heroic concept, simply determining what the outcome of a competitive market would be and then imposing it, bypassing the messy process of people competing against each other? For instance, a government could impose marginal cost pricing and perhaps simulate the costs and standards that would have appeared in a competitive market. If you take the view, as I would, that markets are the prime means by which knowledge is generated and spread, such government action is simply not possible. The outcome of a competitive market arises only through the competitive process: without that process, the knowledge required to achieve the outcome is not produced. So you cannot have the outcome without going through the process. As Hayek pointed out,[21] the essence of knowledge is that it is decentralized, and cannot be gathered together at a central point, such as a Whitehall department or a regulator's office. An inherent problem outside competitive markets is therefore not so much information asymmetry as information shortage. Governments and regulators do not know what market outcomes would be and so, in general, they cannot simulate such outcomes. The main anchor which neoclassical economics provides for government intervention is therefore missing.

In my view, the difficulties I have outlined mean there are massive problems in the way of an energy policy that will be an improvement on the outcome of functioning competitive energy markets. A view commonly expressed is that markets should be allowed to work, for efficiency reasons, but that they should be constrained by government regulation designed to take into account the failings of markets. That is all very well but, in practice, how can governments, lacking any anchor, identify what those constraints should be?

The Importance of Interest Group Pressures

Governments, lacking the necessary expertise and short of information, are highly susceptible to the attentions of pressure groups which move into the vacuum left by the lack of information in politicized markets. As the public choice theorists have pointed out, the actions of interest groups are extremely important influences on government policies which tend to be biased in favour of the organized and to neglect the interests of unorganized small consumers. So rent-seeking behaviour is prevalent.

The economic analysis of this type of rent-seeking behaviour is straightforward. When it is known that government may intervene, as, for instance, when a 'crisis' affects one or more energy industries or when government announces a review of energy policy, interest groups have a powerful incentive to lobby. Any gains they achieve will be concentrated on their members; the costs will be thinly spread over the population at large. So lobbying is potentially a high return activity for the pressure groups, whereas the general populace has little incentive to resist even outcomes which are very damaging to the community as a whole because each individual bears only a small part of the cost. Politicians go along with the pressure groups because they have an incentive to treat people unequally, placing most weight on the views of those who appear able to deliver large numbers of votes and little on the views of the unorganized.

On this view, energy policy is not so much a means by which wise, benevolent and altruistic public servants act for the benefit of the community as a whole: it is a means by which minorities force their views on the rest of the populace via the only organization which has the power to coerce – the government. In the old days of energy policy, the powerful pressure groups which determined policy were British Coal (and its predecessor, the National Coal Board), the National Union of Mineworkers and the very effective scientific lobby which pushed British governments into their ventures in civil nuclear power. The pressure groups had particular power in times of evident 'crisis' when quick government decisions seemed to be required. Recent events at British Energy might suggest that not much has changed. As I have argued elsewhere, the beneficiaries of British energy policy, old-style, were producers not consumers. Policy was not conceived after 'disinterested analysis of the options' but was a product 'of short-termism, aimed at gaining political advantage'.[22]

ENERGY POLICY, NEW-STYLE

Policy: Planned and Unplanned

In discussing new-style energy policy, I can talk only about published documents by government advisers and, in particular, the PIU's *Energy Review*. For all I know, the government may decide to accept few of the PIU's recommendations after its consultation process. Moreover, in practice, policy will probably, as in the past, be determined more by unplanned events and reactions to them than by all this forethought. However the forethought is worth considering as indicative of the way prevailing opinion is moving, not only in this country but evidently also in the United States if the Senate version of the Energy Bill going through Congress is any guide.

I realize there is a danger of reading too much into the PIU's *Review*, which is only an advisory document and which may bear little resemblance to the eventual White Paper. However there is an opposite danger, which impresses me rather more, of neglecting such advisory documents on the assumption that their influence will be limited. The PIU report, in my view, fits the revived prevailing wisdom about energy policy and so it should be taken seriously. One other thing I should say, in case I seem unduly critical of the PIU, is that I realize that part of the unwritten terms of reference of such government review documents is that they should produce proposals for more government action. Statements that most problems now foreseen will be solved through the application of human ingenuity, operating through markets, are not what the sponsors of the report expect or welcome. Consequently there tends to be a bias towards 'activist' solutions. Recognizing that there may be some such bias, how should one regard the PIU's advice?

An Emphasis on Markets: but Qualified

To begin on a positive note, one obvious change compared with earlier statements of energy policy is the emphasis on competitive markets which reflects the much altered economic and political agenda. To quote the PIU report's Executive Summary (third para.), 'The introduction of liberalised and competitive energy markets in the UK has been a success, and this should provide a cornerstone of future policy.' Moreover, unlike previous statements of energy policy, the PIU recognizes the possibility of government failure, so that 'intervention may sometimes make matters worse' (para 3.1). These seem to me important developments in the attitudes of energy policy advisers which reflect the changed climate of opinion about economic policy making as a new 'semi-consensus' has developed.[23] However experience teaches that we should look beyond the words written down in government documents,[24] which (partly because of the influence of 'events' which I have already stressed) are not necessarily a good guide to what governments will actually do. In this case, the PIU document is ambiguous. For all the stress on the benefits of markets, when it comes to considering possible policy measures, the PIU seems overimpressed with the market failure case for intervention and at crucial points loses sight of the flaws in that case.

On another positive note, considering more specific issues, it appears that some of the matters which were prominent in earlier energy policy statements, notably supposed balance of payments problems, fears of sharply rising fossil fuel prices in the long-term future and worries about oil supply interruptions, are, quite rightly, no longer of much concern. A particularly welcome feature is the absence of the crude expressions of concern about the insecurity of imported fuels versus indigenous supplies which used to be so prominent in energy policy statements. The PIU (and the DTI in its *Key Issues* paper) concentrate on two more substantive issues: one is the environmental problems which they believe relate to the energy sector and the other is security of energy supply (which is rather confused in the PIU report with the logically distinct issue of long-term energy price risk).

Of the two, by far the greater space is occupied by discussion of environmental issues. Indeed, the PIU goes so far as to suggest a new objective for energy policy. The DTI's *Key Issues* paper (para. 2.1) quotes, with implicit approval, the PIU proposal (page 52 of its report) that the DTI's energy objective should be redefined as 'the pursuit of secure and competitively priced means of meeting our energy needs, subject to the achievement of an environmentally sustainable energy system'. Institutional change is also suggested. The PIU would like the government to establish a 'new cross-cutting Sustainable Energy Policy Unit to draw together all dimensions of energy policy in the UK' (point (x) in the Executive Summary). Responsibility within government for climate change policy, energy policy and transport policy should in the long run be brought together in one department. The PIU would like government intervention in energy markets to use the 'guiding principle' of 'sustainable development'. I now consider the security and environmental cases for government intervention as set out by the PIU.

Security of Supply

Although the authors of the PIU report believe sustainable development objectives should predominate in energy policy making (para. 4.1), according to them, energy security is a 'cross-cutting' objective where government has a role. After a long discussion of security they conclude (para. 4.111) that there is no pressing need for government action on security but it should 'closely monitor' security risks in future and intervene if necessary. However the PIU does make a case in principle for government action to improve energy security which I find unconvincing, because it does not examine the theoretical case properly, because as in other parts of the report it neglects its own arguments about government failure and because it is silent about the results of past government efforts to promote security.

British governments claimed, in justifications of energy policy in earlier postwar years, that providing security of energy supply is a legitimate function of government. Economists give them some ammunition to reinforce this claim. Security of supply is a quasi-public good. If I supply it, I cannot appropriate all the benefits so I and everyone else will underinvest in it. Thus markets will not supply the optimum quantity of security and governments should step in. The theoretical argument about public goods is correct, and appealing to Nirvana economists, but from a policy viewpoint it is irrelevant because optimum security is not on offer. No one has the knowledge to define what optimum security would be, let alone provide it. So the question becomes whether, if one is seeking a high degree of energy security at low cost, markets or government provide the more likely means of achievement.[25]

Markets will take into account security in the sense that both consumers and producers, when selling and purchasing energy products, realize that security is an important feature of such a product and it will therefore be one of the characteristics of traded energy products which is bought and sold, thus entering into price signals. In a market system, consumers and producers will choose their own preferred degrees of security, rather than having those degrees imposed or influenced by government: freedom to choose in this case, as in others, is a likely benefit of using the market. It is theoretically possible that governments could provide an addition to market-provided security which would yield net benefits (for instance, by holding excess stocks of some fuels, or excess electricity-generating capacity or giving incentives to private companies to invest in additional generating capacity). But it is also quite possible that government action will bring no net increase in security provision (because it will crowd out private provision that would otherwise have been made) or that, if it achieves any net increase, the marginal costs will exceed the marginal benefits.

Reducing security is another possibility, as government interferes in market processes. For example, if energy suppliers and consumers believe that governments will not allow prices to ration demand in the event of a supply interruption, market incentives to supply security will be blunted: potential suppliers of security will not make the investments they would have made had they expected profits to be higher. In that case, it is government failure not market failure which is the problem. We should also bear in mind that, as in other matters, government action on security is likely to be influenced by interest groups.

In Britain, governments have in the past claimed to be trying to improve security, but their record has been extremely poor. During the days of coal protection, it was claimed that British coalmining was being supported to improve security of supply: in particular, to avoid dependence on unreliable foreigners. But, by supporting British coal, governments enhanced its monopoly power. An interruption to coal supplies would be costly in itself but it might also interrupt electricity supplies (since government policy had made electricity generation heavily dependent on British coal). Thus Britain's energy supplies became highly dependent on one source which workers in the industry frequently threatened to interrupt and occasionally did interrupt.[26] Nearly all the important threats to energy security in the second half of the twentieth century came from indigenous coalmining. The CEGB and other consumers were thus forced to maintain costly excess stocks to guard against supply interruptions. Some would maintain that continued support for civil nuclear power was itself a costly insurance policy, designed to offset the perverse effects of government support for coalmining – albeit a flawed security policy, since favouring British-designed nuclear plant encouraged concentration on a narrow range of technologies.

Instead of allowing the natural diversification tendencies of markets to operate, governments, pushed by the then powerful coal lobby and the influential scientific establishment which supported nuclear power, concentrated energy supply, with the perverse consequences just mentioned. In 1989, on the eve of electricity privatization, coal (mainly British) supplied 73 per cent of British electricity, and nuclear another 22 per cent. Since privatization, this undue fuel concentration has been tempered by market diversification so that, in the first half of 2002, the share of coal in electricity supplied (measured in TWh) was 31 per cent (much of it imported), of gas 39 per cent and of nuclear 22 per cent.[27] The coal lobby is no longer so significant but there are other potentially damaging interest groups which will seek to exploit market power granted them by government.

Environmental Issues

Because the PIU gives pre-eminence to environmental issues, the reincarnated energy policy in effect converges on an environmental policy applied to the energy industries. Market failure reasons are used in justification on the familiar grounds that production, transportation and consumption of energy products give rise to external costs which therefore are not taken into account in decision making, thus tending to degrade the environment.

It is not true that markets do not take into account any environmental effects. On the supply side, where property rights in environmental assets have been established, owners will defend those assets against potential polluters as against other intruders. In other cases, the most appropriate government action is to define property rights so that such market effects will operate. On the demand side, markets will work in the sense that, when consumers demand products with certain environmental characteristics, suppliers have an incentive to supply them.

Nevertheless a case can be made, in principle, for collective action (which could include government intervention) in the case of some global environmental effects, where property rights are hard to define. If, as is now generally believed, the major environmental issue is global climate change and if the cause of that change is emissions of carbon into the atmosphere, there are standard economists' prescriptions to allow markets to work better. The PIU report

(Chapter 3) points them out: carbon taxation (fixing the price) and carbon emission trading (fixing the quantity) are alternative ways of using 'economic instruments' to provide carbon abatement incentives.

The use of such general instruments has attractions in principle but, as so often with economists' prescriptions, there are many drawbacks in practice which are centred, not on deficiencies in economic theory, but on scientific ignorance. So far as I can see, the evidence is not clear-cut that climate change is occurring, that carbon emissions are responsible and that world welfare will be reduced by the change (that is, that the loss to the losers will exceed the gain to the gainers, making the heroic assumption that such losses and gains are measurable). Certainly it is not as plain as the PIU report would have us believe. In those circumstances, determining the price (tax) or the quantity of emissions is very difficult and, as usual with such instruments, open to political manipulation.[28] Let me list some of the problems.

First, in accepting that some general economic instrument should be used, we rely on the prevailing scientific consensus that climate change as a result of carbon emissions is occurring and will in future represent a serious threat. Against that scientific consensus are ranged a number of dissenters who question whether there is genuine evidence of climate change, whether any change that has occurred is a trend or a cyclical movement that will be reversed, and whether there is a clear correlation between carbon emissions and change in climate.[29]

I wonder if I am alone in feeling uncomfortable about accepting the scientific consensus when, on so many occasions in the past, the dissenters have turned out to be right. Some 40 years ago, the powerful scientific lobby which promoted nuclear power on the grounds that it would become 'too cheap to meter' persuaded the government to invest large sums in constructing nuclear power stations. Few people would now claim that consensus to have been correct. About 30 years ago, another consensus, accepted by many economists as well as scientists, formed around the view that 'the days of cheap energy are gone for ever', that markets were incapable of adapting to such shattering events as the oil 'shocks' and that only massive government action (for example, big new nuclear energy programmes, government investment in coal production and synthetic fuel plants) could save the world. In the event, there was very little government action but energy markets adjusted in a remarkably short space of time so that, within ten years, world markets were awash with crude oil and prices were tumbling. Just before the decline in crude prices, 20 years ago, the consensus prediction for their end of century level, mainly from economists, was that they would increase from $35 per barrel to $70–100 per barrel in 1980 prices. I mention these predictions not to pour scorn on their authors (we are all shortsighted) but to point out that there is something in the contrarian view that the prevailing wisdom about energy markets is almost invariably wrong and that to base policies on it risks proceeding in the wrong direction.

Second, there is the problem of government failure. If there is a case in principle for applying a carbon tax or some instrument with similar effect, it is naïve to assume that government would implement the required measures perfectly and that there would be no unintended consequences. There is so much uncertainty about what should be done that government would have a great deal of scope to pursue its own agenda, as we saw a few years ago when a Conservative government, followed by New Labour, used the excuse of 'environmental action' to impose arbitrary annual increases in road fuel duties until halted by a citizens' protest movement. A general problem in dealing with long-term environmental issues is that they require an institution which is not only wise and benevolent but is willing to take a very long view. It seems doubtful whether a government in a representative political system where there are frequent elections is such an institution. A good case can be made that political time horizons are shorter than corporate time horizons and it seems generally true that governments are unhappy about incurring costs now in order to produce benefits in the long term for their successors.

For such reasons I have doubts about the carbon tax or emissions trading, though I respect the views of those who argue that, as an insurance policy, we should *assume* that climate change is occurring and that it will have a net negative effect. Nevertheless it is as well to acknowledge that, given our present knowledge and the likely unintended consequences of action taken by real-world governments, the precise nature of what should be done is most unclear.

However using a general economic instrument would at least have some advantages in principle over the mix of interventionist ideas in the PIU report. It would permit markets to work, subject to the constraints imposed by the tax. A curious feature of the PIU report is that, after mentioning carbon taxes and carbon emissions trading in Chapter 3, it then appears to assume, without any supporting argument, that they would be insufficient. On page 93 of the report, it states, 'As well as broad market-based instruments, more targeted policies would be needed, given market failures and other barriers to the development of low carbon technologies.'

As I have already pointed out, some parts of the PIU report emphasize the advantages of markets and point out the problem of government failure. It is not, however, prepared to rely on markets plus some use of 'market instruments'. It wants direct intervention. Indeed in its discussion of environmental issues the PIU report becomes surprisingly *dirigiste* in tone. It is, apparently, quite plain that climate change is happening, that it is damaging, that markets (even if supplemented by taxes or trading mechanisms) will not work and that direct government action is required. It is obvious therefore that all good people must believe that a policy directed by government and heading towards a 'low-carbon economy' must be the right course of action. The criterion by which energy policy proposals should be judged is whether they are consistent with the 'fundamental goal of moving towards a low carbon system' (para. 3.96). There seems no thought here that government might fail: that the objective might be incorrect, that implementation might be poor, that policy might even work perversely, as did energy policies in earlier postwar years. Surely a little more humility might be in order, particularly since the PIU is looking ahead 50 years – a fatal conceit, some might say – though of course the forward look is all in scenario-speak.

The PIU recommends changes in objectives and institutions. For example, it wants government to adopt 'sustainable development' as its guiding principle for intervention in the energy field. That is a principle that requires taking such a long-term view one must wonder what incentive a government would have to adopt it. Furthermore, for a principle to become operational, it must be possible *ex ante* to distinguish actions which are consistent with the principle from those which are not. It must also be possible, *ex post*, to monitor whether such consistency was achieved. Neither the *ex ante* nor the *ex post* condition seems to me to be present. Indeed the principle is so vague there is a clear danger that governments will use it to justify any action in the energy field they wish to take, regardless of whether it has anything to do with environmental improvement.

The institutional changes proposed by the PIU do not look promising either. Given the vagueness of the sustainable development objective, it is hard to see how the proposed 'cross-cutting Sustainable Energy Policy Unit' could have any objective basis for its advice. The suggested new National Energy Research Centre will not seem appealing to anyone who was acquainted with the bloated research activities of the energy industries before privatization. And recent experiences with 'joined-up government' provide little reassurance that having responsibility for climate change policy, energy policy and transport policy in one department would result in improved decisions.

When it comes to specific policy ideas, the PIU gathers together a number of previously suggested ways of moving towards the apparently more benign future it would like and comments on the costs and benefits of each in Chapters 6 and 7 of its report. The government has already embarked on some action, ostensibly on environmental grounds, in the form of the climate change levy – a tax on the business use of energy. The PIU wants more.

It favours continued government intervention to promote energy conservation: it proposes round number targets of a 20 per cent improvement for households by 2010 and another 20 per cent by 2020. There should also be continued intervention to promote renewables: more suspiciously round numbers, this time of 10 per cent of electricity generated by 2010 and 20 per cent by 2020. Dare we extrapolate to 100 per cent by 2100? More electricity should be generated from waste. That old favourite, CHP (Combined Heat and Power) use, should be stimulated. The capturing and sequestering of carbon dioxide from fossil fuels should be investigated. Efficiency in the use of transport fuels should be encouraged, as should a move towards a hydrogen-based low carbon transport system. As regards investment in nuclear power, the PIU wants to 'keep options open'. Ofgem should be instructed to give more help to small generators if present measures do not work.

In sum, the PIU has an interventionist programme in mind for government in the energy market. It wants to play God in the machine. In Chapters 6 and 7 of its report it seems to lose sight of its earlier comments about the possibility of government failure and its remark about the 60 per cent carbon dioxide emissions reduction target for 2050 proposed by the Royal Commission on Environmental Pollution (RCEP). On page 9 of the PIU's report it says, 'It would be unwise for the UK now to take the unilateral decision to meet the RCEP target, in advance of international negotiations on longer term targets.' But by the time it reaches its scenarios and its policy proposals, the PIU seems to regard the RCEP's drastic strategy as the one which should guide action. Consequently, it gives the government the green light for a wide range of interventionist measures. It recognizes there will be costs, and muses about action to help poor consumers and energy-intensive companies (paras 7.105 to 7.109). But the aggregate costs it puts at the equivalent of half-a-year's growth in real GDP over the next 50 years, an implausibly low figure when one considers the amount of government regulation which would ensue and that the major cost of regulation is its dampening effect on entrepreneurship.

To illustrate in a little more detail the basis of the PIU's proposals, consider Appendix 5 to its report, titled 'Energy Efficiency – the Basis for Intervention'. This is a typical piece of Nirvana economics which produces all the old chestnuts about why the government should intervene to promote efficiency (listed in a table on page 183). The 'key barrier' to energy efficiency, it is claimed, is people's failure to 'seek to optimise the efficiency with which they use energy'. Energy costs are too low a proportion of total costs for any but very energy-intensive consumers to worry about them. Hence the government should step in. I describe this as Nirvana economics because it moves stealthily from the correct proposition that market participants do not optimize energy efficiency to the incorrect view that such optimization is possible. Furthermore it leads to a truly startling logical conclusion. If the problem is that, when an input represents only a small proportion of total costs, people will fail to give it proper weight in their decisions and the solution is that government should intervene, it follows that government should examine all those myriad items which represent small proportions of the costs of individuals and companies and, in each and every case, intervene on the grounds that people do not recognize what is good for them. The result would be a nanny state which goes beyond anything so far conceived.

CONCLUSIONS AND THE IMPACT ON ENERGY REGULATION

The reincarnated environmentally inclined energy policy, at least as it appears in the PIU report, seems to me little more appealing than the one which died 20 years ago. The failings of the old policies are there for all to see: one of their principal outcomes was an excessively polluting electricity supply industry with undiversified sources of fuel and technologies and consequent insecurity. Thus in terms of the two most important characteristics of the policy now being recommended by the PIU – security and avoidance of environmental damage – it was a dismal failure.[30]

In some ways, government has moved on. It seems to have turned away from the idea (which had little in its favour) that the energy sector is so important that it must have a policy of its own: what is now described as 'energy policy' is primarily a branch of environmental policy. Moreover, in principle, the government seems to embrace the idea of competitive markets rather than planning blueprints. But, in practice, its advisers are recommending a policy, based mainly on the apparent environmental effects of energy production, distribution and consumption, which could lead to very extensive direct government intervention, with all its associated problems. The authors of the PIU report think, as did their forebears, they can foresee the problems of the energy future. They want to use the government machine to guide us to a 'low-carbon future'. But history shows matters are not so simple. Planners looking ahead many years tend to address the wrong problems, especially in energy markets where they have often been spectacularly wrong. The information required for such planning does not exist and government will generally fail in the design and execution of policies, leaving a trail of unforeseen, often perverse and costly, consequences.

Implementation of a PIU-style energy plan would obviously significantly affect the gas and electricity industries, especially if, as in the past, there was a tendency towards increasing intervention. The reasons to expect such an increase are straightforward: initial measures have unintended consequences, so new measures are applied both in a second effort to achieve the initial objectives and to offset the unintended effects of the first set, and so on.[31] That is how coal protection escalated from small beginnings in the late 1950s to the massive scale it reached in the early 1980s.

Electricity, which was the prime instrument of energy policy in the past, could become so again since the energy sources currently favoured by planners, such as renewables, have limited prospects except as fuels for electricity generation, which means these intermittent sources have to be squeezed somewhat awkwardly into the generation mix. Any plans would be more difficult to implement than in the past when it was a matter of twisting the arm of the CEGB. Now they would have to be more open. Nevertheless the government has already imposed on suppliers an Energy Efficiency Commitment and a Renewables Obligation, as well as taxing business use of electricity and other fuels through the climate change levy.

Then there is regulation of the gas and electricity industries. Could an energy regulator, which has been occupied in opening up markets to competition, coexist peacefully with a government which is pursuing a PIU-style energy plan and is thereby declaring certain areas off-limits to competition? Such a plan could have an impact on two of the pillars of Britain's system of utility regulation, independence from the immediate political process and competition promotion.[32] The British regulatory system, though imperfect as any such system must be, has provided a model for much of the rest of the world and can reasonably be regarded as the most successful system of regulating utilities so far devised. So we should beware of undermining it.[33]

One could take the attitude that democratic governments must always retain the right to constrain 'independent' regulators, setting out the limits within which they can operate as, for example, the government sets the inflation target at which the Bank of England's Monetary Policy Committee aims. Thus, it might be argued, governments can reasonably give regulators instructions on environmental, social and other issues without compromising their independence. 'Independence', on this view, is intended primarily to place a buffer between the regulator and day-to-day political processes. It puts a stop to the detailed intervention for political reasons which went on under nationalization when, for example, at times the Cabinet decided on the prices and investment programmes of the electricity and gas industries, but it does not exclude a policy-making role for government in the relevant field.

The extent to which one accepts this argument depends, I think, on how impressed one is with the case made by public choice theorists. The government failure/slippery slope counterargument is that, in setting these constraints, governments will be neither willing nor able to identify true 'public interest' actions. Thus there is no reason to believe the actions taken will lead to an improvement in welfare. Moreover there will be unintended consequences which will lead to more intervention, more unintended consequences and a rising trend of intervention over time which will increasingly limit the regulator's actions. At the bottom of the slippery slope, government policy dominates and the regulator is reduced to a minor player in the field. I have some sympathy with this argument. I would draw attention to a possible parallel with the belief that existed at the time of nationalization that nationalized corporations would be allowed to manage: governments would just be there to help in the setting of strategic targets. It did not quite work out that way. It is not easy to live with 'partners' which have the power to coerce.

Competition promotion, as well as independence, could be a casualty of government attempts to constrain regulators, because those attempts might well limit the area within which competitive markets are allowed to operate. Fortunately, in this case, Ofgem and its predecessors have gone so far in liberalizing markets that there is, for the time being, less need for active competition promotion than there used to be. The establishment of competitive wholesale and retail markets in gas and electricity in Britain, even if not yet complete, is a remarkable achievement which few economists would have dared predict even ten years ago.

Looking at the matter another way, competitive energy markets can be seen as a defence against government intervention in pursuit of an energy plan. Consumers now have choice and have discovered that shopping around can bring significant price reductions. Interfering governments which, for example, want to influence which fuels the electricity generators use, may therefore face penalties in terms of customer discontent that did not apply in the old days when the costs were hidden in ever-rising gas and electricity prices and in taxes. It will probably be more difficult to reinstitute an interventionist regime in energy than in the other privatized utilities, such as the railways, water and perhaps telecoms, which have not travelled so far down the liberalization road. Electricity and gas consumers, who have become used to competition and have had the benefit of big price reductions, may not take kindly to actions which limit competition and therefore reduce the benefits of shopping around. That is admittedly an optimistic view, which assumes consumers are aware of what is happening and who is responsible.

However there is a way of avoiding the clash between, on the one side, privatized and liberalized markets and independent, competition-promoting regulation and, on the other, government energy planning. Whatever one thinks about the results of privatization in general, in electricity and gas it has through regulatory action led to liberalized markets and big consumer benefits. We should try to keep those benefits. We can, however, avoid the planning which appears to be in prospect. I am sceptical about the case that climate change is occurring and the apparent corollary that there is a major environmental externality which should be internalized. Nevertheless I accept that others see the need for action. If it is to occur, it would be better done by using broad economic instruments rather then embarking on a PIU-style programme of direct intervention which would almost certainly lead to increasing state interference over time. There would be efficiency advantages in letting markets adapt to imposition of the chosen instrument, as compared with intervening to promote this or that fuel or this or that 'energy-efficiency' measure. In terms of our subject in this chapter, it would also allow independent regulation of the electricity and gas industries to continue, with a pro-competition emphasis and without too much hindrance from the kind of government action in the energy sector which has been so unsuccessful in the past.

NOTES

1. Michael Beesley, 'Foreword' to Colin Robinson, *Energy Policy: Errors, Illusions and Market Realities*, occasional paper 90, Institute of Economic Affairs, 1993.
2. Details of the various government publications on energy in 2002 can be found in the energy section of the DTI's website (www.dti.gov.uk/energy).
3. Editor's note: the White Paper, entitled *Our Energy Future – Creating a Low Carbon Economy*, was published by the DTI in February 2003.
4. For example, Department of Energy, *Energy Policy Review*, Energy Paper 22, 1977, and a Green Paper, *Energy Policy: A Consultative Document*, Cmnd 7101, 1978. There have also been many reports from the Energy Select Committee and its DTI successor, from Offer, Ofgas and Ofgem. The 1997–8 review of utility regulation produced the DTI's *Review of Energy Sources for Power Generation: Consultation Document*, June 1998. But there has been no government pronouncement with the status of a White Paper.
5. W.S. Jevons, *The Coal Question*, 1865, reprinted New York: Augustus M. Kelley, 1965.
6. More detailed accounts of the early postwar history of energy policy are in William G. Shepherd, *Economic Performance under Public Ownership – British Fuel and Power*, New Haven, CT: Yale University Press, 1965; Political and Economic Planning (PEP), *A Fuel Policy for Britain*, London: PEP, 1966; Colin Robinson, 'Die Energiewirtschaft in Grossbritannien: Entwicklung und Perspektiven', *Weitschrift für Energie Wirtschaft*, 2/91, 1991, *Energy Trends and the Development of Energy Policy in the United Kingdom*, Surrey Energy Economics Centre Discussion Paper 61, 1992; and *A Policy for Fuel?*, occasional paper 31, Institute of Economic Affairs, 1969.
7. On energy policy in these years see, for example, Robinson, *Energy Policy: Errors, Illusions and Market Realities*. On the nuclear promotion policy, I mention below the possibility that it was not an objective in its own right but a consequence of coal protection.
8. National Coal Board, *Plan for Coal*, 1974; Department of Energy, *Coal for the Future*, 1977. Criticisms of these forecasts are in Colin Robinson and Eileen Marshall, *What Future for British Coal?*, Hobart Paper 89, Institute of Economic Affairs, 1981.
9. Colin Robinson, *The Power of the State: Economic Questions over Nuclear Generation*, London: Adam Smith Institute, 1991.
10. *The Nationalised Industries*, Cmnd 1337, 1961, Cmnd 3437, 1967, Cmnd 7131, 1978.
11. David Heald, 'The Economic and Financial Control of the Nationalised Industries', *Economic Journal*, 90, June 1980.
12. *Fuel Policy*, Cmnd 2798, HMSO, October 1965; *Fuel Policy*, Cmnd 3438, HMSO, November 1967. The two papers are described and criticized in *A Policy for Fuel?*
13. Robinson, *A Policy for Fuel?*
14. Colin Robinson and Eileen Marshall, *What Future for British Coal?*, Prologue.
15. Nigel Lawson, *The View from Number 11*, London: Bantam Press, 1992, esp. ch. 15.
16. For example, Colin Robinson, 'Liberalising the Energy Industries', *Proceedings of the Manchester Statistical Society*, 15 March 1988; and 'Privatising the British Energy Industries: The Lessons to be Learned', *Metroeconomica*, 1–2, 1992.
17. Colin Robinson, 'After the Regulatory Review', in M.E. Beesley (ed.), *Regulating Utilities: A New Era*, Readings 49, Institute of Economic Affairs, 1999.
18. The PIU's 'Energy Review', Chapter 3, suggests that equity issues and 'strategic and political' considerations may also justify an energy policy. Equity matters, however, are not well

addressed by a policy directed at one sector of the economy and 'strategic and political' issues are too vague a basis for policy.

19. R.G. Lipsey and K. Lancaster, 'The General Theory of Second Best', *The Review of Economic Studies*, **24**(1), 1956.

20. H. Demsetz, 'Information and Efficiency: Another Viewpoint', *Journal of Law and Economics*, **12**(1), 1969; *Efficiency, Competition and Policy*, Oxford: Blackwell, 1989.

21. F.A. Hayek, 'The Meaning of Competition', *Individualism and Economic Order*, London: Routledge, 1948. See also Israel Kirzner, *Discovery and the Capitalist Process*, Chicago: University of Chicago Press, 1985.

22. Robinson, *Energy Policy: Errors, Illusions and Market Realities*, p. 48.

23. David Henderson, *The Changing Fortunes of Economic Liberalism*, occasional paper 105, Institute of Economic Affairs, 1998, rev. ed. 2001.

24. Robinson, 'After the Regulatory Review'.

25. Further discussion is in Colin Robinson, 'Depletion Control in Theory and Practice', *Zeitschrift für Energie Wirtschaft, 1/86, 1986*.

26. Eileen Marshall and Colin Robinson, *The Economics of Energy Self-Sufficiency*, London: Heinemann, 1984, esp. ch. 5.

27. Department of Trade and Industry, *Energy Trends*, September 2002, Table 5.1.

28. An attempt to avoid the problem of political manipulation in setting the cap on emissions is being made by the Chicago Climate Exchange (www.chicagoclimatex.com) which evidently has a system of letting participants determine the cap and sets rules for changing it.

29. See, for example, John Emsley (ed.), *The Global Warming Debate*, European Science and Environment Forum, 1996; John P. Weyant (ed.), 'The Costs of the Kyoto Protocol: A Multi-Model Evaluation', *The Energy Journal*, special issue, 1999.

30. The old policies did ostensibly aim at promoting security of supply, but not specifically at environmental improvement.

31. Colin Robinson, *A Policy for Fuel?*

32. The other pillar is the price cap (RPI-X).

33. See, for example, Colin Robinson, 'After the Regulatory Review'.

CHAIRMAN'S COMMENTS

Callum McCarthy

What Colin Robinson says is a rather bracing if understated correction to much that is easily accepted as either sensible or, if not sensible, probably inevitable. I think it is always salutary to be reminded of the frailties of planning. My own favourite reminder is that the CEGB evidence to the Sizewell enquiry forecast that gas would play no part in electricity generation in the year 2000. But one does not have to look that far back to have examples of the 'gapology' that Colin referred to. I was very taken earlier this year that a forecast by the DTI attracted much attention. The forecast was of the danger of a shortfall in gas availability by 2004–5, on the basis of the peak demand that could be expected no more than one in 20 years. I am intrigued to find that, within six months of that forecast, the gap has been put back one year and it has been said to be a temporary gap, which is eliminated in subsequent years. It is just an example of how quickly things change. So I have no difficulty in accepting that the subject of government failures requires just as much attention as market failures. I wonder, though, whether it also requires some degree of sympathy. Many of us who believe in markets as a powerful, albeit imperfect, force are sympathetic to the manifest failures that occur in the perfect model that Colin has been describing. We are concerned to overcome these failings: the search for the second, third or eleventh-best solution. I think we need to approach government intervention in the same way: not to reject it entirely, but to think about how it is best achieved. It does seem to me that, if we are going to have intervention by government, one of the questions to ask is how do we make it as successful (I suspect Colin would say as least harmful) as possible?

I think there are a number of simple rules that are worth discussing in this context. First it seems to me absolutely manifest that there is a rule: to avoid, if you are a government, any attempt to pick winners. If I may give credit to the PIU, it did, at least as a general principle, set out that government should not attempt to pick winners, although I am not sure whether it managed completely to live up to the principle which it so clearly adumbrated.

Second, I think it is quite clear that we should try and adopt, as Colin Robinson suggests, general rather than specific measures, that is general support for R&D rather than support for individual projects, a carbon tax or emissions trading, rather than specific programmes.

And, third, I think that it is sensible to attempt to make measures as comprehensive as possible: hence a carbon tax or emissions trading extending over as much of the economy as possible, not a special approach to gas and electricity alone which fails to give, for example, comparable treatment to the transport industry; still less, attempts to pick a particular technology of generation in the way it is being done at the moment.

There will always, for understandable reasons, be pressures for government to act and we need to help develop some helpful guidance to make the actions as productive as we can. I dwell on this because this is a very apt time for Colin's talk. It is a matter of public knowledge that people are even now beavering away trying to get the White Paper, which is to follow the PIU report, to the prime minister before Christmas. I very much hope that the lessons Colin has pulled out of the experience of the last 40 years, and particularly his emphasis on broad measures, rather than a series of specific initiatives of the sort so obviously liked by individual ministers who can attach their names to individual measures, will be adopted. I was heartened to read something Patricia Hewitt said, namely 'a need to escape from an approach to administration based on a love affair with detail'. That fits in very much with what Colin has been saying.

Index